NORMANDY'S
NIGHTMARE
WAR

Famous for Calvados apple brandy and Camembert cheese, Normandy is a green and pleasant land now dotted with thousands of British-owned second homes. Its coastline is also dotted with thousands of indestructible reinforced-concrete bunkers and gun emplacements that formed part of the Atlantic Wall of Hitler's Fortress Europe.

Tourists passing through the ferry ports like Boulogne, Cherbourg and Dunkirk and inland cities like Rouen and Caen may wonder why there are so few old buildings, but few know that the demolition which preceded the extensive urban renewal of the ancient town centres was effected by British bombs during four years of hell for the people living there. Before its belated liberation three long months *after* D-Day, the sirens in Le Havre wailed 1,060 times to warn of approaching British and American bombers. After one single raid, over 3,000 dead civilians were recovered from the city's ruins, without counting the thousands of injured, maimed and traumatised survivors.

So, whom did the Normans regard as the enemy: the German occupiers who shot a few hundred *résistants* or the Allied airmen who killed as many in northern France as died in Britain from German bombs during the whole war?

Here, told largely in the words of French, German and Allied eyewitnesses, including the moving last letters of executed hostages, is the story of Normandy's nightmare war.

NORMANDY'S NIGHTMARE WAR

THE FRENCH EXPERIENCE OF NAZI OCCUPATION AND ALLIED BOMBING 1940-45

DOUGLAS BOYD

PEN & SWORD HISTORY

AN IMPRINT OF PEN & SWORD BOOKS LTD.
YORKSHIRE – PHILADELPHIA

First published in Great Britain in 2019 by
Pen and Sword History
An imprint of
Pen & Sword Books Ltd
Yorkshire - Philadelphia

ISBN 978 1 52674 581 1

Typeset in Ehrhardt MT Std 11.5/14 by
Aura Technology and Software Services, India

Printed and bound in the UK by CPI Group (UK) Ltd, Croydon, CR0 4YY

Pen & Sword Books Ltd incorporates the Imprints of Pen & Sword Books
Archaeology, Atlas, Aviation, Battleground, Discovery, Family History, History,
Maritime, Military, Naval, Politics, Railways, Select, Transport, True Crime,
Fiction, Frontline Books, Leo Cooper, Praetorian Press, Seaforth Publishing,
Wharncliffe and White Owl.

For a complete list of Pen & Sword titles please contact

PEN & SWORD BOOKS LIMITED
47 Church Street, Barnsley, South Yorkshire, S70 2AS, England
E-mail: enquiries@pen-and-sword.co.uk
Website: www.pen-and-sword.co.uk

or

PEN AND SWORD BOOKS
1950 Lawrence Rd, Havertown, PA 19083, USA
E-mail: Uspen-and-sword@casematepublishers.com
Website: www.penandswordbooks.com

Contents

PART 3: PREPARATION AND PAIN

PART 4: LIBERATION AND DEATH

About the author

Douglas Boyd has lived in France for forty years. A former BBC TV producer/director, he began collecting first-hand accounts of the French experience of war in 1968 while working on television programmes commemorating the fiftieth anniversary of the 1918 Armistice. This book is a fruit of that long research.

This is a revised and updated edition of *Normandy in the Time of Darkness*, first published in 2010.

Also by Douglas Boyd:

Histories:
April Queen, Eleanor of Aquitaine
Voices from the Dark Years
The French Foreign Legion
The Kremlin Conspiracy: 1,000 years of Russian expansionism
Normandy in the time of Darkness: life and death in the Channel ports 1940–45
Blood in the Snow, Blood on the Grass: treachery and massacre, France 1944
De Gaulle: the man who defied six US presidents
Lionheart: the true story of England's crusader king
The Other First World War: the blood-soaked Russian fronts 1914–22
Daughters of the KGB: Moscow's Cold War spies, sleepers and assassins
Agente – Female spies in World Wars, Cold Wars and Civil Wars
The Solitary Spy
Red October – the revolution that changed the world
Lockerbie – the truth

Novels:
The Eagle and the Snake
The Honour and the Glory
The Truth and the Lies
The Virgin and the Fool
The Fiddler and the Ferret
The Spirit and the Flesh

Churchill to Eisenhower, 3 April 1944: 'The Cabinet took an adverse view of the proposal to bomb so many French railway centres, in view of the fact that scores of thousands of French civilians, men, women and children, would lose their lives or be injured.'

Eisenhower to Churchill, 5 April 1944: 'I and my military advisers have become convinced that the bombing of these centres will increase our chances for success. I personally believe that estimates of probable casualties have been grossly exaggerated.'

Since Eisenhower was the Supreme Commander of all Allied forces, Churchill turned to President Roosevelt – the only person who could possibly influence him to change the bombing policy.

Churchill to Roosevelt, 7 May 1944: 'The War Cabinet have (sic) been much concerned about the number of Frenchmen killed in the raids on the railway centres in France. When this project was first put forward, a loss of 80,000 French civilian casualties, including injured, say 20,000 killed, was mentioned. The War Cabinet could not view this figure without grave dismay on account of the apparently ruthless use of the Air Forces, particularly the Royal Air Force, on whom the brunt of this work necessarily falls. It must be remembered that this slaughter is among a friendly people who have committed no crime against us.'

Roosevelt to Churchill, 11 May 1944: 'However regrettable the attendant loss of civilian lives is, I am not prepared to impose from this distance any restriction on military action by the responsible commanders.'

Note: The *Institut National de la Statistique* puts the body count of French civilian casualties killed by Allied air raids 1940–44 conservatively at 60,000, plus another 71,000 injured severely, and uncounted with minor injuries. Other estimates are higher.

List of acronyms

BEF	British Expeditionary Force
CDL	*Comité – Départemental de Libération* committee set up in each *département* to co-ordinate the various Resistance networks' activities and to lay a political foundation for assumption of administrative powers after the Liberation
CGQJ	*Commissariat Général des Questions Juives* – Vichy government organisation for anti-Jewish actions
CIABG	Czech Independent Armoured Brigade Group
COSSAC	Chief of Staff to Supreme Allied Commander
CQMS	Company quartermaster-sergeant (NCO responsible for stores and equipment)
DUKW	Military amphibious transport vehicle
FAFL	*Forces Aériennes Françaises Libres* – Free French Air Force
FFI	*Forces Françaises de l'Interieur* – French in-country Resistance
FTP	*Francs-Tireurs et Partisans* – Communist Resistance network
LVF	*Légion de Volontaires Français*
MGB	Motor Gun Boat (Royal Navy)
MTB	Motor Torpedo Boat (Royal Navy)
NATO	North Atlantic Treaty Organisation
NCO	Non-commissioned officer
NN	*Nacht und Nebel* – prisoners with no records of whereabouts
NSKK	*Nazionalsozialistische Kampfahrkorps* – German transport corps
OKK	*Oberkommando der Kriegsmarine* – German naval high command
OKW	*Oberkommando der Wehrmacht* – German High Command
OTU	Operational Training Unit (RAF)

PCF   *Parti Communiste Français* – French Communist Party

PLUTO   Pipeline under the ocean – several pipelines laid on the bottom of the English Channel carrying motor fuel directly from England to French terminals

POW   Prisoner of war

PT   Motor torpedo boat (US Navy)

SIPEG   *Service Interministériel de Protection contre les Evénements de Guerre* – a French government emergency aid and relief organisation

SNCF   *Société Nationale des Chemins de Fer* – French national railway network

SOE   Special Operations Executive – British organisation for supporting and coordinating subversive activity in German-occupied Europe

SOL   *Service d'Ordre Légionnaire* – Vichy French paramilitary force

STO   *Service du Travail Obligatoire* – Vichy French conscription of military-age males to work in the Reich

TI   Target indicators

V1   German flying bomb

V2   German long-range ballistic missile

V3   German long-range gun

VC   Victoria Cross

WKD   *Wehrmacht Verkehrsdirektion* – German army railway corps

Update

Shortly before the first edition of this book went to press, on St Valentine's Day 2010, the *Euronews* satellite TV channel carried a report of an unexploded Second World War bomb uncovered during construction work on the campus of the University of Caen. Weighing 500kg, with an explosive charge of 265kg, this American bomb had been dropped there on 7 June 1944. It seems that France has an unofficial policy not to talk about, and therefore report, what happened during the German occupation. At any rate, their news editors having decided that yet another unexploded bomb in Normandy was of no interest to viewers, France's national television channels concentrated instead on the medal won by a teenage French girl skier at the Vancouver Winter Olympics.

A 500kg bomb could kill a lot of people. In Caen, 20,000 residents had to be evacuated from the area amid snow flurries under grey skies to a conference centre, specially staffed to receive them. The bomb disposal experts got down on their knees in the freezing slush of the hole where the bomb lay, and which looked uncomfortably like a grave. After several hours' tense and uncomfortable work, with the fuse safely removed, the head of the team took a deep breath and announced that it was safe for removal to a demolition site. Stretching his aching back, he volunteered the information that, given the number of Allied bombs dropped on northern French towns in the Second World War and the rate at which they were being uncovered and rendered safe, it would take *at least* another forty years before they had all been removed.

Exactly six months earlier, British holidaymakers driving into Le Havre on the peak travel day of Friday, 14 August 2009 found diversion signs everywhere and the normally busy St Nicolas district closed to traffic. If some of them picked up the regional daily paper *Ouest France* while killing time in a bar, waiting for their ferry back to Britain, they would have read that Microsoft had just launched Windows 7, that 315kg of cocaine had been seized by French customs police at a motorway tollbooth, and that film director Roman Polanski was fighting extradition from Switzerland to answer a 30-year-old morals charge in Los Angeles.

However, the attention of the locals in the bar was focused on the front page story about the cause of the congestion. A bomb dropped on St Nicolas by the RAF more than sixty years earlier had been unearthed by the driver of a mechanical digger. Considerably eroded at both ends, this lethal relic was 1.3 metres long, weighed nearly half a tonne and contained a 218kg explosive charge. Christophe Darcy, head of the four-man bomb disposal team, declared it 'armed and ready to explode'. He continued, 'In the last six years, eleven bombs weighing between 50kg and 500kg have been discovered during construction work (in Le Havre alone). In addition, each year between ten and fifteen tonnes of dangerous explosive devices from the war are dug up in Normandy.'

St Nicolas was eerily quiet that day as Monsieur Darcy and his team set to work and successfully rendered the bomb safe in three sweaty, nail-biting hours at the bottom of a pit surrounded by berms of earth and gravel to deflect the blast upwards if they made a wrong move and were vaporised in the explosion. Security precautions had involved the police, fire brigade and other municipal services evacuating 2,300 residents from all buildings in a radius of 400 metres. However, those who had lived through the war years in Le Havre were phlegmatic about the drama. One such couple – 84-year-old Denise Mangard and her 89-year-old husband Yves – commented, 'We survived all the air raids on Le Havre, so we're not getting excited about someone de-fusing one bomb.'

Monsieur Darcy was reported in *Ouest France* as stating that more than one in every ten bombs dropped on Le Havre in the war had failed to explode, so that many inhabitants of the city were living above sufficient unstable chemicals to blow them and their homes sky-high if disturbed. Official estimates are that around six per cent of bombs fail to explode, but presumably the intrepid M. Darcy knew what he was talking about, and even six per cent is a worrying thought if you happen to live above them, given the tens of thousands that were dropped in Normandy and along the French Channel coast. Even random samples of the sand and shingle on the invasion beaches have been found to contain about four per cent of metal fragments from shrapnel and bullets. Between 9 and

12 June 2014 off the coast at Fécamp, French and German underwater mine disposal experts brought to the surface seventy-eight American bombs weighing a total of 3.9 tonnes and containing 1.7 tonnes of TNT.

As this second edition goes to press, the *sous-préfet* of the Manche *département* has just announced that his officers continue to receive on average one call every day to deal with dangerous relics of the Second World War. Most bombs are found at depths of four metres below the surface, but some are as low as nine metres down, the depth being determined mainly by the weight of the bomb and the type of ground on which it fell. But you don't always need a mechanical digger to find yourself looking at an unexploded bomb. In July 2016 at Bourg-Achard near Rouen a house-owner doing some double-digging in his own garden dug up ten smaller, but lethal, bombs only a half-metre below the surface.

In February 2017 an American bomb weighing 220kg was removed from a railway embankment at Granville after lying there only a few feet from the main Paris railway line for seventy-three years. People had to be evacuated from homes in a radius of half a kilometre while its fuse was removed so the bomb could be transported and blown up. On 13 April 2017 a 500lb bomb was revealed in a suburb of Boulogne during work to extend a supermarket complex visited daily by thousands of customers. In December 2017 five 250kg bombs were uncovered during construction work in Alençon. And so it goes on.

Of the more observant travellers who wonder why there are so few old buildings in northern French cities, few know that most of the demolition prior to this urban renewal was effected by British bombs levelling the ancient town centres and killing *thousands* of the people who lived there. Why?

Long before any avowed Allied policy of area bombing, inexperienced British aircrews, and eventually American ones too, were sent to bomb northern French towns and cities *for practice* before risking the deadly radar-guided searchlights and night fighters over Hitler's Germany.

Bombing accuracy was always problematic. In one grotesque example, on the night of 30 March 1944 a force of 120 RAF aircraft with experienced crews tasked with bombing Nuremburg mistakenly bombed Schweinfurt *fifty miles away*. And that was when the bomber streams had the benefit of radio guidance systems, airborne radar, improved bombsights, an experienced Pathfinder Force and a master bomber circling overhead. Earlier in the war, most bombs were dropped very wide of the target, killing tens of thousands of neutral French civilians to no military purpose.

At a dinner party in Bordeaux, an elderly Brit who had flown as a bomb aimer in RAF Lancasters confided in the author that the first time he had seen the city was while lying flat on his belly several thousand feet above it. His answer to the question, 'Were you aiming for the reinforced concrete *Kriegsmarine* submarine pens?' was a sideways look and a mumbled, 'With all that Jerry flak coming up at us, I just wanted to get home in time for breakfast.' His motto was *Drop 'em and go.* No wonder French civilians lived through four years of hell – five years in the case of Dunkirk, where the German garrison did not surrender until *after* the end of the war.

Following D-Day on 6 June 1944 the Allied commanders fighting their way across Normandy, and the German forces tenaciously resisting them all the way, were understandably so concentrated on their respective enemies that little consideration was shown to the people whose country had been turned into a battleground by forces outside their control. Conventional histories of the Normandy campaign devote few words to the experiences of the people who owned the fields, orchards, towns and villages across which the Allied armies and air forces fought a total war against the *Wehrmacht* and *Waffen-SS.* Typically, in one recent, well researched 500-page book on the campaign there are just two mentions of civilians trapped in the fighting: a Norman farmer, described as 'disinterested' when his horse and wagon were commandeered at gun-point by British troops; and a 'drunken grandfather' inviting passing British infantrymen to take a swig of brandy from a bottle he was waving at them.

Normandy's Nightmare War puts the record straight and tells the story of what everyday life and death was actually like for the people of Normandy and right along the French Channel coast in the years 1940–1945.

Introduction

In 1935 the expression *total war* was coined by General Erich Ludendorff in his book *Der totale Krieg*.

The idea was not new. Much primitive war involved the killing of all adult males in the conquered people and/or mass enslavement and the laying waste of their land. But civilised warfare, culminating in the set-piece battles of the eighteenth and nineteenth centuries, did not target civilians, although they certainly suffered as the victims of foraging parties or simple robbery at the point of a sword. In the First World War Ludendorff shared with General Paul von Hindenburg the command and control of the German armed forces, reducing the posturing Kaiser Wilhelm II to a figure-head, but this too was not a total war.

Although horrific in scale and suffering compared with previous conflicts, that war was fought on the Western Front by soldiers, sailors and airmen in uniform against opponents also in uniform. There were many instances of civilians being killed incidentally and a few instances of deliberate attacks on civilian targets that caused outrage at the time, but there was no stated policy in the west of slaughtering the population of an enemy country, even less of killing and maiming tens of thousands of neutral civilians. Given the horrific slaughter of the static trench warfare, including the use by both sides of weapons subsequently banned, this was obviously not because of any squeamishness or respect for the 'rules of war'.

Fortunately, the available technology of land and air warfare did not permit the killing of large numbers of non-combatants living hundreds of miles from the field of battle, although Paris and other French cities were shelled by long-range German guns, and Zeppelin airships and aircraft occasionally bombed British population centres. In the war at sea, however, the technology did exist and was inevitably used: Ludendorff was an enthusiastic advocate of U-boat commanders ruthlessly sinking unarmed merchant vessels, and Royal Navy ships blockaded enemy ports to starve the German people into submission.

The evolution of aircraft in the two inter-war decades and its rapid acceleration during the Second World War placed in the hands of military leaders for the first time the power to kill non-combatants on a large scale far from any conflict on land or sea. British Prime Minister Winston Churchill noted that at the beginning of 1942, 'the average bomb load per aircraft was 2,800lb; by the end of the year it was 4,400lb; during 1943 it rose to 7,500lb.'[1] That rapid and continuing increase in destructive power, allied to the appalling inaccuracy of bombing techniques, made inevitable a geometric progression in the scale of collateral civilian deaths.

Few voices were raised in protest when these civilians were citizens of an enemy belligerent, killed as a deliberate policy, supposedly to break the will of the enemy nation to continue the struggle. In France and the other German-occupied countries, however, the long Allied campaign of air raids from bases in Britain claimed the lives of few enemy soldiers, but did kill tens of thousands of neutral civilians. As a European statesman thinking of postwar relations with Britain's continental neighbours, Churchill put on record his desire that these deaths be kept to a minimum. Yet, once control of the Allied war effort lay firmly in the American camp, neither US President Roosevelt nor Supreme Allied Commander General Eisenhower were prepared to limit strategic air raids on German-held areas where large numbers of innocent neutral civilians would be killed. In the run-up to D-Day, and afterwards, there was a deliberate policy in both British and American high commands of bombing flat the major towns of Normandy, regardless of civilian casualties.

Total war means that there are no civilians – as the people of Normandy found to their cost during the nightmare years of the Second World War, when their greatest danger came not from the German armies of occupation, but from their British, and later American, allies. The German-occupied ports of Boulogne, Caen, Calais, Cherbourg, Dieppe, Dunkirk, Le Havre and Rouen were all in the front line – a few minutes' flight for fighters from airfields in southern England and not much longer for bombers, which meant that they could carry less fuel and more powerful bomb loads than when bombing targets in the Reich.

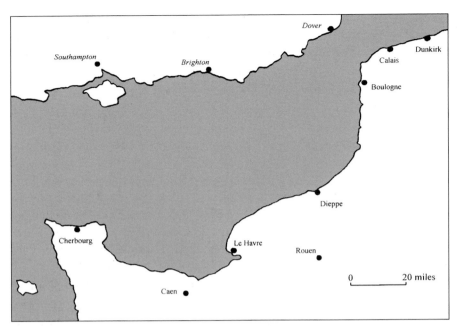

The major French Channel ports.

Throughout recorded history the geographical position of the French Channel ports that brought prosperity in peacetime became a terrible liability in time of hostilities.

Boulogne

Two thousand years ago Boulogne was the home port of *classis britannica* – Rome's northern fleet – and handled most of the traffic between the Continent and Britain, but after the collapse of the Empire the town was repeatedly sacked during the barbarian invasions, most notably by Rollo the Viking during his ninth-century conquest of the duchy of Normandy. William the Bastard's conquest of Britain in 1066 brought a brief prosperity before the town was fought over by Flanders, Ponthieu and Burgundy until Louis XI claimed it for France in 1477.

Three times besieged during the sixteenth century by English forces based in Calais, Boulogne was briefly an English possession until bought back by the French for 400,000 gold écus in 1550. Savage taxation to recover that outlay prompted the Boulonnais to revolt with help from the Spanish Netherlands. The gamble was lost with widespread slaughter and 3,000 survivors were sent to a living death in the galleys. When Napoleon's beady eye settled on the port as an assembly point for his never-happen invasion of England, the harbour was bombarded by the British fleet in a foretaste of 1940.

Caen

Caen's first claim to fame was as the birthplace of William the Conqueror, but after England's King John Lackland lost the duchy, the town was French until re-taken in a bloody struggle by Edward III in 1346. Sustained resistance to their English overlords led to repeated cruel repression of the Caennais, followed by plagues, sieges and sackings. A period of Protestant prosperity was followed by a long decline after the expulsion of the Huguenots. Not until the 14km-long ship canal was constructed in the mid-nineteenth century, linking Caen to the coast at Ouistreham, did the town regain importance.

Calais

The best known of all the ferry ports, Calais was originally a fortified fishing village on an island, besieged by the English for months after the Battle of Crécy in 1346 until starvation obliged the garrison to surrender. Famously, six burghers offered themselves as hostages for the lifting of the siege, but had their lives spared. Duke François of Lorraine captured the town from the English in 1558, after which the region was called *le pays reconquis* – the reconquered land. A brief occupation by Spanish forces from the Netherlands ended with Calais' return to France in 1598. Napoleon assembled part of his invasion fleet there, after which the port was best known in Britain for the cross-Channel sailing packets, to board which Charlotte Brontë had to wait seven days for the weather to permit her crossing on the trip to Brussels with her sister.

In February 1915 Calais had the unenviable distinction of being the first French town to be bombed by German airships, prompting the inhabitants to observe a blackout for the rest of that war. More Zeppelin raids in 1915 and the two following years reflected the importance of the port for the transit of hundreds of thousands of men of the British Expeditionary Force and their equipment.

Cherbourg

The upper town of Cherbourg was an Iron Age hill fort, captured and re-fortified by the Romans. Situated at the tip of the Cotentin peninsula, its natural harbour is protected from all except northerly gales, although Henry II, who welded together the Angevin Empire on both sides of the Channel, preferred to cross to England with his consort Eleanor of Aquitaine from nearby Barfleur, on the lee side of the peninsula. In the Hundred Years War that finally ended the power of the English crown in France, Cherbourg's coveted strategic position meant that it changed hands with much bloodshed six times. After two centuries of relative peace, the English returned to pillage the town in a sneak attack in 1758.

To prevent a recurrence, in 1783 Louis XVI ordered the construction of a major naval base with three seaward-facing forts to defend it. Further expansion was halted by the French Revolution, but Napoleon saw the potential of Cherbourg against his enemies north of the Channel and ordered work on the fortifications to recommence with construction of the long breakwater that created the largest sheltered roadstead in the world.

Dieppe

Dieppe's name probably derives from the Anglo-Saxon *deop*, meaning 'deep'. After 1066 the port prospered from the cross-Channel trade under the Norman and Plantagenet overlords of England. Sacked by the French in 1197, it was sold off by cash-hungry Richard the Lionheart to the Archbishop of Rouen, which did not do his see much good, since Normandy was annexed by France seven years later. After repeated sackings and re-occupations, the town became famous during the Age of Exploration on account of its deepwater captains exploring Africa, the Americas and as far afield as Indonesia.

The revocation of the Edict of Nantes in 1685 saw 3,000 of Dieppe's predominantly Protestant inhabitants compelled to emigrate, many to

England, from the safety of which they may have taken solace in the bombardment and burning of their former hometown by an Anglo–Dutch fleet in 1694. Post-Napoleon, the nineteenth century was more civilised, thanks to Caroline de Bourbon popularising the new fashion of sea-bathing from Dieppe's pebbly beaches. Rushing headlong into tourism with the arrival of a direct railway line from Paris, the Dieppois tore down the old city walls and made their town into one of the first seaside resorts, complete with changing cabins on the beach and the obligatory casino on the seafront to attract the new aristocracy and burgeoning middle classes with money to squander at the tables. British gamblers arriving aboard the newfangled cross-Channel steam packets caused the first golf course in France to be laid out on the cliff top, where they could allay the boredom of afternoons before the casino opened.

Dunkirk

The name Dunkirk is derived from *duyn kerke*, which is Flemish for 'the church in the dunes', around which grew up a lightly fortified herring port in a narrow creek sheltered by the dunes. During the Middle Ages its strategic position saw the port besieged and repeatedly sacked by the Flemings, Burgundians, Austrians, Spaniards, English and French. In 1662 Louis XIV had the port fortified as a base for French privateers attacking merchant vessels beating up-Channel. By the end of the nineteenth century Dunkirk was the third most important port in France, with a large fleet that left each spring for the fishing grounds off Iceland and returned in the autumn, the holds crammed with salted cod – a staple food in the pre-refrigeration kitchen. In the First World War, proximity to the front line saw Dunkirk both bombed and shelled by long-range artillery in 1915 and 1917.

Le Havre

The upper town of Le Havre was, like Cherbourg, an Iron Age hill fort long before the Roman conquest of Gaul when what is now the lower town adjacent to the port was marshland. In the early Middle Ages the modern suburb of Harfleur was a prosperous port-city on the north side of the Seine estuary, besieged by the English under Henry V in 1415 during the

Hundred Years War, providing the platform for one of the most memorable speeches in Shakespeare's plays. King Henry, before Harfleur:

> Once more unto the breach, dear friends, once more –
> or close the wall up with our English dead.
> I see you stand like greyhounds in the slips
> straining upon the start. The game's afoot.
> Follow your spirits and upon this charge.
> Cry 'God for Harry, England and St George!'[2]

Sacked by Henry's forces and with its harbour silting up, Harfleur never recovered its previous importance. In 1517, the reformer king François I kick-started the local economy by ordering the construction of a brand-new port and city around a small chapel dedicated to Notre Dame de Grâce, a short distance to the west of Harfleur. Originally to be grandly titled Franciscopolis, it swiftly became known as Le Havre de Grâce – the haven of grace. Dutch engineers were brought in to drain the marshes, and quick-build timber-framed houses with lath-and-plaster infill sprang up around the chapel.

François' vision was swiftly proven correct. Commanding the estuary of the Seine, leading to the riverine ports at Rouen and Paris, Le Havre was enlarged and fortified by Louis XIV's great military architect Sébastien Vauban. King Louis XV assembled a large fleet there in 1759 for his planned invasion of Britain, as did Napoleon half a century later. Further enlargements to handle bigger vessels during the eighteenth and nineteenth centuries made Le Havre France's premier port for the transatlantic trade and the luxury liner traffic of the twentieth century, as well as a ferry port popular with British tourists crossing to and from Southampton and Portsmouth. In 1939, Le Havre was a major manufacturing centre boasting a population of 164,000 people, for whom the shipbuilding and ship-refitting yards were major employers, as were the trans-Atlantic shipping business, aircraft and automobile factories.

Rouen

Rouen was the second city of the Roman province of Gaul. Decline after the barbarian invasions hit rock-bottom when the town was twice sacked by the Vikings in 841 and 843, but its fortune seemed more secure after Rollo the Viking made it the capital of his duchy in 911 – until a coalition of French, German and Flemish forces saw the town sacked again and its inhabitants slaughtered three decades later.

William the Bastard preferred his native Caen, but did build a castle on an island in the Seine at Rouen to defend this town that was a source of tolls levied on riverine traffic to and from Paris, from which it was only 100km distant as the medieval crow flew. Salt and fish were exported up-river, with wine as the principal export down-river and across the Channel to the English market. In 1150 the merchants of Rouen negotiated their way out of the feudal age by the grant of a charter under which the town was governed by the leading *bourgeois* in organised guilds and trade associations.

The Hundred Years War saw Henry V starve Rouen out in a long siege. Joan the Maid, abandoned by the French to English justice, was imprisoned in the tower that still bears her name and then burned alive as a witch on the Place du Vieux Marché on 30 May 1431 – for which her posthumous reward was to become the patron saint of France, with a statue depicting her dressed in armour adorning nearly every church in France. Recaptured by the French in 1449, Rouen prospered for a century from the import-export trade: wine and grain down-river to Britain; wool and tin up-river to Paris. After the expulsion of the Protestant merchants in 1685, the port went into a decline until the nineteenth century, when the textile trade brought new prosperity. Together with Boulogne, Calais, Dieppe, Dunkirk and Le Havre, Rouen was occupied during the 1870 Franco–Prussian War by German forces, whose advance reached as far south as Tours and Orleans. Far enough behind the front to be spared the fate of French towns occupied or bombarded in the First World War, Rouen and its hinterland nevertheless mourned the death of thousands of men in that conflict. In 1939 it was a prosperous town of 123,000 inhabitants, employed in the port and fluvial traffic, industry and agriculture.

Given their strategic positions on the crossroads of European history that is the English Channel, these northern French ports, so familiar to generations of British travellers as points of embarkation and disembarkation, but little else, have suffered the fortunes of war time and again. Yet, in all the ups and downs of peace and prosperity, bloodshed and brutality over 2,000 years, no desolation was ever so profound as the long nightmare that began for them in the summer of 1940 and lasted, in the case of Dunkirk, for five long and punishing years.

PART 1

DEMORALISATION AND DEFEAT

Chapter 1

Days of desperation

Woken at 01.00hrs on 10 May 1940 to hear the latest intelligence reports from France's north-eastern frontier, where Hitler had been building up his ground and air forces for a massive invasion, the 70-year-old syphilitic French commander-in-chief General Maurice-Gustave Gamelin muttered, 'Take no action,' and went back to sleep. History does not record the wakefulness or otherwise of commanders closer to the impending action, like the C-in-C of the British Expeditionary Force (BEF) General Lord John Gort at his HQ in the Château de Habarcq near Arras, nor that of General Blanchard, commanding the French 1st Army Group, under whose orders Gort was placed.

None of the several million men massed on the German side of the Rhine had much sleep that night. With his eastern frontiers secured for the moment by the Ribbentrop–Molotov Non-Aggression Pact signed before his unprovoked attack on Poland in September 1939, Adolf Hitler had deployed on Germany's western frontiers no less than 135 divisions, including twelve *Panzer* divisions with 2,439 tanks. Close support of these ground troops was to be provided by 3,369 warplanes of the *Luftwaffe*, back to strength after losing thirty per cent of its aircraft in the invasion of Poland.[1]

Facing them were 104 French divisions and the fifteen divisions of the BEF, plus significant reserves. This should have been sufficient to fight a defensive action in prepared positions, without counting the armies of neutral Belgium – through which the German advance was planned to drive – and Holland, the conquest of which was necessary to secure the right flank of Hitler's attack.

The British government of Neville Chamberlain had promised to assist the defence of France by building up the BEF to thirty-two, and eventually, forty-five, divisions – but not before 1941 at the earliest![2] Did Chamberlain think that Hitler would delay the start of the war he planned to give the Allies a sporting chance? With the French government calling up 4,725,350 French reservists in September 1939 to swell the ranks of its 800,000-strong standing army – the largest in Europe – as against 394,165 men in the BEF, many French political and military leaders thought that Britain was under-committed to the alliance in terms of both manpower and equipment on the ground in France. When nothing happened in the months of the phoney war that the French called *la drôle de guerre* and the Germans *der Sitzkrieg*, hundreds of thousands of conscripts from rural areas of France were sent home to prepare the land for the coming year's harvests.

It is not true that the French General Staff placed *all* its faith in the Maginot Line – the chain of technically impressive and allegedly impregnable concrete fortifications that ran from the Swiss frontier opposite Basel northward along the left bank of the Rhine and then north-westward to Montmédy on the frontier with Belgium. However, both British and French general staffs refused to accept that modern weaponry had changed the nature of military conflict from static slogging matches to *Blitzkrieg* – the new warfare made possible by fast-moving armoured columns with integrated air support. Politicians and generals on both sides of the Channel had been persistently deaf to the vociferous protests of a few rebel officers like Colonel Charles De Gaulle, who advocated grouping tanks in mobile columns with their own motorized artillery and close air support. Both the RAF and the French Air Force considered that integration of their fighter arms with ground forces would be an unacceptable subordination to the 'brown jobs', even after Hitler's invasion of Poland proved its terrible efficiency.

Making matters worse in France, forty-one of the best French infantry divisions were immobilised in and behind the Maginot Line, with only thirty-nine divisions plus the BEF on the 300-mile stretch from the western end of the Line to the Channel coast. Of these, twelve infantry and four *horsed* cavalry divisions were tasked with holding the least fortified stretch east and west of Sedan, where the German armies had broken through in 1870 and 1914. General André Georges Corap, commanding 9th Army in that sector, repeatedly protested that he was critically short of men and material, which were pointlessly immobilised in the Maginot Line sector. However, Gamelin stuck obstinately to his

3

conviction that there was no need to reinforce 9th Army because the hilly, forested area of the Ardennes to the north of Sedan was impassable for German mechanised troops.

Accordingly, the defenders on this crucial stretch of the frontier were largely second-rate divisions rotated so often that officers neither knew their men nor which units were on their flanks, while the conscripts they commanded were less acquainted with weaponry than with the picks and shovels they had been issued to construct blockhouses and trenches in a hopeless endeavour to extend the Line westwards in a race against the clock. Here, too, ninety per cent of French artillery pieces dated from the First World War and the troops in the sector of Sedan itself had not a single anti-tank gun capable of stopping a *Panzer* in 1940.[3]

After Gamelin awoke later on 10 May to learn that the German attack had begun at 04.30hrs, the French 7th Army under General Giraud advanced according to plan from its positions on the Channel coast, with

French commanding generals Weygand (left) and Gamelin (right).

the BEF and Blanchard's 1st Army moving up alongside until they reached the Dyle River in Belgium. This move had not been permitted earlier by the Belgian government because they thought it would jeopardise Belgian neutrality – as though Hitler was likely to be deterred by that! Like many ideas that look good on paper or a sand table, yet fail miserably in practice, the new Dyle Line had no effect on the German advance because it was in the wrong place.

In the north, General Fedor von Bock's Army Group B drove on several axes into Holland, forcing the Dutch army back to the coast, after which the terror-bombing of Rotterdam caused the Dutch queen to surrender and flee with her family to Britain. In the south, General Wilhelm von Leeb's German Army Group C stayed opposite the Maginot Line to inhibit any move by the French to re-deploy its enormous garrison. The key to the success of the German master plan was Field Marshal Gerd von Rundstedt's Army Group A, placed in the centre of the three-pronged attack. This comprised more than 1.5 million men and 1,500 tanks in forty-four divisions, with twenty-seven more in reserve. In a classic, fast-moving *Panzer* operation with close air support, planned by General Erich von Manstein, seven armoured divisions drove into Luxemburg and Belgium, aiming at the weakest point in the Franco–British line: Sedan.

Panic in Downing Street saw Chamberlain resigning that evening and Winston Churchill installed as prime minister of a government of national unity. Forty-eight hours later, the German spearheads were across the Franco–Belgian frontier, causing a rout on either side of their advance which made imperative a rapid retreat from the Dyle Line by the French and British forces there, if they were not to be completely cut off.

Hermann Goering's *Luftwaffe* had blown the Polish air force out of the sky the previous year. Neutralising the largely obsolete 1,562 aircraft of the French air force was no harder. From grass runways in outdated aircraft using 70 or 87 octane fuel, the French pilots took off with little but courage and a willingness to die for their country against the battle-tested *Luftwaffe's* cutting-edge Junkers Ju 87 Stuka dive-bombers and Willy Messerschmitt's Bf 109 – then the fastest aircraft in the world. Against these, only the few Dewoitine D-520s and some Hawker Hurricanes among the RAF aircraft of the Advanced Air Striking Force in France stood a chance, for they alone had the speed and manoeuvrability to engage the German aircraft with any hope of success.

After rapidly establishing air superiority, on 13 May more than 1,000 *Luftwaffe* dive-bombers flew a total of 3,940 missions against the French positions on the south bank of the River Meuse, driving back the defenders so that assault troops could cross the river on inflatable boats and rafts. The following day, Guderian's tanks widened the Sedan bridgehead and beat off French counterattacks. On 15 May they were through into open country, swinging westward towards the Channel coast and making nearly fifty miles that day. The sheer speed of this advance caused the German High Command – *Oberkommando der Wehrmacht* (OKW) – to call a brief halt for infantry and supplies to catch up. With more German armour crossing the Meuse down-river from Sedan, the breach in the Allied front was nearly sixty miles wide.

A few individual French commanders like De Gaulle achieved local successes by individual initiative and courage. Elsewhere, panic paralysed the chain of command, with Gamelin informing Prime Minister Paul Reynaud that Paris could fall in less than three days. Generals being sacked all round, Reynaud recalled from French-occupied Syria General Maxime Weygand, who alone seemed a better bet than the demoralised Gamelin, but Weygand could not get back to France before 19 May, by which time the game was lost.

After the *Panzers* of the two northern thrusts re-grouped and swung southwards, they poured through the weakest point in the centre of the Allied line. The German bridgeheads across the Meuse leaving him with an unprotected right flank, Lord Gort judged the Battle of France lost, and considered that the only intelligent course of action was to save as much of the BEF as possible by withdrawing to the coast in the hope of evacuation before the line of retreat was cut. Orders from London obliged him to counter-attack at Arras, but this did no more than momentarily alarm OKW. Guderian's *Panzers* reached the Channel coast near Abbeville on 20 May in a drive that squeezed the outflanked Belgian, British and French forces westwards against the sea, before swinging north to cut them off from the only accessible evacuation ports.

Gort's men nearly missed the boat, literally. Nearing the port of Dunkirk on 24 May, with every prospect of shortly taking a half-million or more prisoners, Guderian received an order, endorsed by Hitler, to withdraw and take up positions outside the town. The order was sent by radio unencoded and was thus picked up by BEF monitors.[4] Historians disagree on the reasons. Some believe that it was to avoid humiliating

Lord Gort indicating to Lt Gen Pownall troop movements on a map at HQ British Expeditionary Force in France.

the British, with whom Hitler still wanted to make peace; others argue that the German tanks were badly in need of maintenance after covering the whole distance from the German frontier on their tracks; others still think that Goering wanted a free hand for the *Luftwaffe* to claim the glory of wiping out Gort's now desperate force. If the last is true, this was the first of a number of critical times when Hitler's trust in Goering proved grossly misplaced.

Despite the horror stories of German atrocities during the invasion of 1914, there were relatively few excesses this time. One took place at Aubigny-en-Artois, between Arras and Boulogne. On 21 and 22 May 1940 the SS Division *Totenkopf* wiped out a small British force defending Aubigny. Suspecting the locals of having helped the British, they selected ninety-eight men and women, the youngest being a boy of sixteen – and shot them at 20.00hrs in a quarry outside the village. On 23 May, they compelled the survivors to bury their victims. Another twenty civilians were shot nearby, for reasons unknown.

When Lucien Vadez, mayor of Calais, was called up in September 1939, he was replaced by 60-year-old regional councillor André Gerschel, who ran a clothes shop in the town. He was a decorated veteran, several times wounded in the First World War and, although strongly left-wing, steered the town quietly through the *drôle de guerre* by persuading the councillors to forget their previous political differences. After the Germans entered Calais on 26 May 1940 he continued to exercise his functions until arrested on 7 July 1940 and locked up in the soon-to-be-infamous prison at Loos-lès-Lille for three months. After release, he returned to his shop, which had been looked after meantime by his wife Odette.

Warned that he risked more serious problems under Vichy's anti-Jewish laws of October 1940, Gerschel fled to Brittany, from where he managed to cross into the unoccupied part of France with false papers, *en route* to the home of relatives in Nice. All was in vain. Once the Germans invaded the Free Zone in November 1942, it was only a matter of days before Gerschel, his wife and her 8-year-old daughter were caught in a routine comb-out. On 11 November 1942 – the twenty-fourth anniversary of the end of the war in which he had suffered so much as an infantryman – they were deported to Auschwitz and death. As a gesture of the town's respect, both his name and that of Odette were symbolically placed on the list of candidates in the postwar municipal elections.

Having been occupied by Guderian's *Panzers* on 25 May 1940, Boulogne had the unwelcome distinction of being the first French town to be bombed by the RAF – on 12 June, while France and Britain were still allies combating the German advance. At 16.53hrs precisely that afternoon, people in the town centre, watching what they thought was a flight of friendly planes bearing the familiar RAF roundels, saw the bomb-bay doors open and bombs falling towards them. The casualty figures were not impressive compared with later raids, but the count of fourteen dead and eighteen injured severely enough to need hospitalisation took the town by surprise. RAF aircraft, flown by British and Polish crews, returned on 18 July and three times in September, with high-explosive bombs weighing up to 500lbs.

Further west along the coast, the geographical situation that had made Le Havre France's great shipbuilding and ship-repair centre and its main transatlantic port, twinned with Southampton, became a terrible liability throughout the occupation. In an attempt to prevent British reinforcements being landed there, the *Luftwaffe* bombed the harbour on 19 and 20 May 1940 during the *Blitzkrieg* invasion of France. During and after the evacuation from Dunkirk, the *Luftwaffe* returned to strafe and bomb the port of Le Havre on 3 and 12 June to interdict its use for further evacuations of British and French troops.

On 28 May Belgium surrendered, prompting this report in the following day's *Manchester Guardian* from its correspondent with the BEF:

> The latest news of the B.E.F in France is extremely grave. It had always been obvious, even before the defection of the Belgian king, that the British force was running risks of encirclement in its heroic efforts to keep the Somme–Arras gap as narrow as possible. It now seems likely that we shall pay heavily in British lives for King Leopold's action. We have to face the fact that the possibility of withdrawing the B.E.F from its present position is small, and the abandonment by the Belgians of their position on its eastern flank has left Dunkirk (the B.E.F.'s port of evacuation) in grave danger of falling to the Germans. The situation is now so clear that military reasons need no longer impose silence. Nothing that we say today can be of the slightest value to the enemy. It is difficult to see how the Germans can be prevented from capturing Dunkirk and cutting off the B.E.F completely. In modern warfare, as all of us now know too late, two things are essential, armoured vehicles and the co-operation of low-flying 'planes. (The B.E.F.) did not have enough 'planes and we did not have nearly enough tanks.[5]

The evacuation from Dunkirk was largely made possible by the 'little ships' owned by weekend sailors, and manned partly by them and partly by Royal Navy ratings, which ferried men out to larger vessels that took them across the Channel. It began under sustained *Luftwaffe* strafing on 26 May. Dunkirk harbour being rendered largely unusable by German bombs, thousands of British, French and Belgian soldiers continued embarking directly onto Royal Navy vessels by clambering along the damaged breakwater, shielded by smoke screens. Elsewhere, men threw away all their equipment and waded out to sea along the corpse-strewn ten-mile stretch of beach within the perimeter, hoping to be picked up by small craft and ferried out to Royal Navy ships, cross-Channel ferries and other large craft standing off-shore. By 4 June, when the evacuation ended, 198,000 British and 140,000 French and Belgian troops had been saved at the cost of abandoning all their heavy equipment in the Dunkirk pocket.

The evacuation was a military miracle, producing such euphoria in Britain that Churchill had to remind Parliament 'not to ascribe to this deliverance the character of a victory (because) wars are not won by evacuations'.[6] Nor are they won by guarding women prisoners, as British ambulance driver Bessy Myers was told by a charming German officer who entertained her and another British girl to a bully-beef dinner with his staff after the Wehrmacht spearheads had swept past them in northern France. The two girls were initially left free to help German and French medical staff care for the wounded of both sides in field hospitals – including an RAF and a *Luftwaffe* pilot, who had managed to shoot each other down. It was all unreal – the word she used to describe the villages through which she drove before the Germans arrived:

> People have left doors and windows open, the streets are littered with objects discarded at the last moment, and there is a general appearance of desolation. We come out on the road where we think we have left the ambulance. To begin with, we do not recognise the road at all, as it is packed, jammed, jammed, packed with soldiers, sheep, carts, refugees, cows, military cars and soldiers on motor-cycles – a never-ending stream of them, some in lorries, trying to force a way through this congestion of humanity and animals.[7]

A further 220,000 Allied troops were subsequently evacuated by British and French vessels from the ports of Cherbourg, Saint-Malo, Brest and Saint-Nazaire. For the thousands left behind in the rearguards with no chance of evacuation – and for the 1.5 million French soldiers cut off, or about to be cut off, by the German advance – prospects were grim. After capture at Dunkirk, Guardsman Terence Prettie and some companions managed to escape from a column of British POWs being marched to captivity in Germany. In several days on the run before re-capture, they experienced the gamut of civilian attitudes. One Belgian refugee told them to give themselves up because the Germans would treat them well; other homeless Belgian refugees insisted on sharing their precious last chocolate bars; a French farmer fed and sheltered the forlorn group despite a foraging party of *Wehrmacht* men politely requisitioning supplies at the same time; a priest procured for them charts and tide tables in the hope they could find a seaworthy boat that had not been confiscated by the Germans, but all to no avail.[8]

When German armoured spearheads reached the coast at Fécamp, just 28km north-east of Le Havre, on 11 June, encircling a pocket of 12,000 Allied troops, including a British general, the military commandant of Le Havre, Admiral Gaudin de Villaine, decided that it was impossible to defend the town. Following the example of national and local authorities all over France, he ordered his troops to leave and proclaimed a general evacuation, panicking thousands of Havrais into fleeing the enemy by any means possible. With trains overcrowded and timetables completely unreliable, several hundred people of all ages headed for the port, hoping for a ship on which they might take passage westwards, away from the approaching enemy.

The collier *Niobe* had been commandeered and loaded with arms and ammunition for delivery by sea to the front line troops on the Belgian border, but with the evacuation from Dunkirk ending on 4 June, the voyage was abandoned and *Niobe* returned to Le Havre in the morning of 11 June, where her captain took on board 800 of the desperate people waiting on the quayside. Given the urgency of the moment, no one apparently considered first unloading the lethal cargo stowed below decks.

At 14.30hrs *Niobe* slipped her moorings and headed cautiously for Caen via the swept channel between the minefields. Reaching the open sea, the passengers realised that they had jumped from the frying pan into the fire. On all sides, warships and merchant vessels were being attacked by German aircraft. Ships that had been bombed and holed were limping coastwards in the hope of beaching before they sank. At 16.55hrs a Stuka dive-bombed *Niobe*, its first bomb exploding on the port side of the quarter-deck. The second bomb penetrated into the hold full of munitions, which then exploded in a virtually simultaneous chain reaction, cutting the vessel in two. The combined blast was so powerful that a ship one kilometre distant was struck so violently by the shock wave travelling through the water that the crew thought they had run aground. Steaming to the rescue, they found only flotsam, empty lifebelts and just nine men, a girl and one small child clinging to the debris.

With the Germans so close, Le Havre's Jewish mayor Léon Meyer resigned on 13 June, not wishing to cause problems between the Germans and the city which he had managed for twenty-one years.[9] Less than twenty-four hours later, motorised elements of the German 15th Army entered the city at 08.00hrs. Immediately, their follow-up troops set about strengthening the defence lines around the city and port which had been dug and built by British and French troops during the phoney war. They re-dug the anti-tank ditches three metres deep and seven metres wide, added minefields and flooded the valley of the River Lézarde for 13km as part of the perimeter defences. On the coastal cliffs and the plateaux of Caucriaumont and Aplemont north of the lower town they constructed casemates for a battery of captured French 155mm guns with ranges of up to 35km, pointing seawards, of course – plus batteries of 94mm and 88mm anti-aircraft guns.

Reynaud's government meanwhile fled first to Tours and then Bordeaux, choked with the hundreds of thousands crossing the River Garonne on the town's single bridge. There, it discussed what to do with the thousands of 20-year-old males who had been called up on 9 and 10 June. Happily some sane person pointed out that there were neither uniforms for them to wear nor weapons for them to fire. One of the young conscripts, a friend of the author, was actually given a uniform, but no one could find him a rifle. He was discharged after a week, entitled to the Mobilisation Medal, sent to him by a grateful government forty-five years later!

Flying several times to France in attempts to stiffen the resolve of the French cabinet, Churchill had little to offer in the way of support, it having

British Prime Minister Winston Churchill.

12

already been decided that the RAF should be withdrawn from France, because it would be needed for the inevitable aerial confrontation that was to become the Battle of Britain. Although Weygand still had 2 million men under arms in the area of conflict, French losses of 92,000 dead and more than 200,000 wounded – against German losses half as severe – meant that Reynaud's cabinet was divided on whether they should fight on or surrender. Six wanted to fight on; thirteen saw the situation as so hopeless that the only sensible thing was to sue for an armistice. That was exactly the advice of the new C-in-C, General Weygand, and of France's most famous soldier, the First World War hero, 84-year-old Marshal Philippe Pétain.[10] Taking over as prime minister after Reynaud's resignation on 16 June, his first act was to ask Berlin via Madrid for an armistice.

Less than three months earlier, on 28 March, the British and French prime ministers had signed an agreement not to negotiate peace terms unilaterally, but Reynaud had signed without the consent of his cabinet, which made his signature unconstitutional and therefore not binding. In any case, the French argued, Britain had not fully committed the RAF at any stage during the campaign and had withdrawn the BEF from France without consultation. On both sides of the Channel there was bitterness, with the British claiming that the French had 'lacked the will to fight' and the French retorting that the British had 'fought to the last drop of French blood before running away'.

In his radio address to the nation on 17 June, the day after becoming head of government, Pétain spoke of the French army's struggle as being 'worthy of its long military tradition, against an enemy stronger in numbers and equipment'.[11] This was a blatant lie: the Allies had enjoyed a numerical advantage and Pétain well knew that it was bad generalship and seven years of political vacillation and vote-catching in France and in Britain, while Germany prepared single-mindedly for war, that had caused the humiliating and costly defeat.

Few people in France actually heard acting general Charles De Gaulle – his substantive rank was colonel – broadcast a call on the following day over the BBC French Service to continue the fight against the invader. Although the text was afterwards circulated clandestinely by leaflets and re-printed in a number of newspapers in areas not occupied by the Germans, fewer still took any immediate action – usually with fatal consequences. In Rouen, the ancient capital of Normandy, Etienne Achavanne was shot on 6 July for cutting a German field telephone line

13

General De Gaulle in 1940.

during a British air raid. For the same offence, two other men were shot on 3 September at Epinal and 7 September at Royan. That was deliberate sabotage, but 'disrespect to the German uniform' was also a capital offence. On 24 August in Bordeaux a Polish–Jewish refugee named Israel Karp shook his fist at the drum-major of a German band, for which he was executed by firing squad three days later.

Commanding the 7th *Panzer* Division, which took the town and port of Cherbourg on 19 June 1940, General Erwin Rommel wrote home to his wife afterwards, 'The war seems to be turning into a peaceful occupation. The population is calm and, in places, friendly.'[12] As they were also in the Channel Islands, demilitarised by London as impossible to defend.[13]

14

Chapter 2

How to kill a republic

To cover up those leaders' guilt for the rout of the army, the destruction of the air force and the disintegration of civil administration, politicians and generals as high as Pétain himself claimed that the Germans had infiltrated trained squads of Swiss and Belgian Nazis who could pass themselves off as French. This invented fifth column – for which there was never any evidence – was alleged to have sown defeatism and confusion among the soldiery and ordered civilians to leave their homes *en masse*, producing the chaos on the roads that prevented any coordinated troop movements to counter the German breakthrough at Sedan.

The real reason for the defeatism of French soldiers was a total collapse of discipline once the incompetence of their leaders was blatantly revealed. Two British volunteer ambulance drivers, Denis Freeman and Douglas Cooper, were stopped north of Paris by a French general trying to rally some troops. He asked whether the two Britons had any maps he could borrow. A general without a map! It was unreal.[1]

All over occupied France, jingoistic posters that had been put up during the *drôle de guerre* promising victory 'because we are the stronger' were swiftly covered up by German posters, printed before the invasion in several languages, of a smiling *Wehrmacht* warrior carrying a small child with two others looking at him trustingly.

Although the language of the caption varied throughout the occupied countries, the message was always the same. In France, it read, *Populations abandonnées, faîtes confiance au soldat allemand!* Abandoned by your leaders, trust the German soldier! Unlikely as that was, who else was worthy of trust at such a time?

As to the mass flight of the millions of refugees, this was provoked by orders from local and regional government. The long columns of refugees

15

passed through town after town and village after village, heading south and west. They came in waves. Firstly rich women in chauffeur-driven cars, then middle-class families in overcrowded saloons, many with mattresses strapped to the roof, as though these would protect the passengers against machine gun bullets. These were followed by workers in old cars or trade vehicles, borrowed or stolen. Peasants worrying about the livestock they had left behind came on carts pulled by weary horses and oxen, reacquainting town-dwellers with the forgotten smell of manure in the streets. Lastly came the poor: pushing prams and wheelbarrows, in which were what few possessions they had and often a child or elderly relative who could not walk. As to where they were going, few had any clear idea of a destination: they were just going *away* as fast as their means allowed.

As the last refugees passed through a half-empty Paris, the sky was black with smoke from the huge petroleum dumps on the outskirts, fired to prevent their use by the Germans. Some houses nearby caught fire by accident, but there were no firemen to combat the flames because they had all obeyed orders to leave ahead of the flood of refugees. Fear of the enemy behind was soon replaced by fear of the one above, with Stukas deliberately dive-bombing convoys and strafing the long columns of adults and children with the aim of provoking such panic on the roads that no French military traffic could progress to the shifting front against the roiling tide of human misery.

One of the French pilots who survived the defeat, to die later in the war, was Antoine de St-Exupéry, author of *The Little Prince*. In his record of summer 1940, published as *Flight to Arras*, he described the scene from the air and on the ground:

> I can see from my plane the long swarming highways, that interminable syrup (of people) flowing endless to the horizon. The inhabitants of the war zone are being evacuated. This, at any rate, is the official version. But it is no longer true. There is a crazy contagion in this exodus. Where are they going? They have no notion. They are going south, but southward there are only villages filled to bursting, men and women sleeping in sheds, stocks of food running out. Scarcely does this caravan come up to an oasis than it ceases to be an oasis, bursts its bonds and pours into the caravan. Faster than the exodus, the enemy moves. Here and there (German) armoured cars roll past the stream. Whole German divisions flounder in this stew.
>
> Only three days earlier, I had seen the village in which we were billeted go to pieces. Coming out of our billet, we found ourselves in the midst of chaos. All the stables, sheds, barns and garages had vomited into the narrow streets a most extraordinary collection of conveyances. There were new motor–cars, and there were ancient farm carts that for half a century had stood untouched under the layers of dust.

There were hay-wains and lorries, carry-alls and tumbrils. Had we seen a mail coach in this maze, it would not have astonished us. Every box on wheels was laden with the treasures of the home. Wrapped in bedsheets sagging with hernias, the treasures that had made up a home were being piled in.

We were staring at sheep who were off in an immense clatter of mechanical equipment. The grate, the grind, the clank of this machinery. Water boiling up in the radiator already. And slowly, laboriously, this caravan of doom stirs into movement without spare parts, without petrol, without spare tyres, without a mechanic. They are mad![2]

Such was the chaos that, after a record 1,212 million francs were withdrawn, the savings banks put up their shutters, provoking more panic. Top officials of the Finance Ministry, finding themselves stuck near Saumur with the Germans fast approaching, paid a street-cleaner on a monthly wage of 400 francs to burn banknotes to the value of 25 million francs. After the Nord *département* was cut off from the rest of France by the German advance, its *Préfet* Fernand Carles demanded several million francs from central government for the immediate needs of his population. The money was loaded aboard two Glenn-Martin aircraft of a new model, whose silhouette was not recognised as friendly by a British ack-ack battery near Lille. The planes were blasted out of the sky; of the six crewmen only one managed to parachute to safety through whirling clouds of banknotes. Millions were lost, Carles eventually signing a receipt for only 240,000 francs.[3]

The most bizarre episode in this wholesale evacuation was set in motion by Minister of the Interior Georges Mandel. He decided that the detainees in the military sections of the capital's two main prisons at Cherche-Midi and La Santé must be moved south so that Communist activists still at liberty could not take advantage of the chaos during the German advance on Paris to rescue their imprisoned comrades. On 10 June the order was given to evacuate the prisoners, initially to Orleans. With no prison transport and public transport completely disrupted, for part of the way the 1,865 prisoners had to march in the midsummer heat, guarded by armed warders and gendarmes. Near Montargis, with the Loire still distant, thirteen or more prisoners who had not the strength to continue were shot out of hand, on the argument that they might, if left alive, give useful information to the enemy. When the column arrived at Bordeaux, ten more men were taken away to be shot – one of them a boy of seventeen – before the nightmare journey continued for the others to the concentration camp at Gurs.[4]

Even that was but a respite. Under Vichy, criminals were released after serving their sentences but political prisoners were kept in preventive detention, as being too dangerous to return to normal life. The number of inmates of French prisons and concentration camps rose from 18,000 in September 1939 to 55,000 in December 1943. Nor were these prisoners safe behind bars because, once the hostage ordinances came into effect, any political prisoner still in detention could arbitrarily be selected for the firing squad in retaliation for a crime that he could not possibly have committed. A total of 2,445 prisoners serving sentences and 1,598 held in preventive detention in this way were handed over to German military justice.[5] But nobody in France was worrying about the long-term future in June 1940, when the main preoccupations were somewhere to sleep and food in one's belly.

Paris having been declared an open city to the advancing Germans, Lieutenant-Colonel Hans Speidel – later to be commander of NATO Land Forces, Central Europe – accepted the surrender of the capital from two French officers at 05.30hrs on 14 June and drove into the city centre without meeting any resistance after travelling through a landscape where crops were ripening in fields abandoned by the farmers and bellowing cows with distended udders were being milked by German soldiers, to give them some relief. He found the streets empty. More than half of the normal 5 million inhabitants had fled and those remaining stayed nervously indoors behind closed shutters.

Closely on the heels of the *Wehrmacht* came Hitler's secret police. On the day following the surrender, a *Gestapo* officer ordered Jean Chiappe, Paris' *Préfet de Police*, to hand over the files of the *Renseignements Généraux* (RG) – equivalent of the British Special Branch – covering foreigners, Jews, spies and Communists. The cupboard was bare, the files 300km away in the Rhône valley. Overtaken by the enemy at Roanne, the RG officers transporting them on two canal barges sank one and refloated it after the German forces had moved on, afterwards requisitioning a disused factory, in which to dry the files carefully, sheet by sheet.[6] Despite their efforts, the files eventually came into the *Gestapo*'s hands after it was agreed by Pétain that the French police services would collaborate fully – in many cases, enthusiastically – with the *Gestapo* in repressing anti-German activities throughout France, leaving the *Feldgendarmerie* – German military police – to deal only with discipline and protection of German personnel.[7]

In the occupied areas, German army chaplains said Mass in churches for congregations whose own priests had fled. The litany being in Latin, the only difference was in the celebrants' accents. From soul food to real food: after empty stomachs got the better of fearful minds, hundreds of thousands of starving civilians queued up for soup and bread at German field kitchens. German bands played in the parks and public spaces – usually some marches, a little Wagner and a token French composition, such as an extract from Bizet's *Carmen*.

There were a few rapes and robberies at gunpoint in isolated places as the infantry and support troops arrived. Elsewhere, especially in towns where the *Feldgendarmie* patrolled, polite soldiers in field grey insisted on paying for their purchases in the shops still open, albeit with German money. This was declared legal tender in the armistice agreement at the rate of 20 francs for one German mark, approximately double its real value. Anyone with anything to sell to the smiling invaders, who had for years been on the Goering diet of *guns, not butter*, had a field day. Perfume, fine wine, silk stockings and dresses headed east in parcels addressed to girlfriends and wives, but so also did cheese and butter. A joke of the time had two English officers on the run in Paris disguising themselves in *Wehrmacht* uniforms. Arrested by German military police and accused of being spies, they asked how they had been detected. 'It was easy,' their captors replied. 'You were the only ones not carrying parcels.'

For the café proprietor and restaurateur, the new arrivals were the only clients with money. It was 'business as usual' also in bed. The *Wehrmacht*'s no-nonsense policy of registering licensed sex-workers and instituting weekly medical examinations avoided the epidemic of syphilis and gonorrhoea that followed the arrival of American troops in 1944. Different brothels were reserved for officers and other ranks. The rules to be observed by the madams were also strict: no Jewesses or coloured girls, condoms obligatory and off-duty snooping to ensure the girls did not work 'on the side'. On leaving a brothel, all ranks were given a card bearing the establishment's stamp, the date and the girl's working name, for medical follow-up if necessary. Thousands of bar-girls and street women had to carry a bilingual ID card permitting them to accept only German customers. They were also regularly checked.[8] Unlicensed women who gave a German soldier VD risked six months in prison. Military personnel were forbidden to have any personal relationship with whores, to divulge personal details or exchange photographs. A loophole in German law that exempted brothel-keepers in the Occupied Zone from tax would be slammed shut after the Liberation when the French taxman insisted on collecting four years' arrears – with interest, of course.[9]

The armistice agreement was signed at Rethondes in the evening of 22 June, after several hours of 'negotiations', in which every French suggestion was greeted with *Nein!* It was finally signed only minutes before the German deadline. That evening, Pétain said on the radio, 'The conditions are severe, but at least our honour is saved. The government remains free and France will be governed only by a French government.'

That was another lie, because he knew that the armistice terms were not 'honourable', but rather Hitler's savage revenge for the humiliation imposed on Germany by the Versailles Treaty of 28 June 1919 – which was itself the French revenge for the harsh demands of the German victors in the Franco–Prussian war 1870–71.

The guns finally fell silent on 25 June[10] as the agreement came into force, *inter alia* requiring the defeated nation to pay an occupation tax

French head of state
Marshal Pétain.

21

of 400 million francs *per day*, allegedly to cover the expenses of the German forces in France. In the event, this money covered such items as rent for requisitioned buildings and vessels, surgical equipment, food for the troops and their draught animals, purchases of foodstuffs sent to Germany and brothels for the exclusive use of the occupation forces.

Thousands of tons of wine and foodstuffs were shipped to Germany in railway trucks that never returned, together with the machinery of entire factories, oil refineries and rolling mills. The initial rigid curfew imposed between 22.00hrs and 05.00hrs was soon relaxed, to start at 23.00hrs and then midnight, as a reward for the population's good behaviour.[11] Another German ordinance imposed punishments for people who failed to keep the space in front of their houses tidy and weed-free. Clocks had to be put forward an hour, so that France was running on Berlin time. To have a semblance of local government through which to administer the occupied areas, the *Wehrmacht* appointed provisional mayors and councillors from the residents who had not fled. Many were reluctant to take this first step towards collaboration until it was made clear that the alternative was a spell in prison.

The caravan of politicians and civil servants that was the national government finally arrived on 1 July in Vichy, a smart spa town in central France. Some guessed that it had been selected because it suited a politician named Pierre Laval, whose home was only twenty kilometres distant. Others more poetic averred that it was because its famous Celestins spring was the only one in the world that gushed water tasting exactly like tears. The true reason was that Foreign Minister Paul Baudouin suggested Vichy to the Marshal because the prosperous spa resort had a modern telephone exchange, a direct railway link with Paris and 15,000 bedrooms in its hotels that could accommodate all the politicians, ministry staffs and hangers-on. Such is the stigma of having been the capital of collaboration that more than a half-century later few people want to be seen taking the cure there and many hotels never re-opened after the war.

All those bedrooms barely sufficed to house and afford office space for a government that historian Robert Aron described as 'a comic opera government adrift in a cataclysm'.[12] Politicians and top civil servants had to use their bedrooms as offices. The secretary of the one-eyed Minister for Ex-servicemen Xavier Vallat took dictation sitting on his bidet. Files were stacked in open drawers between Monsieur's underpants and Madame's lingerie. The chairman of a meeting would get up from time to time to pump up the pressure of the paraffin-fuelled camping stove atop the dressing table, on which the vegetables for lunch were being cooked. Nobody at first worried that most of the hotels habitually closed for the winter season and had no heating systems, because Article 3 of the armistice agreement was optimistically taken to mean that the government would be returning to Paris before Christmas. Four terrible years were to pass before it did.

On 8 July Dr Karl Schaeffer was appointed co-director of Banque de France *ex-officio* as Director of the *Bankenaufsichtsamt*, in which capacity he oversaw *all* French banks, with powers to access and freeze any account. Resistance to what is today normal state intrusion in the banking sector vanished after twelve senior managers of Crédit Lyonnais were imprisoned for attempting to protect clients' accounts from scrutiny.[13] Schaeffer also appointed commissioners to run the Jewish- and British-owned banks in France. Unlike many occupation institutions, his operation was highly efficient, requiring only two German officials to police 80,000 compliant bank employees, thanks to what Schaeffer recalled postwar as generous hospitality offered by, and good personal relationships with, the directors of most of the major banks during his time in France.

However, Schaeffer's attempt to seize all the foreign currency in France for the Reich failed when the Bank of England swiftly invalidated all its banknotes held abroad, unless stamped by a British Consulate before a certain date, with the numbers duly noted. His next move was to open up the safe-deposit boxes of British citizens and confiscate the contents. French citizens needing to open their boxes could only do so in the presence of an official of the *Bankenaufsichtsamt* or another German officer. Family heirlooms were not seized but uncut gems and shares in foreign companies were 'taken into protective custody'.

Starting 9 July, bookshops all over France displayed a cheap French edition of *Mein Kampf* rushed into production by Parisian publisher Mercure de France. On the same day in Vichy 395 *députés* and 229 senators took the first step in making themselves redundant for the next four years by voting to amend the Constitution. Only three *députés* and one senator voted against. After sixty-five years' existence, the Third Republic was being laid to rest, complete with eulogy from one senator, acknowledging that its Constitution had made France a free country. It was, he said, not the Constitution that had failed, but rather its guardians who had not done their duty. They were just about to prove his point.

On 10 July beneath a cloudless sky and a burning sun, 666 soberly dressed *deputés* and senators passed through the massive police cordon holding off a crowd of the curious outside the 1,450-seater opera house of Vichy for a joint secret session. There were no women present, for not until 1944 would they gain the right to stand for public office, or even vote, in France.

Did anyone in the opera house that day remember the text of the Book of Revelation 13:18? *Here is wisdom. Let him that hath understanding count the number of the beast: for it is the number of a man; and his number is six hundred threescore and six.*

One who should have been familiar with the Old Testament was Léon Blum, France's first Socialist and first Jewish premier, the policies of whose Popular Front coalition government of 1936–7 had contributed significantly to the fatal unpreparedness for war. Looking around at his fellow parliamentarians being alternately wooed and threatened by the rhetoric of the charismatic barrister and *député* Pierre Laval, self-appointed gravedigger of the Republic, Blum saw 'all the courage and integrity one knew certain men possessed disappear before my eyes, corroded and dissolved in a human swamp'.[14] As so often when hundreds are confused, one man who knows exactly what he wants to do can win them all over to his side. Thus it was that Laval manoeuvred all the assembled representatives of the people into ending the Third Republic at Vichy and making Pétain a dictator unrestrained by any democratic process. France was no longer *La République Française* but *L'Etat Français* – a national-socialist dictatorship.

Marshal Pétain's first priority, as he saw it, was to rebuild the shattered morale of his nation. For this, more lies were necessary as the stuff of dreams, and the dream he was weaving was that a new France with higher moral values was fortuitously arising from the ashes of the corrupt and inefficient Third Republic. When reality is intolerable, people cling to dreams, and the initial popularity of Pétain's government in Vichy was based on the pretence that the armistice was a diplomatic triumph because it left much of the country under French rule. In reality, this was because Hitler was already planning his invasion of the USSR the following year, and was happy for Pétain to govern under close supervision the two-fifths of the country that had no immediate strategic importance, thus reducing the number of German divisions required to garrison France. The armistice terms also left alone the overseas territories of the

French Empire, for the good reason that they could easily have declared independence had the Germans attempted to seize them.

France was now divided into several jurisdictions, partly to confuse the French government and people as to what was still French and what was not.

Although the German entry into Paris on 14 June was politically symbolic, the most urgent military priority of OKW Chief of Staff General Franz Halder after the breakthrough at Sedan was, for strategic reasons, 'to occupy the Channel littoral (against any invasion from Britain) as far as the Spanish frontier (although) we can accept an unoccupied zone in the south'.[15] The resultant Occupied Zone, comprising all or part of fifty-two *départements*, stretched all the way along the Channel coast and south to the Spanish border – and as far inland as Tours in the west, Bourges in central France and Dijon in the east. In the north-east, Alsace and Lorraine were immediately annexed into the Reich under their old German names of Elsass and Lotharingen, with all adult males of military age immediately conscripted into the German forces. In private, they called themselves *les malgré nous* – meaning, *We don't want to go, but have no choice.*

On 23 July Hitler decreed that the *départements* of Nord and Pas de Calais were to be governed directly by the *Oberfeldkommandantur* in Brussels, and the northern half of the neighbouring Somme *département* became a *zone interdite* – a forbidden zone, to which no refugee might return. The forbidden zone was separated from the rest of the Occupied Zone by an internal frontier running from the estuary of the Somme to the Ardennes via Amiens. To the east of the forbidden zone lay the 'Reserved Zone'. By these devices the oil reserves, coal and potassium mines and the steel industry of the north-east were not available to contribute towards the crippling taxes to pay for the occupation.

Anyone looking at a map after this amputation of France's industrialised and mineral-rich north-eastern *départements* might have guessed that these moves were in preparation for a permanent westward expansion of the Reich after the whole of Europe had been subjugated. Protests by French representatives at the Armistice Commission in Wiesbaden that the territorial decrees ran contrary to the armistice agreement were brushed off by the pretence that they were only temporary. In fact, by incorporating France's major mineral resources into the Reich permanently, Hitler intended castrating the country industrially and preventing it ever again challenging Germany's position as master of Europe.

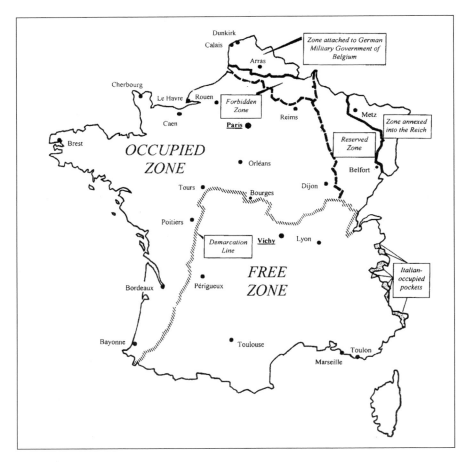

Divided France.

While the government in Vichy theoretically governed the whole of France, its laws were subject in the Occupied Zone to the approval of the German occupation authorities. In the south-east there were also a number of pockets occupied by Italian forces as a result of dictator Benito Mussolini launching a stab-in-the-back invasion just before the armistice to grab some 800 square kilometres of territory while the French defenders were concentrated on the German invasion.

In the so-called Free Zone of the south and centre, Vichy's theoretically unfettered writ was to run in thirty-four *départements* and parts of seventeen others. The Demarcation Line between the Occupied and Free Zones remained permeable in places for some weeks until the necessary patrolling could be organised and the checkpoints and barriers put in place. One woman refugee recalled, 'the demarcation line was still weakly guarded by courteous members of the *Waffen SS*, who were not yet searching the cars. We crossed it at Orthez without incident.'[16] A few weeks later, being caught while trying to cross the Line illicitly could have earned her a prison term or a sentry's bullet. While on the side of the Occupied Zone the frontier guards wore German uniform; the Free Zone side was patrolled by Vichy's rump army entitled *L'Armée de l'Armistice*. A force totalling 100,000 men, it was equipped with small arms and a few outdated 75mm cannons, yet had no transport apart from bicycles and a squadron of eight armoured cars in each 'cavalry regiment'. Its promises of continuing the glorious traditions of famous regiments fooled very few but, for the hungry and jobless, recruitment brought money and better rations than those of civilians.

Correspondence with relatives or loved ones on the other side of the Line was only possible by using 13-line pre-printed postcards with blanks to fill in. The inter-zonal correspondence card read:

> At … on (date) … is in good health / tired / slightly / badly / ill / wounded / killed / prisoner/ has died / is without news of … The family … is well / needs food / money / news / baggage. … is back at / works at…/ will return to school in … / has been received / to go to … on (date) … With love / kisses. (signature) ….

Initially, relations between the occupation forces and the civil population were very calm. A surprising number of German servicemen had brought cine cameras with them and shot films of themselves and their comrades relaxing in a restaurant or on a picnic, enjoying French food and especially the wine – with not a steel helmet or a firearm in sight.

For most French people, getting enough food each day was the prime concern. Those who innocently believed that Marshal Pétain would never allow the Germans to detach permanently from France his birthplace of Cauchy-la-Tour, near Béthune, failed to realise the permanence of the German arrangements in the north-east of the country and the impotence of their head of state. Veterans of the First World War still remembered Pétain as the Hero of Verdun. Younger men thought of him as the man who had been able to halt the fighting that might have cost their lives. Women believed that he would swiftly do a deal with the Germans to release their husbands, brothers and sons languishing in German POW camps. Those with longer memories in the north-east recalled the previous occupation of 1914–18 with its pillaging, atrocities and the deportations of young men and women, and wondered for how long the polite and smiling soldiers in field grey would stay that way.

Foreigners caught in the *débacle* had their own problems. On 6 July 1940 all aliens had their residence permits revoked and found their movements severely restricted. Included among them was the creator of Jeeves and Wooster. Having refused to return to Britain while there was still time because his Pekinese dog would have been placed in quarantine kennels for six months, P.G. Wodehouse was living near Le Touquet. He had arranged with British troops stationed nearby to warn him of the German advance in time to get away, but they decamped in the general rout, leaving him to be rounded up like all male citizens of enemy nationality less than sixty years old. Wodehouse was then interned in a former mental hospital at Tost in Upper Silesia to await his sixtieth birthday, but unwisely made several broadcasts over Radio Berlin's English service that saw him later accused of treason.

On 22 July 1940 Vichy established a three-man Commission for Denaturalisation, whose function was to revoke the protection of French citizenship that had been granted to foreign-born citizens. Its head, André Mornet, was a hard worker, who swiftly revoked nationality from 15,154 persons, including 6,307 Jews, for whom the result was deportation and death.[17] Many cases were brought to the notice of the police, the Commission and the *Gestapo* by letters of denunciation from jealous relatives, neighbours and business competitors – and by the simply mad, like the woman whose letter concluded, 'I would beg you to excuse me from taking fizzy drinks the Jews put the powder from invisible diamonds in its unforgivable it cuts all the fibre of the intestines and the doctors say it's a natural death.'[18] Saner-sounding letters were often signed, 'A French patriot' or 'An honest Frenchwoman'.

The Germans ordered all shops and factories to return to normal working, all prices to revert to pre-invasion levels and all civil servants to return to their posts. All firearms had to be handed in and any sabotage of German property or disrespect to German arms was to be punished. Many of these initial proclamations were *welcomed* by the bewildered population, with people thanking God that someone was in charge again.

In six weeks, Hitler had succeeded in occupying almost three-fifths of France, which included its financial centres and most of its industry. On the German side of the Line, entire factories were dismantled and shipped east. Coal was a big problem. French industry then needed 49.5 million tons a year, but was left with only 3 million tons. To counter the labour shortage due to 1.6 million Frenchmen being locked up as POWs, Pétain and Laval believed that the best course for obtaining their release was by cooperating with the Germans. This policy not only failed – the vast majority remained prisoners until their camps were liberated by the Allied advance in 1945 – but made the names of France's head of state and his first prime minister synonymous with collaboration, earning both a sentence of death for treason after the Liberation. Laval was shot; Pétain, the hero of Verdun, but now incontinent and suffering from dementia, had his sentence commuted to life imprisonment.

Chapter 3

Coming to terms with defeat

The arrival of German spearheads at the Channel coast in May 1940 was the third time in seventy years that the north-eastern *départements* of France had been invaded from beyond the Rhine. The first acts of resistance were spontaneous, with individuals hiding British and other soldiers on the run after Dunkirk in the hope of getting them out of the German-occupied areas and back to Britain via Spain or Switzerland.

It is a measure of the courage and efficiency of these escape lines that from D-Day to the end of September 1944 almost half the Allied aircrew shot down over France were safely returned to Britain. It is a measure of the dangers run by the individual helpers that this was done at the cost of some 500 civilian lives. Reliable sources estimate that, on average, each serviceman returned to Britain cost several French, Belgian or Dutch helpers' lives. This was possibly justifiable in military terms in the case of a trained pilot, but could he be allowed into combat again, with the risk of being shot down and betraying his saviours the first time around? And what military gain justified such a risk for an air-gunner or an infantryman? So why did people do it? Why did they risk their lives when the worst that could befall those they helped was a spell in a POW camp? The only answer is that they were not trying to help the Allies win the war so much as responding instinctively to the humanitarian appeal of a man in trouble. That they knew the penalty for being caught is incontrovertible. As early as 24 August, posters were displayed all over Normandy clearly stating that anyone found helping an escaped Allied soldier would be punished with the death penalty or forced labour, as would anyone who failed to denounce them.

Less risky, but not devoid of risk, was the circulation of crudely duplicated sheets passing on BBC news under names like *La Voix de la*

Nation, La Vraie France, L'Homme Libre and *La Voix du Nord*. So many people listened to the nightly bulletins on the BBC French Service that Cardinal Liénart of Lille felt it necessary to warn the faithful to get their news not from London or the German-controlled Radio Paris, but to tune their dials to Lyons and Toulouse – the voice of the pro-Pétain Church hierarchy. The *Propagandastaffel* mounted a poster campaign showing the BBC as shrewish maiden aunt, *La Tante BBC*, whose initials stood for Bobard–Boniment Corporation – the Corporation of Lies and Humbug. Radio waves were also the medium by which another small group of brave people sent to Britain details of *Wehrmacht* units stationed in Calais, their strengths and weaponry, and of positions of anti-aircraft and coastal batteries – thus inviting the return of Allied bombers to deal with these targets.[1]

However, in the summer and autumn of 1940, the Marshal was by far the most popular figure in French politics for two reasons. He was a great hero of the war France and her Allies had won in 1918 and the man who had stopped the killing in the one she had just lost. In the First World War, from a population of 40 million, French losses were 1.3 million dead and 4.2 million wounded, with half a million taken prisoner. Those figures were twice as high as for all the British Empire forces combined and *eighteen* times higher than casualties of troops from the United States, with a population then two and a half times higher than that of France. With the exception of a minuscule minority, nobody in France wanted tragedy on that scale again, and Pétain was the man who had ended the fighting – at a price.

A phrase in his prime ministerial broadcast of 17 June was, '*Je fais à la France le don de ma personne.*' I offer myself to France … In a predominantly Catholic country, that sounded to many people as though the great hero of 1914–18 was a new Messiah, sent by God in France's hour of need. His elevation to autocratic head of state on 11 July was therefore disapproved by very few. Although his civil marriage to a divorcee was not recognised by the Church, he cultivated its political support by making divorce more difficult for others, attending Mass regularly and re-introducing school prayers, which had been banned under the Third Republic. In those pre-television days when portraits of Stalin, Hitler, Mussolini, Franco, Salazar and other leaders hung in millions of homes and all public buildings in their countries, post offices in the Free Zone sold within two weeks 1,368,420 portraits of the Marshal. Children prayed for him in church and wrote to him as to Father Christmas. Adults addressed 1,200 letters every day to his office in the Hôtel du Parc in Vichy.

Pétain's first *président du conseil des ministres* or prime minister was the manipulative millionaire-lawyer-politician Pierre Laval – a man so opportunistic that when he had earlier changed political allegiance 180 degrees from left to right in the Chamber, his fellow *députés* joked that it was to be expected of a man whose name read the same from the right or the left. Pétain disliked Laval intensely, but needed his political astuteness. At one much-quoted exchange, Laval summed up their relationship by saying, *'Maréchal, nous sommes dans la merde. Laissez-moi être votre éboueur.'* Marshal, we're in the shit. Let me do the shovelling.

Somehow, these two disparate men had to put back on its feet a nation that was reeling from the shame of defeat, with its industry largely destroyed or confiscated. In fairness to Laval, he had been a good

Marshal Pétain (left) and
Prime Minister Laval (right).

friend to Britain during the Thirties until the British government agreed unilaterally to the expansion of the German navy in 1936. He had also worked tirelessly, but unsuccessfully, to bring Mussolini on-side with France and Britain against Hitler's Germany. Calculated ambiguity about the long-term future was a psychological device used repeatedly by the Nazis, who told their victims, 'Do this to our satisfaction and you will be treated better afterwards', without specifying in what way the treatment would be better. Even Laval fell for this line, convincing himself and many other people that the armistice agreement would shortly be replaced by a definitive peace treaty and therefore he repeatedly accommodated German demands in the hope of achieving the best possible bargaining position at the peace conference which never took place.

On both sides of the Line, with 2,500 bridges blown up and 1,300 railway stations unusable, due either to German bombing or demolition by French sappers during the retreat, rail journeys took days instead of hours. Access to the few trains that did run was initially restricted to civil servants, factory workers and the farmers and labourers needed to get in the harvest – under threat. Posters everywhere warned that failing to do it conscientiously would be construed as sabotage and that any shortfall would mean less food for the French, since German requisitions would not be reduced.

Not until the end of July could the millions of ordinary refugees buy a ticket. The armistice agreement placed the French national railway network *Société Nationale des Chemins de Fer* (SNCF) under the control of the *Wehrmacht Verkehrsdirektion* (WKD). Its first order was to run trains enabling 8 million refugees to return home, except those formerly domiciled in the forbidden zone. Already at the end of June 1940 came the first unpleasant demand – for 2,000 km of track with all the necessary sleepers, etc. On 10 August 1940, 1,000 locomotives and 35,000 wagons were requisitioned, followed less than three weeks later by another 2,000 locomotives. For obvious reasons, the management of SNCF delayed complying with these demands, but finally 2,946 locomotives and 85,000 wagons disappeared into the *Reich*, plus another 150,000 wagons that headed east fully loaded, and some of which reappeared in France from time to time.

At official meetings of the *Reichsbahn* (German railways) and SNCF, there were two distinctly different atmospheres: when the WKD was represented or the *Gestapo* present, frigid demands were made; when

SNCF officials met only with *Reichsbahn* colleagues, the atmosphere was more relaxed and on occasions it was obvious that the German railway representatives were trying to moderate the demands of the military, to enable SNCF to continue operations in very difficult conditions.

The German order to run get-the-refugees-home specials was met by a reply that SNCF could transport only 100,000 passengers per week under current conditions. The German riposte was, Try harder! By the end of the week a million refugees had travelled back to the north in the heat of high summer in grossly overcrowded trains, some driven by German footplate crews. On 1 November 1940 organised repatriation was suspended, leaving several million French people far from their homes. Four months later there was still an estimated million refugees spread out over southern and central France whose homes lay in the *départements* of the north-east, or who had reason to fear living under German control and fatally put their trust in the Marshal to protect them if they stayed in the Free Zone.

Whether they went or stayed, everybody found themselves queuing for hours to obtain all the obligatory new paperwork. Outside every town hall, desperate people gathered to scan the notice boards for news of relatives, including children and infants, lost during the panic of a Stuka attack many miles away. By the end of 1942, the French Red Cross managed to return 90,000 children to their anxious parents, but many others were never traced.

The newspaper of *Parti Communiste Français* (PCF) was *L'Humanité*, which had been banned for its defeatist stance – as had *The Daily Worker* in Britain. It now reappeared to toe the PCF line in support of the Soviet–German Non-Aggression Pact with editorials exhorting French workers to welcome German soldiers as fellow-workers in uniform by organising works parties and picnics for them. After thus being pro-German for the first twenty months of the war, the PCF later claimed to have been in the forefront of the anti-German struggle from the very beginning, and spuriously back-dated its first Resistance tracts to 2 July 1940. They were signed by the party's second-in-command Jacques Duclos in the absence of Maurice Thorez, who was safely ensconced in Moscow for the duration.[2] Following the Comintern line into which the Party was locked until Hitler invaded the USSR in June 1941, the predated tracts were in any case simply ranting accusations of British and French politicians for causing and losing 'the imperialist war'.

In 1939 France used up 3 million tonnes of petroleum for transport. With no further importation possible after the defeat, the nation's stock amounted to only 200,000 tonnes – enough for less than a month's normal consumption – plus an annual 50,000 tonnes of petrol substitute that could be produced industrially.[3] Petrol being unobtainable by the average citizen, the price of bicycles soared, as did the number of users until 2.5 million French people who had never ridden a bicycle before used one as their principal transport.[4] Thomas Kernan, the suave cosmopolitan American publisher of *Vogue* magazine, had to cycle to and from his office in the centre of Paris. On the way home in November 1940, he noted one civilian car passing every five minutes.[5] Soon, most of those would be powered not by petrol or diesel fuel, but by gas from charcoal burnt in a specially designed boiler called a *gazogène*, either bolted onto the external luggage rack or towed on a trailer, while bus engines were converted to burn town gas stored in an inflatable reservoir on the roof, refilled at special 'gas stations' as in wartime Britain. With taxis extremely scarce, ancient *fiacres* pulled by bony old hacks reappeared on the streets of French cities, and *cyclo-taxis*, pedalled by men and women, also plied for hire. When it rained, the 'driver' had only a cape for protection, but the covered trailer compartment might hold as many as three dry adult passengers. Some independent spirits, who before the occupation would never have walked more than a few paces if they could help it, took a pride in ignoring these expedients and going everywhere on foot.

With no diesel fuel for tractors, farmers repaired ancient steam traction engines and used horses and oxen to pull the plough, the harrow and the reaper – their consolation being the higher rations to which they were entitled by their Category C ration cards. Other heavy workers were in the privileged Category T for *travailleur*. With entitlement varying with age, sex and type of work, Category A for *adulte* covered all other adults between twenty-one and seventy, while those over seventy were Category V for *vieux*. Infants were E for *enfant*, but children from three to twenty-one were graded J1, J2 or J3 – the three categories of *jeunes*. Babies were entitled to milk; conversely, the old received a larger bread ration. The average adult received 350 grams of bread per day – reduced on 14 April 1941 to 275 grams. To prevent people stockpiling their entitlement, the coupons could only be used on the date printed on them. The bread itself was not what it had been. Before the war, 100kg of wheat produced 75kg of flour; by November 1940 the same amount of wheat had to produce

82kg and eventually 98kg of flour by April 1942.[6] The difference was made up by including husks, sawdust and whatever else could be made to look like flour.

The meat ration was initially 350 grams per adult per week, with Wednesday, Thursday and Friday declared meatless days. Even horse meat became so scarce that queues formed outside every shop with anything edible on sale. Unrationed locally caught fish was much in demand at markets. With a monthly allowance of 500 grams of sugar, 300 grams of coffee and 140 grams of cheese, rations were supposed to have been calculated as sufficient for good health, but medical records show that boys maturing in 1944 were seven centimetres shorter than those the same age in 1935, while girls were eleven centimetres shorter than their older sisters had been at the same age. Dental health especially suffered greatly.[7]

To break completely with the past, Marshal Pétain replaced the Revolutionary slogan *Liberté, Egalité, Fraternité* that was carved on every public building in France by *Travail, Famille, Patrie*. Work, family and the fatherland. It sounded harmless enough as a national motto. As head of state, the Marshal communicated with the population via a stream of *Paroles aux Français* – printed tracts, broadcasts and public speeches couched in the tone of a stern but caring father of the nation. In them, he held up the honest peasant as the hero of his new-model France. As early as 23 June 1940, he compared the defeat and occupation to a freak hailstorm that had devastated a farmer's fields. 'Did he despair? No,' said Pétain. 'He rolled up his sleeves and set to, re-ploughing and re-planting to ensure the harvest.'

Posters everywhere showed grizzled old peasants proudly passing their ploughs on to their sons with the message, 'This is a fine weapon, my son. Use it to fight the good fight.' To encourage a return to the land, the Marshal introduced a system of start-up loans. To qualify for this, a couple had to have at least one child and the expectation of more. Partly because they also had to sign up for a ten-year stint, only 1,561 couples took up the offer, dashing the Marshal's hopes of rural renewal. More domestically, *Le Journal Officiel* of 18 September announced a special subsidy of 150 francs for seeds and tools, to encourage everyone to take an allotment and grow their own food in anticipation of severe shortages to come.

Pétain was fond of saying, 'I keep promises, even those made by others,' but it eventually sank in with the general population that his promise to 'bring the boys home' was not going to be kept, because officers and men alike were being held as hostages for the good behaviour of the population and Hitler had no intention of liberating 1.6 million French POWs, most of whom were working as unpaid labour in the Reich, officers alone being exempted.

Life was cruelly hard for their wives back home. Against a factory worker's salary of 1,200–1,800 francs a month, the allowance to a POW's wife with one child was 630 francs, increasing to 830 for two children and 1,030 for three children, but this was still far too little as inflation bit.[8] Hunger, exacerbated by the sight of their increasingly undernourished children, motivated many women in the Occupied Zone to find a German lover who could provide extra rations. For favours, food or cash, war-widows and wives whose husbands were POWs in Germany, went 'on the game'. At Blainville-sur-Orne near Caen the gendarmerie commandant advised his superiors, 'Immoral behaviour by wives of POWs is to be seen wherever (German) troops are stationed. Girls still in their teens are becoming prostitutes. This behaviour is difficult for (my) officers to control, given the German protection certain women enjoy.'[9]

The newspaper *La Gerbe* commented ambiguously, 'For certain people, the principal charms of being here (in France) are to be found in nicely rounded backsides.'[10] Still, if many off-duty Germans frequented the licensed brothels and nightclubs, others sat quietly painting in the old quarters of Rouen and other Norman cities or listened to serious music in the concert halls.

Cabaret clubs and music halls knew a boom with popular singers like Maurice Chevalier, Charles Trenet and Edith Piaf happy to perform for the lonely men in field grey far from home – and to accept engagements for lucrative tours in the Reich, as did whole theatre companies and film stars.

Since coming to power in 1933, Hitler had based his plans for the conquest of Western Europe on the premise that the continental super-power of the victorious Reich could co-exist with the maritime power of the British Empire because they in no way threatened each other.[11] Assuming that the British government would continue appeasing him and end by accepting Nazi domination of the Continent was to prove one of the Führer's major mistakes. As a result, neither the *Kriegsmarine* nor the *Wehrmacht* had planned the construction of the fleet of vessels necessary for a seaborne invasion of the British Isles. One month after the

A different image of the *Wehrmacht*: two off-duty soldiers in Rouen.

French surrender, after a few tentative peace feelers from both sides that stood not a chance against Churchill's determined stand, on 16 July Hitler ordered OKW to prepare an amphibious invasion of Great Britain. *Fall Seelöwe*, or Operation Sealion, had to be executed before the autumnal gales, but transporting a million or more men, plus tanks, artillery, trucks, munitions and motor fuel across the Channel with its four strong tides each day and unpredictable weather was a far more complicated logistics exercise than the river crossings in continental Europe for which the *Wehrmacht* was trained and equipped.

All around the French Channel and Atlantic coasts, schoolchildren on holiday watched German soldiers undergoing a crash course in amphibious landing techniques. For most, this involved being pushed off boats into two metres of water, to test how well they could swim or wade ashore with full pack and weapons weighing them down. Improvised landing barges dropped their ramps for trucks to be driven into the shallows towing a dozen bicycle-soldiers on a rope. If the truck did not stall in the water, most of the riders fell off in the soft sand, to the gleeful amusement of the children watching.

There was little for their parents to laugh at. Coming to terms with all the difficulties of living in an occupied country, where every day brought new regulations and prohibitions, most adults consoled themselves with the thought that things would have been far worse if France were still at war. Those living in the north of the country were, however, about to find that they were still at war – a one-sided war that would eventually make the whole of France a target for yesterday's allies. At first intermittently, and then daily, RAF aircrews crossed the Channel in a few minutes' flight to unleash death and destruction upon the towns and ports of the French Channel coast – especially Dunkirk, Calais, Boulogne, Dieppe, Le Havre, Rouen, Caen and Cherbourg.

Chapter 4

Under the German yoke and British bombs

In 1940 Adolf Hitler was not yet totally deaf to reactions to his plans within OKW. Its less than optimistic assessment of the *Seelöwe* project led him to make what was seen in Germany as an appeal to reason in a speech to the Reichstag on 19 July. He said:

> A great empire will be destroyed, a world empire which it was never my intention to destroy or damage (and) the continuation of this war will only end with the complete destruction of one of the two warring parties. Mr. Churchill may believe that this will be Germany. I know it will be England.

He was sounding out Britain's attitude to recognising German dominion over Europe and the restoration of the former German colonies in return for a cessation to hostilities. Any other British prime minister than Winston Churchill might well have pursued this overture at such a desperate time. However, despite a number of exploratory negotiations by Britons of various political hues in Italy and neutral countries with the connivance, if not the open approval, of the Foreign Office, Churchill would have no truck with Berlin.

Since *Seelöwe* had not been planned in advance and few seaworthy purpose-built invasion vessels existed, tugs and self-propelled barges were requisitioned throughout the occupied countries to tow long lines of river and canal barges from all over northern Europe to assembly points in the French and Belgian Channel ports. The first requirement for an invasion of Britain by this motley fleet was control of the skies of southern England, for which reason air supremo *Reichsmarschal* Hermann Goering summoned senior *Luftwaffe* commanders to his luxurious hunting lodge/palace of Karinhall, north-east of Berlin, on 2 August and issued his *Adlertag* or *Eagle Day* directive, afterwards boasting to the Führer that his *Luftwaffe* aces would annihilate the RAF in a few days' combat.

In the Battle of Britain which began a week later the famous 'few' proved Fat Hermann wrong. While the glamorous 'Brylcreem boys' of RAF Fighter Command grabbed all the headlines for blasting the *Luftwaffe* out of the sky, Bomber Command was tasked with the less glamorous destruction of the invasion fleet and the harassment of the hundreds of thousands of German troops being assembled for *Seelöwe* in the ports of Normandy. Given the gross inaccuracy of contemporary bombing techniques, implicit in that decision was the killing of unspecified numbers of neutral French civilians who lived there. Not until late 1941 was Churchill's scientific adviser Professor Frederick Lindemann able to 'raise doubts' in the prime minister's mind about bombing accuracy. In Churchill's words:

> I authorised his Statistical Department to make an investigation at Bomber Headquarters. The results confirmed our fears. We learned that although Bomber Command believed that they had found the target, *two-thirds of the crews actually failed to strike within five miles of it.* The air photographs (taken afterwards) showed how little damage was being done. It also appeared that the crews knew this and were discouraged by the poor results of so much hazard.[1]

Behind that bald paragraph was an examination by D.M. Butt, a civil servant at the Air Ministry, of 4,065 photographs taken on 200 raids by cameras fitted to bombers flown by experienced crews. Butt found that, even on the two-thirds of missions when the pilots reported having bombed the target on moonlit nights with good visibility, only one aircraft in four had bombed within five miles of the target; on nights with no moon, only one in twenty got even that close.

The resultant heated debate in Cabinet and at the Air Staff and Chiefs of Staff meetings was restricted for security reasons and the only outward sign that something had been terribly wrong was the replacement at the head of Bomber Command of Air Vice Marshal Sir Richard Peirse by Air Chief Marshal Sir Arthur Harris, with no noticeable improvement in bombing accuracy.[2]

Air Chief Marshal
Sir Arthur Harris.

Before this, in the three months beginning with the end of June 1940, Dunkirk, already badly damaged during the evacuation, was raided six times, as was Boulogne. Calais was hit twelve times and Le Havre once. With neither the aircraft nor the far more powerful bombs available later in the war, these raids were not on the later scale of destruction, but still claimed French lives and destroyed French homes.[3]

During the Battle of Britain (10 July–6 September 1940), Le Havre's airfield at Octeville, protected by batteries of 20mm anti-aircraft guns, was a crucial forward fighter base for Goering's aces. Aircraft on the ground for re-arming or undergoing maintenance were concealed in barns on nearby farms because the field was so vulnerable to reprisal raids, being only a few kilometres from the coast. Bomber Command paid visits to Octeville and Le Havre, dropping 100lb, 200lb and 300lb bombs, not only on the port, where the invasion fleet was being assembled, but also in residential districts, killing scores and causing thousands more Havrais to flee into the countryside for safety. Some stayed there until the advent of cold weather drove them home. As with those returning after the panic evacuation in June, many found that their homes had been broken into

42

and belongings stolen during their absence. This experience, and their reluctance to undergo it again, was to cost thousands of lives at the end of the war.

In Dunkirk, where eighty-two per cent of homes had been destroyed in the May fighting and only 12,000 of the prewar population of 31,000 had a roof over their heads, the first RAF raid in July 1940 was followed by a massive raid on 8 August. German troops took priority in the shelters, leaving most civilians finding what shelter they could in cellars beneath the ruins of their homes. Few people in Britain knew or cared that innocent French civilians were being killed and seriously wounded by bombs which bore cheeky messages scrawled in chalk like *Here's one for Adolf.* [4] The addressee was for the time safe; each mis-directed delivery merely adding to the misery of his French victims, cowering in their cellars.

With Germany hungry for both raw materials and manufactured goods, the big French companies were sniffing out new opportunities. To impose a semblance of order on this latter-day gold rush, a law of 16 August 1940 obliged each sector of industry and commerce to form a *Comité d'Organisation Nationale*, through which the government could control all business transactions, update business methods and re-equip factories to prepare French firms to compete in a German-dominated United States of Europe. The acronym CON was unfortunate, since *con* is both a female sexual organ and a rude word for 'silly' – as in English. After this was pointed out to the presumably humourless administration in Vichy, the official abbreviation was shortened to CO.

Humour was anyway in short supply, particularly in the occupied north. Edmond Perron was a Dunkerquois philatelist who had been profiting from the occupation by posting to himself envelopes with stamps over-printed *Besetzes Gebiet Nord Frankreich* in the rather optimistic hope that these would become rare. He also kept a diary, in which he recorded the RAF raid on 14 September:

> At 22.00hrs we heard the (anti-aircraft) guns and hastily got dressed to go outside and watch the aircraft caught by the searchlights and targeted by lines of tracer. Suddenly, the crash of bombs bursting nearby made us hurry inside to take refuge inside a cupboard under the stairs. The noise was infernal. More bombs. A colossal explosion and the windows were blown in, the cardboard that had replaced the panes

being ripped out. We took mattress and blankets down to the cellar. It went on until 05.00hrs. When a succession of four explosions came closer and closer, I had never been more afraid. At dawn, we went upstairs and lay down, while the children went back to their room and my wife made coffee. What a night![5]

The victims of that raid who were not killed outright were taken to the hospital in Rosendaël, where most of the 400 beds were still occupied by civilians who had been injured during the fighting in May. That was the last night the Perron family spent in their home, moving from one address to another twelve times before the end of the war – which came in long-suffering Dunkirk a day *after* the official German surrender on 8 May 1945.

Le Havre was overflowing with *Wehrmacht* and other German units due to land in the first wave of the invasion between Brighton and Selsey Bill. On 15 September a dinner was given in the Casino for VIPs who had arrived from Germany to inspect the growing fleet of patrol boats, torpedo boats, mine-layers and other craft being assembled in the port. A number of French ladies, both professional and amateur, were present to entertain the visitors. After dessert, as coffee and liqueurs were being enjoyed, the arrival of twelve RAF Blenheims taking advantage of the full moon was heralded by a barrage from the anti-aircraft batteries. Running outside to watch the raid, the officers and their ladies were just in time to see a hail of bombs descending, which killed forty of them. French rescue worker Léon Gillet was forbidden access to the scene, where body parts were liberally scattered on the terrace, but found an ear, complete with earring, lying in the road some distance away.[6]

By 15 September 1940 everyone holding a bank account had to provide proof of Aryan descent before being allowed to access their money. Safe-deposit boxes of all Jews were opened and contents confiscated. The result was a harvest for the Reich because in 1939 Paris had had the largest Jewish population of any city except Warsaw and New York, including 150,000–200,000 stateless refugees from Nazi Germany and Poland.

Goering came to inspect the invasion preparations, as did Hitler's deputy Rudolf Hess and other high Nazi officials. In an attempt to prevent the population sending intelligence to Britain, the Boulonnais were forbidden to go more than 5km from their homes. After a raid on the night of 17 September sank two tugs and a number of barges in the harbour, the Boulonnais rejoiced but it was hard to know on whose side they were when their erstwhile allies killed ten civilians and wounded the same number, leaving twenty-seven major fires burning in the town. It grew harder still as 126 further raids produced the grim tally of 726 civilians killed, some 700 seriously wounded and eighty-five per cent of homes uninhabitable.[7]

By the middle of September, the worst fears of pessimists were proven true. In Calais, Georges Dauchard went for an afternoon walk on 15 September and noted in his diary:

> The invasion fleet was getting larger with each day. (On one stretch of the port) there were 150 small craft of all kinds, in the Carnot dock about the same number. Coming home, we could see several laden oil tankers moored at the Quai du Commerce, which made us apprehensive, because by now we had learned that air raids were not something to take lightly.[8]

That night, starting at 21.30hrs, waves of bombers came in at rooftop height at regular intervals and damaged the town more than the port, dropping a number of delayed action bombs that claimed the lives of rescue workers. Dauchard's eyewitness account of the scene next morning reads:

> Houses and apartment buildings had been completely destroyed or made uninhabitable. One bomb landed twenty metres from the Town Hall, blowing out all the stained glass and other windows. In the central station one German and three French railway workers were killed. Several bombs fell on the hospital, decapitating one patient in his bed and killing two others. A Franciscan nun died of her wounds the following day, after promising to request, on arriving in heaven, that hers should be the last death (from bombs) in the hospital.[9]

Dauchard noted next day a growing anglophobia among his fellow-citizens, due to so many bombs landing in residential areas. The Germans did not neglect this propaganda windfall, displaying posters all along the Channel coast depicting a British bomber over a ruined French town, with a caption asking, *And these were your allies?* The RAF, however, could compliment itself that the raids were successful. Indeed, a signal had already been sent from the *Kriegsmarine* HQ in Paris to Berlin: 'Moorings at Calais, Boulogne, Dunkirk and Ostende are now unusable due to air raids, raids by swift surface craft and shelling by (British) long-range coastal guns.'[10]

After his baptism of fire on 15 September, Georges Dauchard described his fear two days later when he heard the sound of aircraft engines at 22.00hrs:

> We hurried to get across to the cellar opposite, but it was too late. Bombs falling all around. Terrible noise. Faint ack-ack fire audible. A raging fire somewhere near the Carnot dock. The district is getting unsafe.

The following night he heard bombs falling further away, the explosions and ack-ack fire making it impossible to sleep before 02.00hrs. On the night of 19 September, he noted:

> A continuous passage of troops along the boulevards, with weapons and baggage and some tanks. (German) sailors are becoming more numerous. Heavy ack-ack. We stayed in the cellar until 01.30hrs but bombs continued falling further away until 04.00hrs.[11]

The bombing continued on 20 and 23 September, after which the RAF claimed to have destroyed twelve per cent of the impromptu German invasion fleet. By the end of the month, the Calaisiens heaved a collective sigh of relief as the raids ceased for the time being, now that *Seelöwe* was cancelled and the intended invasion troops redeployed.

On 1 October the RAF bombed the Graville district of Le Havre, scoring a lucky hit on a whole train of munitions which blew up in a chain of secondary explosions, badly damaging homes in a wide radius. Cruel as was the suffering of the civilians living there, in Vichy greater agony was being prepared for a whole class of citizens. That same day, Foreign Minister Paul Baudouin noted in his diary that Pétain had been at his most intransigent in Cabinet when drafting the first *Statut des Juifs* that morning. On 18 October 1940 *Le Journal Officiel* published the text of the new law, backdated to 3 October. With all the thoroughness of the German racial laws, it defined who was, and who was not, a Jew. All Jews had to register their addresses at the nearest Hôtel de Ville. Even those who were French citizens found a long list of occupations from which they were henceforth barred, ranging from head of state to the humblest teacher, by way of the civil service and any elected office. Léon Meyer had seen this coming: had he not resigned as mayor of Le Havre, he would have been deprived of office automatically. Nobel Prize-winning philosopher Henri Bergson, a sick 81-year-old who had converted to Catholicism long since, went to register as a way of expressing solidarity with the community among whom he had grown up.

In particular, the statute specified that no Jew was allowed to serve in the educational or judicial systems, the armed services, the civil service, press and entertainment, nor to present himself for election to public office. Jews were also forbidden to queue, without doing which they could not buy food. They had to hand in their radios and were forbidden to use telephone kiosks in case they made them unclean for subsequent Aryan users. The state-run telephone service was instructed to disconnect Jewish subscribers and remove their handsets. Since Jews might no longer teach in schools, the Director of Education in each *département* sent to all head teachers a circular, from which this is an extract:

> The Law of 3 October regarding the status of Jews stipulates as follows:
>
> Art 1. 'Jew' in the context of this law means any person having three grandparents of the Jewish race, or two grandparents if married to a Jew.
>
> Art 2. The following public service employment is barred to Jews:
>
> Art 3. Members of the teaching profession.

Article 7 continued:

> The Jewish state employees affected … will cease to exercise their functions within two months of the promulgation of this law. They will be permitted to claim their pension rights, providing they have sufficient pensionable years of service or be entitled to a proportional pension if they have served at

least fifteen years. Those who fall into neither category will have their cases settled within a period to be determined by the administration.

By his circular of 21 October, the Secretary of State for Education has informed me that by 'teachers' is meant all civil servants whose professional activity brings them into regular and direct contact with pupils and whose authority affects the teaching and indirectly the pupils, viz. primary school and other teachers, heads of schools, etc.

Shortage of paper caused the circular to be issued on paper headed *République Française* with the old revolutionary slogan *Liberté, Egalité, Fraternité*, which was hardly appropriate in the circumstances.

No less ominously, the *Préfets* who control regional government in France were given power to intern foreign Jews. The concentration camp at Gurs, where refugees from the Spanish Civil War had been held, was among those taken over for 'foreign undesirables'.[12] Three days later, Algerian Jews were deprived of citizenship, which had been theirs by right since 1871. Towards the end of the year Jewish-born Catholic priest Abbé Glasberg managed to get into the camp at Gurs and reported the 'inhuman conditions' to his superiors. On the instructions of Cardinal Gerlier, Monsignor Guerry went to Vichy in December to in a protest at this un-Christian treatment of the detainees to the Minister of the Interior, but got no further than the minister's *chef de cabinet*.

On 12 October Wehrmacht sappers blew up the monument in Reims to the African colonial soldiers who had died for France in the First World War, exposing in the granite base a document acknowledging their important contribution to victory. In Paris, the sappers also dismantled the statue in Denys-Cochin square of General Charles Mangin, a hero of the first war. The reason? When commanding his regiment of Senegalese soldiers occupying the Rhineland in 1918, Mangin had ordered towns in his area to supply whores for military brothels and over-ruled the protests of the mayors by saying, 'Don't worry, *meine Herren*, German women are none too good for my Senegalese soldiers.'

A series of laws dated 18, 20 and 31 October and 9 and 16 November 1940 completely revised French corporation law. As in the European Community which Britain joined in 1973, young and ambitious businessmen snatched the opportunity to enhance their careers by working for the COs. In the absence of trade unions and parliamentary democracy, considerable power accrued to them, largely through their authority to impose sanctions on companies who failed to march in step with the New Order. The inherent problem from the start was one endemic in totalitarian economies: a proliferation of 'organising bodies' whose members had to pay the costs of a flood-tide of time-wasting paperwork. Some companies belonged to more than one CO; others had no idea to which they belonged. Many companies believed they were being discriminated against when the restricted resources were carved up. Whilst major companies could keep abreast of all the bureaucracy, smaller ones found that they were pawns being moved now by German orders or lack of them, now by the OCPRI – the central office for distribution of industrial products. It was a dream-world, in which German agencies often insisted on placing orders direct, reducing the staff of the COs to collecting statistics and filling in forms.

On 22 October Laval met Hitler at Montoire on the Demarcation Line in central France, to prepare the way for Pétain's meeting with the Führer two days later. Hitler was on his return journey from a meeting with Franco, at which his expectation that the *caudillo* would repay German help in the Spanish Civil War by offering military support against Britain had foundered on the German refusal to promise Franco in return suzerainty over French North Africa. Laval later told some dinner guests, 'My meeting with Hitler at Montoire was a moving surprise. Rejecting any idea of vengeance, Hitler is prepared to admit France into the (New Europe) he will create when the war is over.'

At the meeting with Pétain, the Führer was at his affable best, having been advised how docilely the Marshal was leading his people into the occupation.

Photographs of the two leaders shaking hands at Montoire made the front pages of newspapers all over the world. In a letter thanking Cardinal Baudrillart for supporting him, Pétain wrote, 'I want (the people) to trust me blindly, as three million of them did when I was their commander when they faced the enemy (in 1914–18). Later, they will come to understand what my plan was.'[12] On 30 October, Pétain broadcast an appeal for collaboration as a way of 'making the best of it':

This first meeting between victor and vanquished marks the recovery of our country. I accepted the Führer's invitation of

Marshal Pétain (left) meets Hitler (right) at Montoire.

my own volition and was subjected to no *Diktat* or pressure.
I accept the principle of a sincere collaboration between our
two countries. This policy is mine and I alone shall be judged
by History. I went freely to talk to the Führer. A collaboration,
which I accept in principle, has been planned between our
two countries. It must be sincere. This policy is mine. It is me
alone that history will judge.

What 'collaboration' meant was becoming clearer with each passing day.
Proving that Jews were not the only internal enemies, on 9 November
the confederation of trades unions was abolished, as were all existing
political parties. This was the final straw for the discontented miners in
the Nord/Pas de Calais coalfield, already smarting under the German
pressure on the mine-owners, keen to increase productivity by twenty-
five per cent as required by the *Reich* because of the profits this would
bring them.

Disillusioned with Pétain and Laval, desperate for their families because wages had been frozen but food prices were soaring, and defying the wishes of Moscow although they were largely Communists, the miners chose the symbolic date of the 1918 armistice to call a strike. On 11 November more than a fifth of the work-force in the north-eastern coalfield did not turn up to work. Refusing to believe that the men had organised themselves without any outside direction, the mine-owners and the German authorities suspected some mysterious conspiracy at work and began hunting down the 'saboteurs'.

Governments depend on the fact that most citizens quickly accept new rules and regulations. Already France was effectively two countries: to the west and north of the Demarcation Line the population was subjected daily to the sight of armed German soldiers and the rhythm of life was set by the Occupation authorities; in the predominantly agricultural Free Zone, most people had yet to see their first German soldier.

As the first winter of the Occupation closed in, country folk were better off than townspeople because they could grow their own fruit and vegetables and their heating and cooking was mostly by wood from the forests hauled home, sawn and split by hand. With French coal requisitioned at the pit-head for the Reich, town-dwellers all over France faced a bleak, cold winter. The Christmas of 1940 was for everyone a sad travesty of prewar celebrations. The average food ration for adults totalled 1,800 calories per day, equivalent to a slow starvation. Swedes were traditionally grown in France as animal fodder. Now, they became for millions the only vegetable obtainable. With the black market not yet organised on any great scale – and anyway accessible only to those with money – this winter was known as *l'hiver des rutabagas*, or 'the winter of swedes'. The general misery was summed up in a parody of a Christmas carol. No one knew where it originated, but all the many versions went something like this:

> Christmas has been cancelled,
> the Virgin and Child evacuated.
> St Joseph is in a concentration camp
> and the stable has been requisitioned.
> The angels have been shot down.
> The Wise Men are in England.

The cow is in Berlin, the ass in Rome,
and the star has been painted blackout blue[13]
by order of the Blokleiter.

On 31 December the French service of the BBC asked every patriot to keep off the streets at 15.00hrs the following day. Radio reception, despite German jamming, being better in Normandy than further south, not only was the pre-war roar of traffic absent from the streets of the Channel ports that afternoon, but from five minutes to the hour Germans sobering up after their *Sylvesternacht* celebrations found themselves alone in a deserted world. This uncanny demonstration actually broke no laws and therefore went unpunished.

PART 2

OCCUPATION AND HUNGER

Chapter 5

Dig, or die!

On 1 January the German authorities extended by thirty minutes the length of miners' shifts in the Nord/Pas de Calais coalfield. Since the mine owners had already cancelled the improvements in working conditions they had been forced to grant under Léon Blum's Popular Front government, this latest move so angered miners in one pit that they downed picks and shovels on the following day half an hour before the end of their shift in retaliation. With organised trade unions banned by Vichy, this passive resistance spread rapidly from pit to pit through impromptu *comités d'unité syndicale et d'action* – solidarity and action committees.

Tension escalated rapidly. On 7 January the men were formally ordered by *Préfets* Fernand Carles in the *département* of Nord and Amédé Bussière in neighbouring Pas de Calais to comply with the new rules; on 9 January German posters warned of the sanctions to be imposed; on 16 January orders were given to arrest two PCF activists at each pit. Forty were arrested and nine detained in prison.

The most familiar images of the German war machine show *Panzers* pulverising the opposition, yet much of the *Wehrmacht*'s heavy equipment was horse-drawn. With most leather requisitioned for uniform boots and belts and for harness for those hundreds of thousands of draught animals, shoe rationing came into force in France on 5 January 1941, after which storekeepers attempted to convince customers that wooden-soled shoes and clogs were a new fashion, with compressed cork a quieter alternative for those who could not stand the clip-clop noise that made them sound like horses as they walked along the pavement.

The novelist Colette, whose husband was Jewish, kept a relatively low profile during the occupation years, but she did go public with her recipes for salads of edible weeds. She also recommended rubbing swede juice on the skin to prevent wrinkles, and stitching a layer of newspaper into one's winter underclothes to cope with the lack of central heating. Whether working class French people appreciated her advice to wear gold jewellery for additional warmth is doubtful; the luckier ones bought an over-vest of cat-skin or any other fur, and hardly needed her counsel in *Paris de ma fenêtre*: 'Go to bed. Get the meal over and done with and the household chores finished, and go to bed with a hot-water bottle for your feet.'[1]

A rhythm that haunts the sound-track of every film set in wartime France was first heard when programme producer Victor De Laveleye of the BBC Belgian service used the Morse code for letter V, which is dot-dot-dot-dash– standing for *victoire* in French and *vrijheid*, or freedom in Flemish – in his programme of 14 January 1941. The same rhythm being also the opening bar of Beethoven's Fifth Symphony, the BBC adopted this played on timpani as the signature tune of its broadcasts to occupied Europe from 22 March onwards. When an announcer took this one step further and asked listeners to display the V sign, there were a spate of Vs chalked on walls all over the occupied countries. Nervous or anglophobic French people finding one on their house wall added two more strokes to make an M, said to stand for *Vive le Maréchal* but his popularity was beginning to wane – especially with the young after a decree of 18 January 1941 which obliged young French males to register for compulsory service in *Les Chantiers de Jeunesse*, or youth work camps.

The modern concept of re-cycling was foreshadowed by a Vichy decree dated 23 January, which made it an offence to throw away metal, paper, skins, rubber, feathers, bones, animal skin and leather. All had to be put out for collection by municipal employees driving horse-drawn carts. Made from traditionally secret and presumably unrationed ingredients, perfume continued to be the luxury present always obtainable by those who had the money: Schiaparelli, Guerlain and the other great names enjoyed a boom due to all the Germans seeking a special present for the ladies in their lives, whether in France or back home.

Marching on in step with the German drum, on 1 February Vichy approved the formation of a single new political party under the title *Rassemblement National Populaire* (RNP). Also on the German model, and in an attempt to deprive the growing black market of its foodstuffs supplies, at the start of the year Vichy instituted *le Service du Ravitaillement* to control the cultivation of crops, the raising and slaughtering of domestic animals and the transportation and distribution of food supplies. Unfortunately, the new bureaucracy had all the failings of every command economy: in January 1941 the 135,000 inhabitants of Le Havre were sent 279 beef carcases, twenty-three veal calves, three sheep, ninety-one pigs; while Rouen's smaller population received 555 beef carcases, 302 veal calves and 365 pigs.[2] Like all bureaucracies, the service grew larger and larger: on 1 January 1941 it employed 50 people in Le Havre; two years later their number had risen to 140.

Those with a nose for profit sniff every wind. The business community rapidly came to terms with its new super-client across the Rhine. Starting February 1941, increasing numbers of senior executives went on expenses-paid trips to glean know-how and technology in Germany – especially in the use of artificial substitutes for natural products in short supply. On 17 March the Stock Exchange re-opened in Paris and knew a continuous upward trend in share prices over the next two years. Boards of management took advantage of Vichy's fixed low interest rates to refinance loans and take out new ones.

But for the man – and especially the woman – in the street, life was grim. The handbag of every shopper was now stuffed with the ration coupons for each foodstuff, clothes, textiles, tobacco, garden seeds, wine, with special coupons for work clothes or a bathing costume, for a pair of shoes or washing powder or metal household goods, schoolbooks, etc. The list was endless, but possessing all the necessary papers was only half the game. Local newspapers carried announcements of foods and other rationed goods that would only be available on a certain day at the supplier with whom one was registered; if that was missed, it was back to square one. Pregnant or breast-feeding women and mothers of large families were issued the *carte nationale de priorité* theoretically entitling them to go to the head of any queue. Bafflingly, queuing was forbidden by various edicts, none of which had much effect when long-awaited food supplies were available in a shop.[3]

In these nationwide conditions, there was little to alleviate the deep distress of the miners' families in the coalfield of the north-east. On 21 February Michel Brulé, a young activist at Dourges, was arrested. Like a flash of fire-damp underground, strikers *demanding* his release refused to work throughout the coalfield. Amazingly, he was released four days later, which got the men back to work, in a mood that required little to spark another wholesale protest.

In February 1941, *Préfet* Carles asked the German administration for permission to convert the citadel of Doullens into his own concentration camp for both male and female PCF activists and sympathisers. Permission granted in July, the camp opened in September and operated until March 1943, when the 350 male prisoners were deported to Buchenwald, Dachau, Mauthausen, Neuengamme and several score female prisoners to Ravensbrück women's camp, which has been described as ' a crime against women'.

It is estimated that 2,700 people were deported from the *zone rattachée* to German concentration camps during the occupation, some after sentencing by a German military tribunal, others on simple suspicion. For most of them, the alleged crimes were failing to hand in a hunting gun, helping downed Allied aircrew on the run, distributing Communist propaganda, minor acts of sabotage or lack of respect to the German uniform. The others were more or less common criminals who had committed thefts of German property or perhaps those who had the bad luck to injure or kill a German soldier in a traffic accident. Surprisingly again, nearly one-third of these were released and allowed to return home after serving their sentences in German prisons. However, those still considered hostile were despatched at the end of their sentences to concentration camps, where more than 200 died from various causes, including Allied air raids. Forty-three of the men and three women were executed after being condemned in a Nazi People's Court.

Open acts of resistance were more summarily dealt with. In 1942, 123 *résistants* were shot in the moat of the citadel of Arras, mostly being PCF members arrested by the French police and handed over to the Germans. In 1943 sixty-one more were executed, with a peak in 1944 when 212 were shot, mostly in the ten weeks between D-Day and liberation. In the same period, some 2,100 *résistants* were deported to prisons and concentration or death camps in Germany, 700 of them under the ultra-strict *Nacht und Nebel* (NN) regime, apparently inspired by Hitler's adoration of Wagner's music. In the opera *Das Rheingold*, a character curses another with the words, *'Nacht und Nebel gleich!'*, condemning him to disappear on the spot into darkest night and fog. The families of NN prisoners could not find out where they were, or even if they were alive or dead, because they officially ceased to exist. They were at the mercy of any sadistic guard who felt like beating them up or killing them, their rations were even worse than for other prisoners and they were not entitled to any medical care. In many camps, as at Natzwiller in Alsace, the NN prisoners were brutally worked to death in quarries.

Left and below: The former concentation cap at Natzwiller is now a memorial to the prisoners killed there. The huts have been cleared away, but on the parade ground where they were forced to watch executions, the gibbet has been preserved.

By early 1941, even smart middle-class people had been reduced to keeping rabbits and chickens, feeding them on scraps and taking them for walks on a lead to scrabble for worms and snails in the parks. Birdseed for more exotic avian species was all but unobtainable, so they got eaten. March was a black month for those with big appetites: fish, chocolate, tobacco and wine were all rationed. On 5 March all the oats in many northern *départements* were requisitioned, with the exception of the amount calculated to be necessary for sowing the next season's crop, and an allowance of three kilograms per day per workhorse. Feeding oats to any other animal or eating them oneself was an offence, the denunciation of which led in the occupied zone to a charge of sabotage being judged by a German military court.[4]

Denunciations for these and other infringements flowed in, both to the Vichy authorities and the Germans. A former *Abwehr* major told the author that he estimated at 30 million the number of anonymous denunciations of all kinds made during the occupation.[5] He also said that, in his office, many letters were never opened because there would not have been time. Judging by the handwriting and spelling of those that were, he thought that the majority had been written by the poor and underprivileged to get even with those above them in society or enjoying some advantage they lacked. Specific motives varied from the desire to be rid of an inconvenient wife, a violent husband or a business competitor, to settlement of family feuds. A high proportion of the anonymous letters came from women seizing the power of life and death over spouses and neighbours. When those denounced were male, one might argue that in a country which denied women the right to vote and any representation in government, the writers were collectively teaching a lesson to the men who had voted for the men who had voted for Pétain in the casino at Vichy.

The denunciations always acted on were those against Jews. To ensure this, the energetic ultra-right politician Xavier Vallat was appointed General Commissioner for Jewish Questions on 29 March, to set up the machinery to deal with them. The fact that not all the population now approved of its new government is borne out by Pétain feeling it necessary on 11 April to condemn 'the intellectuals, teachers and politicians who promote anti-government propaganda by futile gestures like writing (Gaullist) slogans on walls'. There were also many clandestinely duplicated news sheets, like the one satirising a pro-German broadcast by Catholic politician Philippe Henriot, known as 'the French Goebbels' for his war of the airwaves against Gaullist transmissions from London. It read, *Laval Productions present an exclusive and hysterically funny performance by the great fantasist of Radio Paris, Philippe Henriot. For one night only!*

After France left the League of Nations on 18 April, Vichy tightened the screw one more turn by informing newspaper editors that they must conform fully with the government's internal and foreign policies because those who did not would 'lay themselves open to severe penalties, and may be banned from publication'.

Pétain sailed sublimely onwards in his belief that his new, patriarchal style of government was good for all, announcing in a speech on 1 May that, 'May Day has hitherto been a symbol of division and class hatred. From now on, it will be a symbol of union and friendship, because it celebrates work.' The Communist newspaper *L'Humanité* published a special edition calling for closer links with the USSR and accusing General Charles de Gaulle, leader of the Free French forces in Britain, of serving, not French interests, but those of international capitalism.

The miners in the Nord and Pas de Calais *départements* showed what they thought of both *L'Humanité* and the government by displaying red flags and the forbidden *tricolor*. More importantly, they had used the time since the previous strikes to organise what they called *le téléphone arabe* – a word-of-mouth communications network using clandestine couriers travelling from one coal town to the next. On 27 May the afternoon shift refused to go down No. 7 shaft at Dourges and the news spread like an explosion throughout the coalfield. The following day, the strike committee at Dourges under Michel Brulé delivered a letter to the mine owners demanding *inter alia* the release of imprisoned comrades, a return to normal working conditions, an increase in wages and increased rations of meat, and soap with which to wash their soiled work clothes.

Thinking themselves less likely to be arrested than their menfolk, wives of miners were demonstrating in front of town halls and picketing mines in protest at the German ordinances extending the miners' working week and forbidding the traditional snack breaks, without any additional payment. To show them just how wrong they were, these demonstrations were broken up by armed force and the women's leaders were arrested, two being sentenced to hard labour for two and three years respectively, and another becoming a martyr for the cause. Arrested by the *Gestapo* and deported to Germany, Emilienne Mopty was executed by beheading in Cologne on 18 January 1943.

At *Oberfeldkommandantur* (OFK) 670 in Lille, General Niehoff decided to break the strike by condemning eleven miners and two wives to deportation into the *Reich* on 3 June. On the same day, 30,000 posters were displayed all over the coalfield, warning miners that failure to return to work made them liable to 'the severest penalties' after trial in German military courts. To Niehoff's surprise, this provoked a widening of the strike that brought 100,000 of the 143,000 miners in the coalfield out in sympathy. His reply was to place the coal towns in a state of siege with armed patrols in all towns, public buildings closed

Gestapo mugshot of Emilienne Mopty.

and demonstrations forbidden. Miners' wages were suspended and ration cards not issued to their families. Cafés and cinemas were closed and any kind of assembly forbidden.

The enthusiastic collaboration of *Préfets* Carles and Bussière was a tremendous help to the German authorities: all activists arrested by their police and gendarmerie under 'administrative internment' – which required no justification other than a suspicion of 'anti-state' activity – were immediately handed over to the German security services for torture and execution or deportation to camps in Germany. Between them, the French police and the *Feldgendarmie* arrested more than 500 PCF members or sympathisers in the area. The result was that prisons were so grossly overcrowded that two barracks had to be converted into internment camps.

On 4 June, 100,000 miners were still on strike, defying the local French administration and *Oberfeldkommandantur* 670 in Lille, but the violence of the reprisals was such that the strike was weakening, General Niehoff having instructed the employers that, although some concessions could be made, they should not be made immediately, because this would encourage further industrial action. Feeling betrayed by the return to work, and acutely aware that his high profile made him a target for both French and

German security forces, Brulé disappeared and lived with false papers as an active Resistance fighter until he was captured in November 1941 and shot at Wambrechies on 14 April 1942.

A spate of sabotage of German property and especially telephone lines brought death to the apprehended culprits. Even accidental damage was punishable by imprisonment. To prevent activists damaging pithead installations, armed German soldiers occupied the pits, ready to pounce on any go-slow as an act of sabotage. At the very moment when some concessions might have aborted the movement, the Germans decided to impose 'payment by team' so that every miner would suffer pay cuts for each go-slow or act of sabotage by anyone else in his team. Understandably, the strikers caved in and went back to work on 10 June after what was the most significant industrial action in the four years of the occupation. Their reward was an increase in wages, special food allowances and distribution of work clothes. The concessions did not include pardons for 244 of the detainees, who were deported without trial to Sachsenhausen concentration camp on 23 July and onwards to camps at Natzwiller-Struthof in Alsace and further east to Dora, Buchenwald, Auschwitz, Dachau and Mauthausen. In an attempt to pour oil on the troubled waters of the coalfield, sixty-five of them were released in 1942 and 1943 after signing an undertaking not to make any complaint about their treatment in the camps or to discuss their detention.[6] More than 130 of the other deportees died in the camps.[7]

During this period of violent industrial unrest, one law-abiding section of the population was also suffering. On 11 May the first round-up of foreign-born Jews, guilty of no offence except being born outside France, took place in Paris. French police and gendarmes despatched to concentration camps at Beaune-la-Rolande and Pithiviers, south of Paris, more than 1,000 men with French wives and families, as the first stage of their journey to the crematoria at Auschwitz. On 2 June 1941 Pétain issued his second *Statut des Juifs*. This obliged *all* Jewish heads of families everywhere in France to register their addresses with the local Town Hall, providing records that later proved invaluable to the SS and its accomplices in the *Milice* for scooping up victims. The list of professional activities barred to Jews was now so long that it effectively left them unable to earn a living. The only exceptions were for those who had rendered exceptional service to the French state – which was an ambiguous term by then – or whose family had been in France for at least five generations and rendered exceptional service to the French state during this time. All account holders received letters from their bank managers in the week of 13 June, requiring them to send an attestation of racial purity or risk their money being seized by the state.

On learning that Jews might no longer be officers in the armed services, one of France's senior lawyers, Maître Pierre Masse, wrote to Pétain:

> I should be obliged if you would tell me how I withdraw rank from my brother, a lieutenant in 36th Infantry Regiment killed at Douaumont in April 1916; from my son-in-law, a second-lieutenant in the Dragoons killed in Belgium in May 1940; from my nephew, Lieutenant J-F Masse of the 23rd Colonial Regiment, killed at Rethel in May 1940. May I leave with my brother his *Médaille Militaire*, with which he was buried? May my son Jacques, second-lieutenant in the *Chasseurs Alpins*, wounded at Soupir in June 1940, keep his rank?[8]

Courage availing nothing, Masse was arrested for his effrontery and deported to Germany, where he died.

Some COs did work. Banking, then with no need of expensive machines, was enjoying a boom in export credits to cover orders from the *Reich*. Henri Ardant, MD of *Société Générale*, considered it so vital for French banking to integrate itself into Hitler's united Europe that he jumped at the chance to run the banking CO established on 13 June 1941. His connections with the SS hierarchy were so close that *SS-Standartenführer* Helmut Knochen said at his post-war trial, 'He gave us all the information we wanted from the point of view of both banking and finance.' That bedfellows are not always lovers is demonstrated by the management of the *Banque Nationale pour le Commerce et l'Industrie* complying with the *Bankenaufsichtsamt* regulations while protecting Jewish employees from the second *Statut des Juifs* in June 1941, finding work for them to do at home and continuing to pay their salaries.[9]

In those days, popular songs became popular by catching a mood. One hit was *Attends-moi, mon amour* – wait for me, my love. With 1.6 million men locked away in POW camps, it was a plea for a distant lover to wait until reunion was possible. Another popular title was *Si loin de toi* – so far from you – and needs no explanation.

On 21 June those French people whose duties brought them into contact with Germans heard whispers that they should listen to the radio next day, when the hot news was of Hitler's invasion of the USSR, codenamed Operation *Barbarossa*. Earlier that year, 3,040 managers and 3,630 German railway operatives were embedded among French personnel at important junctions, marshalling yards and stations. Despite their on-the-ground presence, the 180-degree change in PCF policy meant that Communist staff of SNCF now obeyed orders from Moscow to delay German military trains and mis-route important cargoes whenever possible by detaching the consignment note from a wagon and shunting it into a siding, where it might stay untraced for weeks, or by painting new numbers on the wagons. More daring methods of hindering the German war effort included the introduction of sand into lubrication systems and using acid to corrode brake tubes. The German reaction was predictable. When the perpetrators were caught, they were shot. When they were not found, increasing numbers of prisoners in French and German prisons were selected and shot in their place.

Where direct sabotage was impossible, train timetables were transmitted to London, so that air raids could be timed for maximum effect. In addition, sympathetic footplate men hid Jewish and other refugees in water tenders and transported intelligence across the Line hidden under the coal. One of the safest places was aboard the special train that regularly conveyed Laval each week between Paris and Vichy without the usual strict controls. Thus began an ambivalent period for French railway workers, epecially the footplate crews, for it was they who drove the deportation trains of political hostages and Jewish and other women and children suffering intolerable thirst and hunger on the first leg of their one-way trip to the camps. Yet, short of reporting sick – which would only work once without exposing them to reprisals – what else could they do? This was often the dilemma of those later accused of collaboration.

On 30 June 1941 Pétain followed Hitler's lead by severing diplomatic relations with the USSR, but most French people were far more interested in the introduction of clothes rationing the next day, with a national appeal for them to hand in unwanted or outgrown garments, in return for which they would be given extra clothing coupons. Most people with surplus clothes, however, kept them to trade for a few eggs or a loaf of bread.

In the towns of Normandy, as elsewhere in the Occupied Zone, the sex-workers raking in money serving the needs of the German garrison troops were now walking around in the latest Paris fashions and platform shoes made from wood, straw and synthetic leather. For other women, who had not the money to buy the few new clothes available – especially the wives of absent POWs – one solution was to take Monsieur's suit to the 'little dressmaker around the corner' and get her to re-model it for Madame. New or re-cut, the skirt-culotte was the garment smart women wore on their bicycles. This had the advantage that they could bend down to pump up their tyres without fear of an importunate breeze revealing their stocking-tops to male eyes. A more inventive solution was the knee-length skirt by the house of Paquin which had a lower skirt that press-studded on after arrival at a smart event. Cycles there were, everywhere – and, like everything else in France, each one had to be registered.

The shame of the defeat, demoralisation and despair in September 1940 had prompted a teacher at Le Havre's boys' secondary school named Morpain to get together a group of trusted friends to collect information about German activities in the port, including the construction of a bomb-proof submarine pen – to be sent to London. Betrayed in June 1941, Morpain and two members of his group were arrested and shot on 7 April 1942. Even under torture, they appear to have given little away, because the other members of the group were not arrested, but went underground and reformed early in 1943 as the H-Hour network.

Pétain's announcement on 8 July 1941 that his regime was 'authoritarian and hierarchical' was quite superfluous. Three days later, two right-wing politicians launched *La Légion des Volontaires Français*. Officially recognised by Vichy on 3 August, the LVF had the support of the *Institut Catholique*. Monsignor Jean Mayol de Lupé enrolled himself as its chaplain general with the SS rank of *Sturmbannführer*, and took to greeting his Sunday congregation of legionnaires: *'Heil Hitler! Et un pieux dimanche, mes fils.'* Heil Hitler and a devout Sunday, my sons! And he was politically correct, for had not Marshal Pétain himself stated in public that Nazi Germany was Europe's bulwark against godless Marxism?

Pétain's National Socialist government praised motherhood as a career and turned Mother's Day into a national feast day, with the enthusiastic support of the Church. Three months after the Armistice, one of many magazine articles signed by the Marshal stated, 'The rights of families precede and override those of the State and individual rights.

The family ... is the essential unit of social structure.'[10] The strong Marian cult in the Church naturally approved. Benevolently smiling priests were photographed for the press with children reciting prayers they had written, asking Jesus to protect the Marshal. The image of the Good Shepherd was applied to him by bishops. On 24 July 1941, the Church bestowed its final blessing on Pétain and all his works in a statement read out in every church:

> We venerate the Head of State and ask that all French citizens rally round him. We encourage our flock to take their places at his side in the measures he has undertaken in the three domains of family, work and fatherland.[11]

No head of state could have asked for more.

Not everyone agreed, by a long way. Even Pétain, in his cloud-cuckoo land surrounded by sycophants at Vichy, felt it necessary on 12 August to denounce on radio those who refused to collaborate:

> In 1917 I ended the mutinies. In 1940 I put an end to the rout. Today, it is from yourselves that I wish to save you. I have been aware for some weeks of an ill wind blowing through several regions of France. People are being disturbed by London radio and contest the authority of my government. It will take a long time to suppress these enemies of the new order. So, my friends, we must seek out their leaders and break them.[12]

Although delivered in the Marshal's usual calm tones, the words were worthy of Hitler at his most bullying. How many people took the risk of listening to the BBC French Service at that stage of the war is unknown but, as from 13 August, none of them were Jewish because all Jews had their radios confiscated. On the same day, PCF demonstrators came to blows in Paris with French police and German *Feldgendarmerie* units. To show them who was boss, the sober, bespectacled Minister of the Interior Pierre Pucheu expanded the *Service de Police Anti-Communiste* (SPAC) next day by the formation of *brigades spéciales* under the aegis of the *Renseignements Généraux*. This was effectively a nationwide machinery for tracking down and sentencing Communists with no appeal system and only one verdict: death. Seeking to justify himself at his trial for collaboration in Algiers during 1944, Pucheu claimed that he had accepted the Interior Ministry under compulsion, and selected hostages to be shot from lists of known Communists in order to spare the lives of 'good Frenchmen', but those who knew him at the time saw a man eaten hollow by the worm of ambition.

For a mixture of motives, soon after the Germans' arrival, a few brave patriots started feeding military intelligence on the Germans' activities back to Britain's SOE and De Gaulle's *Bureau Central des Renseignements et d'Action* (BCRA) based in London. But, as the first small groups of friends involved gradually came into contact with more extended Belgian and French networks, they were vulnerable to penetration by French police and German agents. In the four years of the occupation, military courts pronounced more than 450 death sentences and several thousand prison sentences on civilians living in the *zone rattachée*, those longer than one year being served in Germany. Such bland statistics take no account of all the psychological and physical torture inflicted on those caught and their families. Even for those 'fortunate' enough to serve their sentences in France, all over the occupied zone prisons were divided into French and German sections, the former being staffed by the Vichy prison service and the latter under direct German military rule.

With Hitler's *Panzers* driving, apparently invincibly, into the USSR, the Comintern ordered the PCF to launch a campaign of assassinations of German personnel with the aim of ending the relatively peaceful relations between the population of the Occupied Zone and the German garrison forces, which in turn would oblige OKW to keep on occupation duty in France whole divisions that could otherwise be sent to the eastern front. On 13 August two Communist activists hacked an off-duty German soldier to death with a chopper and a bayonet near the Porte d'Orleans in Paris. Twenty-four hours later, the French equivalent of the notorious Nazi People's Courts was created by Vichy's establishment of special tribunals to pronounce death sentences on Communists and anarchists. To rout them out, a new department was created inside the Paris police force, which fulfilled its *Gestapo*-type functions with ruthless efficiency, effective immediately.

Five days later a German firing squad executed two men arrested during a PCF demonstration, who were also accused of thefts of explosives. On

A rare photograph of a German firing squad in France.

21 August during the Paris rush hour a 22-year-old Communist veteran of the Spanish Civil War assassinated a *Kriegsmarine* lieutenant on a Paris Metro platform – allegedly to avenge their deaths. On the morning after the assassination, the German hostage ordinance was proclaimed by bilingual posters in German and French warning that, on and after 23 August, any French person under arrest for whatever reason would be considered a hostage, and that in future a number of hostages corresponding to the gravity of such crimes would be shot.

In this case, forty-eight hostages were shot at Châteaubriant, Nantes and Paris. Although many innocent people were randomly executed during the next three years in reprisals for sabotage and attacks on German personnel, a large number of those shot were Communist activists held in prison. On this occasion, following the logic that the PCF activists ordering and executing the assassinations were mainly Jewish immigrants, the Jewish community was fined 1 million francs.[13] Hard-line PCF members acclaimed the assassinations as heroic and patriotic, but most French people disapproved both the murders and the consequences they entailed. Journalists of all shades except the PCF openly condemned them, author Pierre Audiat commenting:

> It was by no means clear how the elimination of a German soldier, who was only here in obedience to military discipline, might influence the outcome of the war. Had some truly heroic gesture been made, the murderer should have demonstrated his patriotism by staying on the scene (to be arrested for it).[14]

As other journalists remarked in print, there was nothing heroic about assassinating an off-duty German and running away, leaving other people to be shot in reprisal. However, the Comintern's plan worked well, leaving the German occupation authorities no option but to fight terror with terror. From now on, increasing numbers of hostages – both arrested PCF activists and innocent people caught in the net – would be shot for every assassination of a German. Arthur Brunet had been active in the miners' movement and was picked up by the *Gestapo* on 21 September. Shortly before being shot in the citadel of Lille, he wrote to his wife: 'You know that I am innocent. All I ask is that you keep my memory in your heart forever. Be brave for the sake of our dear children.'[15]

Alfred Delattre had been a PCF activist since 1929 and was a leading figure in the miners' strike, as was his wife Aline. On 07.00hrs on 8 September 1941 he wrote to her parents, who were looking after his four children:

> They have just told us that our appeal has been dismissed. We are to be shot at eight o'clock. Dear ones, give a kiss from me to my beloved Aline and look after her when she is released. You will have to give her courage. I have asked that everything in my cell be delivered to you so that you will have something to remember me by once I am gone. Now I leave you for ever.[16]

He was executed with two other activists of his group in the citadel at Arras. Another prominent PCF member, Jean Catelas, was condemned by French judges at the La Santé prison in Paris and guillotined there with two others on 24 September, after writing to his defence counsel: 'I fall as a soldier fighting for a cause that is French and just. I pardon my judges who did not judge, but only obeyed orders.'[17]

Chapter 6

Dear Mummy, I am going to die

It was not only German and French firing squads, Gestapo torturers and the blades of the guillotine that people had to fear. In Le Havre, for example, several hundred civilians had already been killed by RAF bombs and many more injured. On 12 September 1941 the daily paper *Le Petit Havre* published this article under the title 'The Night Exiles':

> Starting at five o-clock every evening, they leave their homes and walk up the hill, sweating and gasping under the weight of bedding, food and all the precious things they dare not leave behind – official papers, photographs, letters.
>
> These are the night exiles, fleeing their homes to escape the bombs and the threat of being buried alive or dying a pointless death. They are not going far. As soon as the last No. 8 tram has passed, they crowd into the tramway tunnel and, under its dripping roof, cram themselves and their shapeless bundles wherever they can, waiting for sleep that does not come.
>
> It is uncomfortable and cold in the tunnel, with violent draughts sweeping through. And there's too much noise, although the police try to keep the level down. Above the whispered rumours and a thousand other irritating sounds, a husband shouts at his wife and another wife accuses her husband of forgetting to turn off the gas when they left home. Smoking is forbidden, but some people ignore the notices. Those who cannot keep still push their way through the crush. Someone plays an accordion badly.

Just when sleep seems possible, the sirens wail for the Alert. People sit up, listening to *them*. They are overhead. No, they're over the town centre. No, they're over the port. No, they're over Graville. The argument is joined by an old soldier, showing his wound and telling everyone how he copped his packet at the battle of Chemin des Dames in the last war. When the raid is over, people scramble back to their places, seemingly indifferent to the awful tragedy outside which may right now be destroying their homes so that tomorrow morning they will possess only the few belongings they have with them.

Even for the toughest, there is no peace in these sleepless nights, troubled by fleas, with the smell of oil and the dampness everywhere. In one place, a 15-year-old boy is looking after his sick grandmother. In another, a mother breastfeeds her little one, while three other small children squabble around her. The very young have at least the advantage that they do not understand what is going on. Another young mum sits with her baby and the few things she has been able to bring with them after finishing a hard day's work. Occasionally some good soul helps her get to the tunnel, but good souls are becoming rarer. Yet somehow she manages to get there each night, to sleep as best she can in the dirt and the dust on the tram lines for the sake of the child in her arms and of her husband, far away in a POW camp in Germany.

There are so many of them in the Sainte Marie tunnel – between 5,000 and 10,000, depending on the night. They are young and old, poor and rich, but they keep coming back to grab a pitch under the dripping roof because it is better to spend the night there in the dirt, damp and discomfort than to die beneath the bombs.[1]

Four days later, the dirt, the smells, the damp and the draughts of the tunnel all seemed a small price to pay. When the night exiles emerged at dawn on 16 September, they found the city centre ripped apart, with the major stores like Monoprix and Au Printemps reduced to smoking husks by a raid starting at 21.30hrs the previous evening, in which waves of RAF bombers had dropped bombs for three solid hours.

Contemporary newspaper photograph of people sleeping in the tram tunnel.

In these early raids, although each casualty was a tragedy for those involved, the total numbers were not too great for the local police, fire and ambulance services to cope with, but as the RAF gained larger bombers carrying heavier bomb loads, the number of dead and injured began to exceed what the existing services could handle. The Pétainist civil defence organisation *Secours National* and the French Red Cross organised nationwide collections of money, of food, of clothing and shoes for those made homeless, as did the Catholic and other churches. Food and clothing had to be stored near the towns at risk, but not in them, and emergency kitchens were equipped and staffed to feed and care for those rendered homeless. Later, the Red Cross also purchased large stocks of condensed milk in Switzerland and distributed them strategically around the country.

A small number of children were even evacuated to safety in neutral Switzerland, but evacuating homeless children from bombed towns was rendered administratively difficult by the division of the Channel coast into three zones with different administrations. Altogether thirteen centres providing accommodation for evacuated children were set up in safer parts of France, in some cases by the requisitioning of chateaux with extensive grounds. The National Lottery issued special tickets, from which the profit went to evacuation of children, its posters showing happy girls and boys looking out of the windows of trains. Reality was sometimes very different. As in Britain, some children responded well to the arrangements made for them; others were deeply unhappy and impossible for their host families to handle. Until the entry of the USA into the war made this impossible, the American Friends Service Committee in France financed and ran reception centres in the Free Zone, and the American Red Cross shipped in through Marseille whole cargoes of baby clothes, nappies and milk.

Evacuating the adult population was more difficult. One solution discussed in Vichy was to construct resettlement camps for the entire populations of towns at risk, but this was discarded for a complex of reasons, including the impossibility of finding work for hundreds of thousands of displaced people near such camps without placing an intolerable strain on the local economy. In any case, many people refused to go and live among strangers who had enough problems of their own. Cherbourg was forcibly evacuated twice and St-Malo no less than four times, but each time most people returned as soon as they could, preferring to be in their own homes despite the dangers. Local authorities also had to take into account the need for people to stay in the towns and cities at risk in order to run the municipal services there, staff the public utilities, man the factories, teach in the schools, drive buses and trains and serve in the shops, so priorities were far from clear-cut.

The job of a mayor in France is traditionally very hands-on. In these difficult circumstances, it called for very special qualities. On 29 September 1941, after Vichy's replacement for Léon Meyer had died and his replacement proved unsuitable, Le Havre got the new mayor it deserved. Pierre Courant was a 43-year-old lawyer, who proved to be the right man to see his city through the rest of the occupation, setting up emergency services in collaboration with the various charities and acting as go-between with the occupation authorities. With the increasing scarcity of motor fuel, it was often from German fuel dumps that the fire service filled its tanks. Courant's town hall became the coordinating headquarters of fire-watching teams reporting outbreaks to the municipal fire service and for the rescue teams with lifting equipment, stretcher bearers and first aid workers, and the liaison with local doctors and hospital managements. The Vichy youth movements supplied both girls and boys to help the professional rescue workers. Even the town morgue had to be reorganised and staffed to cope with at first dozens, then hundreds of dead and severely injured after a single raid. Because local services could not handle disaster on that scale, provision was made to lend spare capacity to nearby towns and conversely to 'borrow' their spare capacity in the hour of need. Happily, no planner then dared voice the thought that the death toll from one raid would eventually be in the thousands, for this was inconceivable at the time.

That September saw mysterious fires damaging crops in the Occupied Zone. When the arsonists were caught, the penalties were severe because this was treated as sabotage. In any case, whom did it harm? The government distributed posters to make the point that German requisitions remained unchanged, so burning crops simply reduced the food available for French people.

On 4 October 1941, Pétain's plan for industry became clearer. His *Charte du Travail* or Labour Charter banned strikes, made free trade unions illegal and obliged all employers and employees to join a new, government-approved trade union.

The legend reads: 'Less corn means less bread.'

On 22 and 23 October two more attacks on German officers led to the execution of ninety-eight hostages, personally selected by Interior Minister Pierre Pucheu. When appointed in July, Pucheu had boasted of his intention to execute 20,000 Communists. To spread the terror country-wide, the ninety-eight were shot in Bordeaux, Nantes and Châteaubriant. Roughly half of this batch of victims were Jews taken from Drancy concentration camp, enabling Pucheu to justify his action by claiming that otherwise the Germans would have shot French veterans.

Evidently, to his way of thinking, being Jewish cancelled out status as a veteran: among sixteen hostages shot at a firing range near Nantes was one of the decorated heroes abandoned by the government of the country they had served in one or both world wars. Léon Jost was a director of the biscuit company Lu who had lost a leg in the first war and since devoted much time to ex-servicemen's and other welfare work. Arrested on 15 January, he had been sentenced on 15 July to three years' imprisonment for helping to organise an escape line to Britain via Douarnenez. Selected by Pucheu, he was among those driven to the firing range. As there was a three-hour delay in arranging the transport, Jost added a series of postscripts to his last letter, all neatly numbered like the minutes of a meeting. In the first, he apologised for his handwriting, having given up his spectacles and pen. In the last, he asked his wife to write for their children a memorial of his life with her. 'I was marked out by fate,' he wrote, 'but we loved each other greatly, didn't we, my darling?'[2]

Like all the other terror machinery of the Reich, the hostage executions generated their own bureaucracy. Désiré Granet, shot at Châteaubriant on 22 October, wrote just before his death to his 11-year-old son Raymond, 'I ask you to keep the promise you made me, to work hard at school and to love your mother, who has loved me and whom I love so much.'[3] The widow asked one favour only of his killers: to be able to bury the body of her husband in a local cemetery. A confused and anonymous *Oberleutnant* (signature illegible) in the *Feldkommandantur* at Nantes replied on 9 December, the envelope being addressed in error to the dead man instead of the widow:

> In reply to yours of 28th inst, the Kommandantur informs you that your husband, shot as a hostage at Châteaubriant on 22 October, was buried in the cemetery of Russigne (sic).

Your request for re-possession of his effects has meanwhile been passed to the *Préfecture*. Your request to remove the body has been refused.

A form letter from the mayor of Châteaubriant advised her in scarcely warmer tones:

It is permitted to place flowers on the graves. It is not permitted to remove the bodies, nor to place a gravestone on the grave with the deceased's name. Any pilgrimage or demonstration is forbidden.[4]

Some of the questions one cannot help asking oneself about these executions are answered in an eyewitness report of the execution of Granet and twenty-six other men, written immediately afterwards by Abbé Moyon from Béré-de-Châteaubriant:

It was a warm and sunny autumn day. Being a Wednesday, the town was bustling with the activities of the weekly market when my lunch was interrupted by Monsieur Moreau, director of the concentration camp at Choisel. Hearing that the hostages were to be shot, I agreed to go with him to be with them in their last hours. At the camp, the hostages had been placed in a special detention hut, surrounded by both German soldiers and French gendarmes when I arrived. The *sous-préfet* had already given the men the news and suggested they should immediately write last letters to their families.

I had the feeling that some of the men only truly believed they were going to die when they saw me arrive (wearing my *soutane*). I told them that I had come not only as a priest for the believers, but to give what consolation I could to them all and carry out any last wishes. For forty-five minutes I listened to them talking of their families, their hopes and cares, but I was unable to answer their most urgent question: when, where and how they were to be executed.

The door of the hut, which I had closed to give us some privacy from the guards, was thrown open to admit French gendarmes with handcuffs for all the condemned men, as well as a *Wehrmacht* chaplain, who told me to leave. All the other prisoners had been locked in their huts, and from every hut came the sound of men singing the *Marseillaise*. The handcuffed hostages were led into waiting trucks, joining in the *Marseillaise*, some singing the *Internationale*. I tried to keep up with the execution convoy in my car, but was left behind, my last contact being the sound of the condemned men singing. At the quarry chosen for the execution they were divided for execution into three groups of nine, all the men refusing to be blindfolded. The youngest, a boy of seventeen, fainted before the volley rang out.[5]

Désiré Granet was a left-wing activist, interned because of his political activities, but not a terrorist. Out of solidarity for his fellow-prisoners he had refused the offer of a former comrade who had changed sides to intervene on his behalf with Pierre Pucheu, for whom he now worked. But Guy Môquet, the 17-year-old hostage who fainted, was just a boy who had been arrested on 15 October 1940 while indiscreetly distributing leaflets at a Paris Metro station. Ironically, at that date the PCF was still pro-German and Môquet's tracts blamed equally German and French big business interests for causing 'the capitalist conflict', as the party line went. His arrest was made under a French law of September 1939 which made it an offence to distribute propaganda by the then illegal PCF. His last letter to his family read:

> Dear Mummy, my dear little brother and beloved Papa,
> I am going to die. You especially, Mummy, I ask to be brave. I am trying to be as brave as those who have passed this way before me. Of course, I should have liked to live, but what I want most of all is that my death serves some purpose. I hope that all my things will be sent back to you and hope that (my little brother) Serge will be proud to wear them one day.
>
> Papa, please forgive me the many problems I caused for you and Mummy. Know that I have done my best to follow the path you showed me (of left-wing politics). I am saying goodbye – a last goodbye to all my friends and my brother whom I love very much. May he work hard at school and

grow up to become a man. At seventeen and a half, my life
has been short, but my only regret is to have to leave you all.
I am going to die with my friends. Please, Mummy, I want
you to promise me to be brave and get over your grief. I can't
write any more.
Goodbye to you all, Mummy, Serge, Papa. Courage!
Your loving Guy.
P.S. My last thoughts are that you should be worthy of us
twenty-seven who are going to die.[6]

Abbé Moyon was careful to keep a neutral tone in his account of the
execution, for this was still the honeymoon period for Pétain and the
Church hierarchy, with religious schools eligible for State subsidy and
teachers once again allowed to hang a crucifix on the classroom wall,
which had been forbidden for thirty-five years as part of the separation of
Church and State under the Third Republic. While other demonstrations
and mass meetings were forbidden, formal pilgrimages and other religious
assemblies were tolerated.

Firing squads were not the only danger in France that October:
newspapers carried announcements headed *Attention, all those who are
eating cat-meat!* The warning boiled down to advice to cook the cats well
to avoid being fatally contaminated by microbes from rats they had eaten.
What food was obtainable depended on geography. A politician called
Yves Bouthillier, who held several ministerial positions under Pétain,
summed it up thus:

'The south of France has no wheat, no sugar, no potatoes, no seeds,
no coal and very little barley and oats; the north has no wine, no oil and
no soap.'[7]

In November food shortages led to a rapid expansion in the black market,
condemned by both Vichy and the Church. However, for hungry people
the morality was obscure, with Bishop Dutoit of Arras telling his flock:

When a producer has furnished at the legal price the quantity
of foodstuffs or merchandise he is required to produce, it
seems to us that it is not against the law to ask a *slightly* higher
price for his surplus. But justice and charity are opposed to
any increase in price that constitutes an exploitation of the
need or credulity of the buyer.[8]

As in Britain, so also in France, many right-wing intellectuals had long been infatuated with Hitler's New Europe. In November, Pierre Drieu La Rochelle and Robert Brasilach, respectively a contributor to, and editor of, the far-right newspaper *Je Suis Partout*,[9] were living it up at a writers' congress in Germany. A more commendable motive for travelling there was that of Colonel Hans Speidel. Despatched by *Militärbefehlshaber in Frankreich* General Otto von Stülpnagel to Hitler's HQ in East Prussia to request permission to relax the Hostage Ordinance because the scale of reprisals was playing into the Communists' hands, Speidel returned empty-handed and later commented, 'Von Stülpnagel was too correct for the Party.' For his 'correctness', the unfortunate *Militärbefehlshaber* was to pay a double price, deprived of office the following year and accused by the Allies of war crimes after the war, awaiting trial for which he committed suicide in February 1948.

On 16 November 1941 six Communist activists were shot in the citadel of Lille, not as hostages, but for crimes they had committed, and six others sentenced to forced labour. Heading the list, Félicien Joly had been found guilty of fifty sabotage missions and other anti-German activities. After being extensively tortured at Valenciennes, he was still able to think clearly of his loved ones' future as it would be. To his fiancée, he wrote, 'When the rhythm of life overwhelms memories of me, embrace the future, be happy in another man's arms and do not weep for what we have done together.'[10]

And so Moscow's contribution to France's misery went on and on: hit-and-run assassins killing unsuspecting off-duty Germans, making no contribution to the war effort, and sabotage that caused the deaths of increasing numbers of hostages shot in cases where the perpetrators could not be found.

In Paris and major towns in the provinces high street stores were taken over by the *Office de Placement pour l'Allemagne* – a German labour exchange staffed by French-speaking staff who dangled the promise of better rations and higher wages before workers disillusioned with Laval's empty promises. Where a single parent, or both parents, volunteered to work in the *Reich*, their children were accommodated in special children's homes, like the *Manoir de l'Enfance* at Rouen.[11]

After the departure on 19 November 1941 from Paris Gare du Nord station of the 100,000th French volunteer worker for Germany, one might think Goering would be all smiles on meeting Marshal Pétain a week later at St-Florentin. Yet, blocking all the Marshal's quietly-voiced

Laval's 100,000th volunteer does not look too happy when being sent off to Germany.

requests, Goering shouted, 'Tell me, Marshal. Who won this war? You or us?' Visibly shaken by this gross discourtesy, Pétain replied with a quiet sarcasm that escaped Fat Hermann, 'I had not previously been quite so aware how badly we had been beaten.'

He must have been the only person in France still unaware. All over the country, his people were in mourning – for the defeat, for the million and a half POWs still languishing in German camps and for their own self-esteem. As during a period of formal national mourning, public gaiety was frowned upon, especially dances, which were banned as being frivolous and inappropriate, their passing celebrated with a popular song *Depuis que les bals sont fermés* – meaning, since the dance halls closed. But you cannot stop young people seizing the excuse to hold and be held. In place of public dances came *les bals clandestins*, organised by word of mouth. Friends whispered of a rendezvous in a house with a room large enough for a dozen or so couples to get together to the music of a portable wind-up gramophone and, for an hour or two, the war was forgotten in the arms of one's partner.

In December 1941 Hitler decreed the construction of a Gürtel von Bollwerken – literally, a girdle of bulwarks – running 5,000km along the coast from Norway to the Spanish border. Along the way, each port was to be turned into a fortress to withstand attack by land, sea and air, while the intervening coastline was to become a death trap sprinkled with anti-tank ditches, minefields and gun emplacements. At least, that was the idea. The emphasis on the ports was consistent with his obsession that the Allies would have to capture one in the first hours of an invasion in order to re-supply the bridgehead. Le Havre, with its deep-water facilities and ship-building and repair yards, was to receive particular attention. The labour force was supplied by conscripting local men as *requis*, paid a minimum wage for constructing the thousands of reinforced concrete bunkers, blockhouses, strongpoints and submarine pens. Was that collaboration? With most of these constructions still regrettably intact – in some cases despite falling down cliffs that eroded beneath them and there being assaulted by the tides for six decades and more – it does not seem that the *requis* deliberately sabotaged their work.

Life inside the fortresses – and indeed all across northern France – was a series of miseries for most people, with the official rations furnishing only 1,200 calories or less than half the daily requirement for an adult male.[12] To make up the shortfall on the grey and black markets, with salaries frozen at the 1940 level, seven-tenths of average monthly income was devoted to food, according to a survey by sociologist Patrick Dourdin. At 876 francs, it was approximately the black market price for two kilos of butter. Deaths from malnutrition, hypothermia and lack of medicine pushing civil mortalities to 169 per cent of pre-war levels so alarmed the *Propagandastaffel* that it recommended a forced exodus to remove 1,000,000 'useless mouths' from the capital to the provinces where they could be more easily fed.[13] Aperitifs, tobacco, bed linen, shoes, torch batteries and shaving cream had become unobtainable in shops. The money economy was failing; barter became the rule, with people rhyming:

> The cobbler's got some ribbon, the hairdresser's got cheese.
> Everybody's got to swap in times like these.

On alcohol-banned days, known as *les jours sans* or 'days without,' regular patrons at a café or restaurant ordered their 'usual coffee' with a wink to the waiter and found in the cup a black market *digestif* or *apéritif*.

Cartoonist Aldebert drew a smirking waiter whispering in a client's ear, 'In the soup, Monsieur, you'll find a whole chicken stuffed with two mutton chops.' People joked, 'Save paper! Don't throw away your used Metro ticket, but use it to wrap your weekly meat ration after sealing the perforations, so the meat doesn't fall through.'[14] Behind the jokes was a national propaganda campaign against the black market, with severe penalties for small operators when caught. The big operators rarely were.

Nobody lucky enough to have cigarettes threw away the dog-ends, which were kept to re-roll for another smoke. Extraordinary *ersatz* tobacco mixtures were sold, the most bizarre being 'Belgian tobacco,' a concoction of gossamer spider silk said to resemble 'the pubic hair of Venetian blondes'![15] Real soap had disappeared; on contact with water the substitute blocks disintegrated to a gritty paste. Workers in dirty jobs had the right to extra 'soap,' but the repeated queuing to collect it took up a working day, which they could ill afford. The depression that all these shortages and restrictions produced got steadily worse, until a report by the Lyon *gendarmerie* in July 1943 openly affirmed: 'The mood of the population is very negative. People criticise every initiative of the government and listen favourably to English radio. They consider the Germans to be the main enemy.'[16]

Not that most people were prepared to do much about it. One of the few very active espionage networks collecting information on German activities in and around Cherbourg for London was named *Interallié*. It was founded by handsome 30-year-old Major Roman Czerniawski, who fought in the Battle of France as intelligence officer of 1st Polish Division and escaped after the defeat from a German POW camp at Lunéville in Lorraine, making his way with false papers as far as Toulouse.

There he formed a relationship with petite, well-dressed, green-eyed law graduate Mathilde Carrée, who had escaped from a boring marriage by enlisting as a nurse in a military hospital. For whatever reason, his new lover seemed to Czerniawski the right partner with whom to found an underground network collecting intelligence for forwarding to London, with the help of some contacts he had in the *Deuxième Bureau* at Vichy. There, curled up like a cat on the sofas in the smart hotels, Mathilde acquired the code-name by which she was to become infamous, *La Chatte* – the she-cat or 'pussy'. Czerniawski, who spoke faultless French, took the *nom de guerre* Armand. Their network of agents was designated F1 in London. Part of its initial success was Mathilde's ability

Major Roman Czerniawski in
his Polish uniform.

to persuade people who could be useful, but sadly she often neglected the
cut-outs and checks vital for security.

Armand's use of fellow Poles in France to transport microfilms across
the Line to Marseille and thence to London was critical. So good was the
quality of the material that, early in 1941, *Interallié* was sent a transmitter
to speed things up. Each message began, 'No 55A to War Ministry,
London, this is *La Chatte* talking.' Over-confidence led to a fatal error
in October 1941, when a docker in Cherbourg was asked by a female
member of *Interallié* to provide information and instead denounced her
to the *Abwehr* – German military intelligence. In her home were found
compromising documents and a list of twenty names, including that of
Raoul Kieffer, an ex-officer who transported information on the first leg
of its journey, to Paris.

Realising the importance of the network, the local *Abwehr* officer
requested a first-class interpreter to help in interrogations, and was
sent a 42-year-old failed pianist. Having been held prisoner in a British

POW camp in France during the first war, Sgt Hugo Bleicher spoke excellent French and good English. He also had a flair for interrogation, swiftly recognised by his secondment to the *Abwehr* for the rest of the war. After turning Kieffer, he set about penetrating the network all the way to the top. On 17 November, he arrested Armand, who had been betrayed by a Breton fisherman he was trying to persuade to smuggle messages across the Channel.

Relations had lately been stormy between Mathilde and Armand, who had meanwhile taken up with a former mistress. After Mathilde was arrested, whether from sexual jealousy or sheer terror on being locked up for her first night in the German wing of La Santé prison in Paris, on the following day she was out of her cell and in the bed of *Interallié's* nemesis, joining him in a sing-song around the piano of her new lover with a group of German officers, by whom she was re-christened *das kleine Kätzchen* – the little kitten.

Bleicher, who was never promoted, although using the *nom de guerre* 'Colonel Henri', was a gifted, but not brutal interrogator – as proof of which, two of his British prisoners, Odette and Peter Churchill, actually invited him to their wedding after the war. He persuaded Armand to collaborate by promising that his agents would be treated as POWs and not spies. The promise was not honoured: those who refused to be turned were tortured and deported, most never returning from the camps.

In one of the most successful *Funkspiele* of the war, Bleicher used a former *Interallié* radio operator to feed false intelligence to London. Confident that Mathilde was now his agent, he released her to troll for her contacts still at liberty, whom she betrayed one by one. At her trial in 1949, where she based her defence on the claim that a woman did not have the same choices as a man after being captured, Armand accused her of being 'a dangerous nymphomaniac'. Her death sentence was commuted to life imprisonment because, by then, people in France were tired of all the killing. In her memoirs, written during the twelve years spent in French and British prisons before her release, Mathilde admitted to having been 'driven by the animal pleasures of the body which my soul disdains'.[17]

Most people preferred to shut their eyes and escape with the help of popular songs like *Douce France, cher pays de mon enfance* – Sweet France, the dear land of my childhood – an unashamedly nostalgic yearning for the happier past, to which virtually everyone looked back. Charles Trenet had a hit with *Couché dans le foin avec le soleil pour témoin.* Ostensibly about a carefree tumble in the hay with a girlfriend 'where only the sun could see us', it touched a chord in people fed up with being spied on.

By the end of 1941, 7,000 French companies were accepting and fulfilling German orders for both civilian and military products. It was a figure that would double before the end of the occupation, when virtually all firms with fifty or more employees and many smaller companies were working exclusively for the Reich. In some fifty major corporations, German directors were forcibly installed in the boardroom, where they intervened directly in management decisions.

What was the alternative? French industry was in a vice. Since the occupation administration controlled the allocation of raw materials, any firm that refused German orders would have been obliged to lay off its workforce. Not only did working for the occupiers mean business, German contracts also made for a truce between management and labour, since the single-union representatives could literally see on which side their bread was buttered: the occupation authorities released extra food for factory canteens where the workers were behaving the way they wanted. A full stomach being a powerful argument, any initial reluctance of management and labour to deal with the only client in the market dwindled rapidly. Commercial giants like Paribas, Rhône-Poulenc, Ugine, Crédit Lyonnais, Société Générale and many others were, according to historian Annie Lacroix-Riz, more than eager to do business with the Reich.[18]

Yet, a few refused to compromise. At the top of the scale, the giant Michelin company had both the advantage of being based in the Free Zone and the clout to keep the German agencies at arm's length. When Germany offered to release supplies of artificial Buna rubber to replace the no longer available supplies of natural rubber from Indo-China in return for shares in the company and taking over subsidiaries in Belgium and other Axis-occupied countries, Michelin found a thousand ways to wriggle out of such a deal because its management shrewdly foresaw the impossibility of a *final* German victory, whatever the next few years might bring. The price for such resistance in more vulnerable companies was often harsh: when the President of the *Crédit Commercial de France* bank refused to hand over to the Germans 440,000 shares in the *Galeries Lafayette* department store formerly owned by a Jewish shareholder, he was fired.

To understand the policies of the biggest companies requires mentally sitting for a moment in their boardrooms, where the war and the occupation were seen as temporary complications that required only modification, and not abandonment, of long-term policies. Louis Renault, the otherwise shrewd head of the automobile empire, guessed wrongly that Germany and Britain would soon make peace to avoid weakening themselves by a prolonged conflict that would leave them both wide-open to Soviet invasion or American economic domination. His decision to accept orders for vehicles from the *Wehrmacht* was to cost his life after the Liberation.[19] Yet, how could he have refused, after making trucks and tanks for the French army and having both the skilled work-force and the necessary production lines? Getting into bed with the enemy required a delicate balancing act: the Peugeot family supported Pétain for the first two years of the occupation and accepted orders from Germany, yet refused such blandishments as extra food for its workers, because of the German propaganda that came with it.[20]

Even without extra doses in the workplace, German propaganda was organised in every town by an office of the *Propagandastaffel*, whose functionaries not only censored anti-German stories in the newspapers, reduced to a single sheet by the shortage of paper, and repressed any mention of the growing differences between Berlin and Vichy, but also ordered editors and publishers to print Hitler's speeches in large typeface, to promote pro-German films and books and carry Berlin's version of the war news in every issue, omitting Allied successes. Even Pétain's speeches were censored. Because the French take a delight in playing on words, papers published in the Free Zone were not allowed to be imported across the Line, in case they contained some subtleties that the German censors had missed. Even within the Occupied Zone, editors took risks with tongue in cheek, as when *Le Petit Havre* was obliged to salute Hitler's birthday in 1941, but did so with none of the enthusiasm the censors might have desired. The editorial read:

> For the present, our role is simply to be an organ of information. We do not intend in the present state of things to meddle in internal or foreign politics. Let everyone have his own opinions. We therefore acknowledge the fact that Adolf Hitler was born in 1889 at Braunau, in Lower Austria, and it is his birthday today.

Among the forty-six rules for the media published on 18 February 1943, editors were informed that it was forbidden to use the expression 'Alsace-Lorraine'; 'Anglo-Saxon' had to be replaced by 'Anglo-American'; what the French called 'the Free Zone' must be referred to as 'the unoccupied zone'; and so on. Occupation costs were not to be mentioned, nor were deaths of POWs in captivity. And Rule No. 7 was Nazi geography writ large:

> Do not in future use the terms 'Austria', 'Poland', 'Czechoslovakia' or 'Yugoslavia'. Austria is part of Germany. There is no longer a Czechoslovakia, but the province of Ostmark. There is no longer a Poland, but a *'gouvernement général'*. Yugoslavia does not exist; use the terms 'Serbia' and 'Croatia'.

An inside-page story about vandalism caused an explosion at the weekly meeting in the *Propagandastaffel* in Orleans, swiftly enshrined in yet another nation-wide edict: 'No further use is to be made of the word "vandalism" when referring to destruction. Reason: the Vandals were ancestors of the German people.'[21]

Chapter 7

Shameless women and guilty men

In 2009 President Nicolas Sarkozy announced that it was time to rationalise the country's forces of law and order, France having been policed nationally for two centuries by two quite separate national forces. The division of responsibility gave the *Police Nationale* jurisdiction in large towns and cities, with the *Gendarmerie Nationale* looking after the countryside, villages and small towns. Even at the site of major disasters, the two forces shared no common radio frequencies and local units of one force had no authority to liaise with the other. On a personal level, relatives of traffic victims picked up, or people arrested, by the *gendarmerie* were wasting time trying to trace them through the police and vice versa.

Why the strict segregation? While filming in Armentières some years ago, the author put that question to the *Commissaire de Police*, who replied:

> Remember that modern France began with the Revolution. All revolutionary governments are paranoid. The *Police Nationale* is controlled by the Minister of the Interior and the *Gendarmerie Nationale* comes under the Minister of Defence. Every head of government makes sure that those two ministers are personal enemies who would never share power with each other. Thus, no one man can control both forces. Since they are roughly equal in size, neither of these two large paramilitary forces can be used to stage a *coup d'état* without being counterbalanced by the other.

Nevertheless, on 13 January 1942 the officer commanding the *Gendarmerie Nationale* in Paris ordered all units under his command to adopt the system of repression practised by the Paris police, to give all assistance to the police in case of terrorist attacks, to pursue the aggressors by all means and capture them dead or alive.[1]

Words, however, were not enough for the Germans or the government in Vichy. Two months previously, the Pétainist ex-servicemen's organisation called *La Légion des Combattants* had been transformed into *La Légion des Combattants et Volontaires de la Révolution Nationale* with membership open to all who approved Vichy politics, whether veterans or not. It thus became in effect a far-right political party.

The Vichy regime wanted to take the war to the enemy by creating an ultra force of volunteers prepared to stamp out the left-wing Resistance by using its own undercover methods of kidnapping and murder, so members of the new-style *Légion* were invited in January 1942 to join a new paramilitary force called *Le Service d'Ordre Légionnaire* (SOL). Members wearing SS-type uniforms surmounted inevitably by berets enjoyed torchlight oath-taking ceremonies and marched around on parade with waving banners. A far-right Pétainist ex-serviceman with a distinguished record in both wars was appointed Inspector-General of the SOL. The enthusiasm which Joseph Darnand put into his new job was to earn him honorary membership of the SS in 1943 and a death sentence after the Liberation.

On 12 February 1942 a group of schoolboys walking home for lunch from Boulogne to Wimereux had a grandstand view of something for which the RAF and Royal Navy were searching high and low. Various Resistance sources had warned London that the much bombed pocket battleships *Scharnhorst* and *Gneisenau* and the heavy cruiser *Prinz Eugen* were being readied in the harbour of Brest for a dash through the Channel to safety in a German port, and that *Luftwaffe* bases all along the Channel coast were on standby for some special operation that was most likely the provision of an aerial umbrella for the battleships. The submarine HMS *Sealion* was on station in the Channel to intercept the three capital ships and their escort of destroyers and minesweepers, but failed to see anything. Nor did a Coastal Command Hudson. The weather was on the German side that day, with low cloud, a gale blowing and thick sea mist.

The boys first heard the sound of powerful engines out at sea. Reaching the crossroads at Honvault, they saw a swarm of Messerschmitt and Focke-Wulf fighters between the sea and the cloud base. Then, like grey ghosts, the minesweepers loomed up out of the mist, followed by several destroyers and three larger warships – all going flat out, so close in-shore that they seemed to be skimming the mole of Boulogne harbour. Within a few minutes, the fleet and its aerial umbrella had disappeared into the greyness. Among the boys was the young Guy Bataille, later a journalist and historian, who only appreciated what they had seen years later, when the exploit of Admiral Otto Ciliax in Operation *Cerberus* – the famous 'Channel dash' of the three capital ships to a safer port in Germany – was a matter of historical fact.

Assassinations of German personnel brought increasing misery to uninvolved people shot or deported in reprisal. After an attack by a Communist *Francs-Tireurs et Partisans* (FTP) group on German soldiers near the arsenal of Le Havre, more than 150 men were rounded up on 23 and 24 February 1942. Of these, thirty foreign-born Jews from Poland, Romania and Lithuania were transported by the *gendarmerie* to Rouen prison, from there to the German-run concentration camp at Compiègne, to be herded into cattle trucks in June and July, destination Auschwitz-Birkenau. None returned.

In the same month, the underground newspaper *Défense de la France* – which would re-brand itself as *France Soir* in 1944 – published a prophetic tirade against women who slept with the enemy:

> You so-called French women who give your bodies to a German will have your heads shaved, with a notice pinned on your backs *Sold to the enemy!* Likewise, you shameless girls who trip around with the occupiers will be shaved and whipped. On all your foreheads a swastika will be branded with hot iron.

Who were these shameless women and girls? If some were amateur prostitutes, others were single mothers needing a protector, a source of money or extra food; others again were just young girls seeking some fun in the dark years when a new dress or a pair of pretty shoes was otherwise only a dream. But a good number were respectable women employed in hotels, restaurants and other places reserved for a German clientele. Even those who at first never smiled or replied other than frigidly to questions, found from daily contact with German personnel that most of them had no more desire to be in Hitler's armed forces than the French had to see them in France. From there, Nature took her course.

Raymonde Z worked in an abbatoir near St-Malo, plucking and gutting twelve chickens an hour. It is easy to see why she fell for her elegant lover Fritz, in his smart dark-blue *Kriegsmarine* uniform, but there was a price to pay. As the Bible has it, 'the sins of the father shall be visited on the sons'.[2] In this case, it was the perceived sin of the mother that had to be expiated. After the Liberation Raymonde's son Gérard grew up with the other children at school singling him out as *le fils du Boche* and his abusive mother punishing him daily as the incarnation of her shame. Interviewed for *L'Express* aged sixty-plus in 2004, he said bitterly, 'She ought to have aborted me, or given me away'.[3]

Perhaps some of these women sought an escape from Pétain's crushingly patriarchal *Etat Français*, in which the female citizens had no political rights, no representation and no influence of any kind outside the home. But many others genuinely fell in love, never thinking that there would be a price to pay for the hours, weeks or months of happiness before their lovers were posted away at short notice to the eastern front. Thérèse Y worked in her mother's bar at Lillebonne, halfway between Rouen and the coast. After closing time, her mother slept with Germans for cash, and turned a blind eye to what her 17-year-old daughter was up to with Josef, in civilian life a music-loving pharmacist who sang operatic arias to her after the bar was closed. To have a sexual relationship with a racially inferior French women outside an approved brothel was an offence under military law, so Thérèse's dreams of romance ended when she told him she was pregnant.

After he stopped seeing her, she found a job a waitress in a requisitioned château where, among the men she served at table was her ex-lover, pretending not to know her. His regiment posted elsewhere, Josef vanished, only to reappear in Lillebonne three days after the lonely birth, apparently full of remorse. After briefly holding in his arms the daughter who had been christened Marie-José after him, he vanished forever, leaving a baby girl who grew up wondering, 'When will Daddy come back for me?' Unlike many of France's war babies, Marie-José was told the truth by her mother when young, but it was not until 2002 that they travelled together to the WASt – the Wehrmacht Archives Service – and there, among 18,000,000 files they found that of Josef, who died unmarried in 1984.[4]

Illicit affairs with German personnel during the occupation resulted in 30,000 declared births. To this figure must be added all the children who were fathered on paper by an unwitting or consenting French partner of the mother. Conservative estimates put the total above 70,000, but it may well be higher. This compares with 5,500 known births to German fathers in Denmark, whose population was one tenth the size of France's. According to a report of the Propaganda *Abteilung* dated 14 September 1942 some 3,000 children had *already* been fathered by German personnel in Normandy alone. [4] Whichever figure one takes, if pregnancy resulted in only five per cent of cases, there must have been several hundred thousand emotional liaisons with 'the occupier'. Viewed by the French as the ultimate national shame, this is only now being discussed and written about openly, two generations later.

In Malo-les-Bains, a suburb of Dunkirk, Marcel Petyt was a man who defied the full rigour of the occupation from April 1941. His activities included organising escape routes for British airmen shot down and the collection of intelligence that might be useful to London for planning an invasion. Sentenced to death by a German court martial, he was reprieved and sentenced to hard labour for life in October 1941. The reprieve was revoked when he was randomly selected as a hostage to be executed in reprisal for sabotage by unknown persons and was shot at Loos-lès-Lille on 30 April 1942. He wrote to his wife a few hours before the execution:

> I prayed that we should be saved the horrors of war, but the Good Lord decided otherwise and we must bend to his will. I should have liked to give you more happiness but the Almighty does not permit it. I ask one promise that you must not refuse. Keep your faith, my love, and if you think you can remake or improve your life by marrying again, you must do so. Forgive me all the little pains I have caused you in twenty years of marriage. You know I didn't mean them, for you have been the ideal wife and the sun of my life – far too good for me at times. Goodbye, my love, dry your tears as possible (sic).
>
> (signed) Your husband who will think of you until his last breath. [5]

At the beginning of May, under pressure from *Hauptsturmführer* Theodor Dannecker, Adolf Eichman's representative in France, Xavier Vallat was sacked from the euphemistically named *Commissariat Général des*

Questions Juives (CGQJ) – the General Commission for Jewish Questions. Although quite prepared to draft laws making even French-born Jews second-class citizens and expropriating their assets for the state, Vallat's Catholic beliefs forbade him to sanction round-ups of men, women and children for despatch to concentration and death camps.[6] So he was replaced by Louis Darquier, a virulently anti-Semitic 44-year-old journalist with an English wife, who styled himself Darquier de Pellepoix. As the new head of the CGQJ, his first speech to the nation left no doubt where he stood:'The people of France must realise that the chief cause of their present misfortunes is the Jew.'

So that there would be no ambiguity about who was a Jew, eighteen days later every Jewish person aged six and above living in the Occupied Zone was required to wear a *mogon dovid* – a star of David the size of a man's palm that had to be obtained from their local police station.

Three of these were issued per person and cost one precious coupon from the clothing allowance. Entrance to cafes, restaurants, cinemas and museums was forbidden to Jews. By the same 'logic', they were confined to the last coach on trains in the Paris Metro. On 6 June the theatre, cinema and music businesses were added to those professions henceforth barred to Jews.[7]

Dérogations, or certificates permitting people defined as Jewish under Vichy law not to wear a star, were hard to come by even by bribery or personal connections. When leaving her country home – her husband rarely allowed her to come to Paris – the wife of Vichy's ambassador to the German occupation authorities Fernand De Brinon was careful to carry everywhere with her a pass bearing the magic formula: 'The Commandant of the SIPO and the SD … hereby certifies that Madame De Brinon, née Jeanne-Louise Franck, born on 23 April 1896 (the place of birth was diplomatically omitted) is excused from … wearing the Jewish star, until final clarification of her origins.'

She was in very limited company. Rich or well-connected Jews could ask a friend like entertainer Sacha Guitry to intervene with German ambassador Otto Abetz in Paris or some other high functionary. So, for example, Colette's husband, the son of ex-Premier Georges Clémenceau, and the wife of General Alphonse Juin, the C-in-C of French forces in North Africa, were all racially 'purified'. Pétain personally intervened on behalf of three friends; eight fixers working for the German procurement offices were exempted; the *Gestapo* and anti-Jewish police gave out thirteen other certificates to turncoat Jews who worked for them tracking down co-religionists in hiding. Jews with neutral nationality were not required to wear stars.

Félix Cadras was not Jewish but a member of the PCF and thus equally guilty in the eyes of the Vichy regime and the occupation forces. Born in Calais, he was only nine years old when his father was killed at the front in the First World War. He studied textile design before becoming a local organiser of the textile workers' union during the Depression of the 1930s. Called up in September 1939, he served in the artillery until the defeat, after which he went underground, paying brief visits to his little daughter Mary and his wife under various aliases. Arrested in February 1942 by the *brigades spéciales* he was held in the cellars below the *Palais de Justice* in Paris and tortured both by French police and *Gestapo* operatives before being transferred to the high-security wings of La Santé and Fresnes prisons in solitary confinement, chained to the wall day and night. Allowed two visits by 7-year-old Mary, he smuggled a letter out in the lining of her coat. Before he was shot by a German firing squad on 30 May 1942, he wrote to his wife and mother about his joy on being told by Mary that he was now also the father of another daughter, named Georgette after his sister, who had been arrested shortly after Félix and deported to Ravensbrück women's concentration camp. Glossing over his own imminent death, he begged the family to send any food they could spare from their scant ration not to him but to her.[8]

Raids on targets in northern France were now being flown by pilots in RAF uniform from Poland, the former Czechoslovakia and the 'white colonies' of the British Empire. Men of De Gaulle's *Forces Aériennes Françaises Libres* (FAFL) were also flying missions against their own country in the knowledge that thousands of French women and children were among their victims on the ground. One of the most famous was Pierre Clostermann, who became an RAF Wing Commander and wrote several best-sellers about his experiences after the war. The standing orders for these pilots on missions over occupied Europe included the sentences:

> It is important to remember that the priority and the choice of targets are established with great care for the well-being of the population in these countries. Pilots failing to observe these rules lay themselves open to severe penalties.

That was the theory. In practice, especially in the heat of combat, things could not be so clear-cut. On 20 June 1942 René Mouchotte, Clostermann's commanding officer, was escorting RAF bombers raiding Le Havre. Watching the sticks of bombs fall, not on the Germans in the port area, but right along the main street shopping area, he felt a surge of guilt:

> I thought with horror of the poor people buried in the ruins of their houses, destroyed by their former allies (and I wondered) whether they knew that the monsters who were ravaging their homes were protected by Frenchmen (flying the escorting fighters).[9]

One of De Gaulle's close advisers, Georges Gorse, summed up the general's impersonal view of casualties, military or civilian:

> If we want to liberate France, we have to grit our teeth and accept that the British bomb occupied French towns. We have to accept that French people are killed by Allied bombs, just like those killed by the Germans in 1940 and like the hostages shot in Nantes and Paris. The workers at the Renault factory in the Paris suburbs consider the raid of 3 March as a promise of liberation.[10]

The factory in question was turning out 18,300 trucks for the Germans in 1942 and repairing damaged tanks, but did those workers agree with him? In the raid 223 aircraft dropped 475 tons of bombs on and around the factory, killing only seven shift-workers with a timing that smacked of inside information. But – and it was a big but – the usual inaccurate bombing of most crews caused the death of 600 civilians, buried in mass graves, and seriously wounded another 1,500 men, women and children living in the workers' homes close nearby. Did the victims and their families see those deaths and injuries as a promise of anything?

How did other pilots of FAFL feel about what they were doing? One of them was Pierre Mendès-France, who went on to become De Gaulle's postwar Minister of Finance and later the prime minister who ended the

Part of a mass grave after the raid of 3 March.

French war in Vietnam. He confessed to having second thoughts about killing French civilians:

> You can't shut your eyes to it. I too have killed French people because obviously there were some in the factory (that we bombed yesterday). It's painful, but my conscience is clear. They died for a purpose because the objective was achieved. And they were adults – probably all men – whereas hitting dwellings is killing women and children to no direct purpose. One day, I am bound to do that. (Near misses are) unavoidable, otherwise do we why send forty aircraft to bomb one target?[11]

Hitler's Minister for Armaments Albert Speer was complaining that the manpower shortage in the Reich was critical as the high casualty rate on the eastern front sucked more and more German men into uniform. Playing on the unemployment artificially created in France by their requisitioning of machinery and whole factories, the Germans printed colourful posters

German recruiting office on the Champs Elysées.

showing smiling French wives and children whose husbands and fathers were working across the Rhine. Some 200,000 French citizens signed up for work in Germany voluntarily, including 70,000 women, many of whom returned after the end of the war to have their heads shorn and be publicly humiliated, allegedly for sleeping with their German workmates or bosses.

However, many of the stories told by those returning on leave contradicted the recruiting propaganda. Few German women would have anything to do with single French men, who slept on straw mattresses in barracks or warehouses adjacent to the factories where they worked, and which were later the targets of regular visits by the Allied air forces. The working week – and these were not slave labourers – varied from sixty to eighty-four hours. They worked alongside forced labourers from Hitler's eastern conquests, with whom they had no common language. Washing, toilet and laundry facilities were appalling. The list was endless, including the difficulty for French workers, accustomed in peacetime to a main meal of soup, hors d'oeuvres, meat and cheese all served separately, to adapt to German food, which was usually a single plate of *Eintopf* stew of indifferent quality. Despite what they had been promised, rations were even worse than in France.[12]

Added to all that, the foreign volunteer workers were subject to surveillance by the *Gestapo* and liable to end in a concentration camp for anything that smacked of sabotage or even an anti-German remark or joke. The organisation of former conscripted French workers in Germany claims that 60,000 of those who went to Germany failed to return and that 15,000 were shot for 'acts of resistance' to the German war effort. More conservative estimates of French workers who lost their lives there range between 25,000 and 35,000. But even in such unlikely circumstances some French workers formed lasting friendships with fellow-workers. A neighbour of the author was drafted to an aircraft factory outside Vienna where he made a lifelong friendship with his foreman. When the Russians approached in 1945 the foreman helpfully signed a compassionate leave pass for the Frenchman to go home to his allegedly dying mother – who was in perfect health. The friendship forged in adversity lasted fifty years, with summer holidays of the two families taken together alternately in France and Austria until the death of the Frenchman in 1995.

Scraping the barrel, Hitler's insatiable labour boss Fritz Sauckel had 250,000 of the French POWs redesignated 'foreign workers'. But still the Nazi war machine needed more men. Under the impression that one POW would be sent home in return for each man volunteering to work in the *Reich*, Laval convinced himself that this was the way to 'bring the boys home'. In May 1942 he signed a protocol covering, as he thought, the supply of 500,000 workers. After a second meeting with Sauckel, Laval tried to sell this to the nation on 22 June by announcing:'There is new hope for our POWs. In the knowledge that we can always rely on their generosity, I turn today to the French workers, on whom the fate of the prisoners depends.'

His deal, as now presented to the nation, was that one prisoner would be returned to his home and family for every *three* workers signing on. Called *la relève*, or 'the relief shift,' the scheme was a dismal failure for many reasons. Only skilled workers counted for the exchange and it was not possible to volunteer in order to obtain the release of any particular person, such as a father or brother. The scheme fell flat, with only 17,000 volunteers by the end of August.

With Darnand and Darquier heading the SOL and CGQJ respectively, all that was needed for a 'final settlement of the Jewish question' in France was an energetic and like-minded Secretary General for the *Police Nationale*. René Bousquet, a young civil servant with a brilliant record, had formerly been *préfet* of the Marne *département*, and had been decorated with the Légion d'Honneur at the age of twenty-one for saving lives there during severe floods. He had also won the *Croix de Guerre* during the Battle of France in 1940. Leaving the Marne with a reputation for being anti-Masonic and anti-Communist, but with no taint of anti-Semitism, he claimed to have organised food parcels for the detainees in the German concentration camp at Compiègne.

On 2 July 1942 Bousquet met his German opposite number, *SS-Brigadeführer* Karl Oberg, the *Höherer SS- und Polizeiführer Frankreich*. They got along fine, even when Oberg insisted on introducing into the French legal system the Teutonic principle of *Sippenhaft* – the punishment of a whole family for the misdoings of any member. Posters all over France stated clearly that male relatives over eighteen, including cousins and brothers-in-law, would be shot; female relatives would be sentenced to forced labour; and children younger than seventeen would be sent to special punishment schools.

Minutes of the meeting taken by Oberg's interpreter record Bousquet's point that Pétain disliked using French police for arrests in the Free

Bousquet enjoying a joke with SS officers after a roundup in Marseille.

Zone, while not protesting about the arrests *per se*. Less than a week later, Eichman's 'man in Paris' *SS-Hauptsturmführer* Theodor Dannecker cabled to Berlin the good news that Laval would allow Jewish children to be deported from the Free Zone with their families, and had said that the fate of Jews in the Occupied Zone and other 'enemies of the regime' was of no interest to him at all.[13] One of them was Valentin Feldman, a naturalised, Russian-born philosophy teacher in Dieppe. Arrested on 5 February 1942 not only because he was a Jew, but also an active *résistant* who had participated in several armed attacks, he was shot in July. His last words to the firing squad were, 'You fools! It is for you that I have to die.'

After Bousquet and Oberg made their compact, the stage was set for the most monstrous single outrage of the four years' collaboration. Meetings on 8 and 10 July between the *Gestapo* and Jean Leguay, Bousquet's deputy for the Occupied Zone, saw 5,000 Paris police mobilised on 16 July to round up 12,884 foreign-born Jews living in Paris and the suburbs. *SS-Obersturmführer* Heinz Röthke proudly cabled details of the 'body count' to Berlin: 4,051 of those arrested were children and 5,802 were women. Herded into the largest covered space in Paris – an indoor cycling stadium called Le Vélodrome d'Hiver – in conditions of indescribable squalor and filth where several people committed suicide and a woman died in

101

childbirth, they were afterwards transported to the concentration camp at Drancy guarded by French *gendarmes*, where mothers were separated from their children, even toddlers. All were eventually herded into cattle trucks at Le Bourget station, destination Auschwitz, but guarded by *gendarmes* as far as the German frontier. In all, eighty-five transports from Drancy fed the gas chambers and concentration camps with 75,721 victims, of whom less than 3,000 survived. In addition, transports from other camps dotted all over France fed a constant stream of victims to camps in the Reich.

Concentration and deportation camps in France, November 1942.

Among the many protests and pleas for help that were addressed to Pétain was a letter dated 25 July from 18-year-old Gilberte Leroy in Amiens, who courageously asked him to intervene on behalf of a neighbour, arrested despite having fought for France in the First World War. His wife had been hospitalised with a nervous breakdown after the arrest, and was unable to care for their 13-year-old daughter. Because Pétain's sinister doctor Bernard Ménétrel acted as his personal secretary and decided what letters the Marshal should see, letters like this received no reply.[14]

On 11 August 1942 Laval agreed to send 150,000 skilled workers to Germany. The Germans would eventually bring their requirement for French workers to the astonishing figure of 1,575,000 plus the POWs out of a total population around 40,000,000. However, it is estimated that only 785,000 men and women actually went to Germany, and half of those deserted on their first home leave.[15] By 1 September only 17,000 skilled workers had signed a contract, instead of the 150,000 Laval had promised Sauckel, so he undertook to find the shortfall by 25 January 1943.

But there were more immediate problems than that in Normandy. Just after 17.00hrs on 17 August 1942 the population of Rouen heard the warning sirens wail for the fourth time that day and the fifty-third time since the start of the war. No one took much notice because no bomb had fallen inside the town limits since June 1940, but those with keener ears recognised something different in the sound of the aircraft approaching. This was to be the first raid on occupied France by the Eighth US Army Air Force based in Britain – for whose inexperienced crews it was just a practice run before tackling better defended targets in Germany. Their mission was to bomb 2,000 wagons photographed by reconnaissance aircraft on the three kilometres of track in the Sotteville marshalling yard, on the left bank of the Seine. Although this was a daylight raid, accuracy of the B17 crews was no better than in the RAF's night raids. Roughly half the bombs fell somewhere near the target, the rest on residential districts, killing fifty-two Rouennais and injuring 120 more.

Chapter 8

The jinx on *Jubilee*

After the entrance into the war of the United States in response to the Japanese attack on Pearl Harbor in December 1941, President Franklin D. Roosevelt sought to placate Soviet dictator Josef Stalin by promising that Hitler would be forced to withdraw many divisions from the Russian front by an invasion of Europe being planned by the Western Allies for August 1942.

Roosevelt had no appreciation of the logistics problems involved. Churchill was well aware of them, but because he did not want to appear reluctant to get back into the fight, a compromise code-named *Jubilee* was worked out, in which a mainly Canadian force would be landed at Dieppe, tasked with taking and holding the port as either a rehearsal for a full-scale landing in the future – the official version – or a proof to the American allies that the capability to mount a successful invasion was, not months, but years away.

If the latter reasoning sounds cynical, Britain's senior general Montgomery shrewdly distanced himself from the fiasco, leaving Chief of Combined Operations Acting Vice-Admiral Louis Mountbatten in charge. As Montgomery commented later:

> The chosen main force was not an elite battle-hardened British corps, but a Canadian division that had done no fighting and which was commanded by a major-general who had never even commanded a battalion in battle.[1]

The Canadian commanders and their men were as little experienced in modern war as the man in the White House, and confidently expected a walk-over, despite several rehearsal landings on the British coast

General Bernard
Montgomery.

having proven that there were then more problems than solutions to a
large-scale amphibious invasion.

Why the choice of Dieppe? At that time both the British General
Staff and Adolf Hitler were convinced that a successful invasion required
the capture of a deep-water harbour in working-order within the first
hours of the landing. Hitler continued to think this for days after the
Normandy invasion across open beaches in June 1944. Although the
sea crossing to Boulogne, Calais or Dunkirk was shorter, they were
considered too heavily defended to tackle and the Channel ports to the
west of Dieppe – Le Havre, Caen and Cherbourg – too far from the line
of advance into Germany to be useful jumping-off points. In April the
Gestapo had arrested a network of eight *résistants* in Dieppe, since when
no fresh intelligence on the German dispositions in the town had been
sent to London, although it was known that the Dieppe garrison was

of poor-quality troops, many of them East Europeans wearing German uniform only because they had been given the choice of a labour camp or enlisting in the *Wehrmacht*.

Their C-in-C von Rundstedt had a dry sense of humour, remarking:

> Often I would be informed that a new division was to arrive in France direct from Russia, or Norway or central Germany. When it finally made its appearance in the west, it would consist in all of a divisional commander, a medical officer and five bakers.[2]

Of the reinforcements who did arrive, he observed philosophically that it did not take an Aryan superman to operate a machine gun inside a concrete bunker. Von Rundstedt also ensured that three *Waffen-SS* divisions, one parachute division and 10th *Panzer* Division were stationed near enough to rapidly reinforce the defenders in Dieppe in case of need.[3]

At 03.00hrs on 19 August RAF aircrew at dozens of airfields in southern England were roused for the overture to *Jubilee*.[4] In addition to missions targeting airfields at Boulogne and Abbeville, a limited amount of softening up was planned for Dieppe, where the invasion fleet and its screen of fighters was planned to be the bait that would draw the *Luftwaffe* into an all-out confrontation with the RAF.

The strange invasion fleet of some 250 landing craft and cross-Channel steamers with escorting minesweepers and destroyers was only eight nautical miles short of its landfall at Dieppe at 03.47hrs, when it collided with a German convoy shepherded by fast motor gunboats, which immediately attacked the invasion force, sinking several craft, causing casualties and disrupting the order in which landing craft would arrive at the beach. More importantly, the element of surprise was lost before the small-boat force of Commandos had landed the west and east of the main group to take out gun batteries and a radar station on the cliffs above the town.

Ashore, at 05.00hrs, the sirens wailed as waves of RAF aircraft flew in just above rooftop level, triggering the anti-aircraft batteries, to whose noise was added the sound of bombs exploding. The German security services instructed the population to take shelter from what looked like just another air raid. Ambulances and fire trucks roared through the streets, heading for the bombed areas near the seafront. People on their way to the nearest shelter picked up leaflets in French, whose message was similar to an appeal broadcast by the BBC French Service shortly before the electricity and telephones failed:

> French citizens! This is not the invasion. We ask you not to take part, and to do nothing that might invite reprisals by the enemy. We appeal to you to keep calm and sensible. When the hour of invasion does come, we shall tell you. Then we shall act together for our common victory and your liberty![5]

As the Canadians' landing craft neared the shore in the full light of day and with the sun in the men's eyes, some German artillery opened up on them, but this was nothing compared with the hail of fire that met the first men and tanks emerging from the landing craft on the beach, which was steeply sloping and consisted of pebbles, almost impossible for a man to run on or for tanks to negotiate because their tracks could not get a grip on anything solid. Canadian Bud Buchanan was one of nine cousins from the same family on the raid. Of their arrival off the French coast, he wrote:

> (It was) as if the whole place was on fire. You could see tracer bullets landing in the sea in front of you, skimming the water, and shells were going off, and planes were overhead and doing a lot of damage too. By the time we got onto the beaches, it was pretty hot, in fact it was damned hot. We were put out of the boats about fifty feet out to sea and we had to make our way ashore. We lost a lot of men right there on the beach.[6]

Another man recorded the scene even more vividly:

> I've done a lot of landings since then – Sicily and Italy and so on, but never anything like that. There were bodies floating everywhere. There were what looked like hundreds of Canadians lying on the beaches dead or injured. The beach was being raked with gunfire. The Colonel was killed and the adjutant was killed and the coxswain was killed. We were drifting near to the beach and there weren't many of us left.

107

So I said, 'Every man for himself. Abandon ship!' I remember saying to my young skipper, Lt Over, before we jumped, 'Well, cheerio, Derek. See you in Pompey (Portsmouth) and whoever gets there first puts up the pints.' He was killed as we jumped overboard. When I looked, I think his head was pretty well gone.[7]

Of fifty-eight tanks that left England, only twenty-nine ever reached the beach. Of them, five made it as far as the promenade, where two managed to circumnavigate the anti-tank obstacles and were immediately shot up. One by one, all the others slewed out of control on the pebbles, to be 'brewed up', most with the crews inside. Some landing craft that grounded on the beach never disgorged a single man, since all were dead before or shortly after the ramp was lowered.

After the signal to withdraw was given at 10.22hrs, Buchanan was one of those who got onto a boat, but it was overloaded.

So I swam across to another one and I got onto that and my cousin Jackie Hunter was on it. He got hit, partially cut in half. He said there was no hope for him, so he threw himself into the water.[8]

By 13.30hrs the last men to get back to Britain that day had been taken off the beach, where their comrades left behind faced years in POW camps. Of the roughly 5,000 men who sailed from Britain in the evening of 18 August, 906 lay dead on the beach or floated lifeless in the shallows, and 2,195 were taken prisoner. The scale of losses in some units was such that when Private John King of the Royal Hamilton Light Infantry went on parade back at base the following morning, instead of hundreds of men, there were ten who, 'had to go round and collect (their) mates' personal gear and put it in envelopes to send back home.' Another soldier in the Royal Regiment asked to be directed to his regiment after being de-briefed at a naval base near Portsmouth. Finding only two men in the hut indicated, he protested that he was looking for the regiment. A Canadian MP said, 'That's it, buddy. That is your regiment.'[9]

Total casualties on the German side were 591 wounded, killed and missing, with eight prisoners taken back to Britain for interrogation. Hitler's personal interpreter Paul Schmidt was sent to Dieppe to interrogate Allied prisoners and returned to tell his master that the ordinary soldiers had fought well, but that their commanders were incompetent. If added proof of that were needed, the senior Canadian officer to land, Brigadier William

Southam, had brought with him in a waterproof bag his copy of the Top Secret *Jubilee* orders. During the surrender, his signals officer suggested that he throw it onto a bonfire that was destroying other, far less important, papers. Southam refused. Although he tried to bury it under the pebbles just before he was personally taken prisoner, it was recovered and read by his captors. The instruction that German prisoners taken during *Jubilee* were to have their hands tied behind their back was later used to justify Hitler's order that British and Canadian prisoners be shackled, at first with rope and later with handcuffs – a practice that was abandoned after German POWs in Canada were similarly handcuffed in retaliation.

In his history of the war, Churchill called *Jubilee* 'a costly but not unfruitful reconnaissance in force', of which 'the results fully justified the heavy cost. The large-scale air battle alone justified the raid.'[10] A substantial body of senior military men did not agree, one brigadier writing to another that there was:

> ... a school of thought which considers that Dieppe was a howling success because we managed to bring (the *Luftwaffe*) into the air and shoot down 200 German aircraft at the expense of 100 of our own plus, of course, 5,000 (sic) good soldiers.[11]

Allied losses were closer to 112 aircraft shot down and a further fourteen written off.

Six hours after the withdrawal, although the beach was littered with corpses, shot-up and burning vehicles and discarded equipment, and more corpses were floating in the shallows, shops were already open again in the town. Women shoppers watched long columns of prisoners, some lacking even trousers and boots, and carrying their wounded, as they were marched by *Feldgendarmerie* guards to a makeshift barbed wire 'cage' at a football ground outside the town. By the following morning life was back to normal for the civilian population – or as normal as could be with all the debris on the beach, corpses washing ashore and occasional explosions as ordnance was cleared. For once, the French inhabitants had got off lightly with forty-eight dead and 100 wounded. Some families even had cause to rejoice: Dieppe was labelled 'the martyred town' and the military governor handed the mayor 10 million francs for distribution among those who had suffered during the raid.

When the mayor appeared insufficiently grateful, the *Kreiskommandant* asked, 'Are you not satisfied?'

Taking advantage of the moment, the mayor replied, 'What about our POWs?'

'How many?'

'A thousand?'

German propaganda claimed that the Dieppois had supported the garrison during the landings. In fact, they had done nothing but keep out of the way. Yet, to give credibility to the propaganda message, 1,200 Dieppois POWs were released to return home.[12]

Mountbatten attempted to justify his raid on Dieppe afterwards by saying that the Normandy invasion of June 1944 succeeded because of the lessons learned at Dieppe in August 1942. One 'lesson learned' was that it was militarily a mistake to refrain from heavy pre-invasion softening-up bombing and naval bombardment, no matter how many civilians were killed in the process. This was a lesson that would cost many innocent French lives.

Pétain's next move was to placate the Germans by a law of 4 September, which compulsorily conscripted some 250,000 workers in six months, mainly in the Occupied Zone. By now, the Marshal's popularity was plummeting. General Weygand told Laval to his face, 'Your policies are a disaster. Did you know that ninety-five per cent of the French people are against you? And, anyway, you've backed the wrong horse: Germany will lose this war.' Laval replied, 'You're wrong. It's not ninety-five, but ninety-eight per cent who are against me. Despite that, I am still working for them all.'

On 5 September Rouennais journalist Georges Pailhès saw B17 bombers and their escorting fighters flying so high that only their contrails were visible, which he took to mean that they were *en route* elsewhere. But these were American aircraft, bombing from altitude. Seventy tonnes of bombs fell in the next ten minutes, half on the railway marshalling yards in the lower town, but with 108 hits on residential areas. Only then did the stunned Rouennais realise that they lived in the front line, and start to organise emergency services, which would be sorely tried in eight more American raids and the catastrophic RAF raid on the night of 18–19 April 1944 that no one who lived through it would ever forget.

On 6 October 1942 the naked body of a woman was found in the forest of Rambouillet, west of Paris. At first treated as a routine murder of a prostitute working the woods, the trail led to the leadership of the PCF under its wartime head Jacques Duclos. On the model of the murder squads among the international brigades in the Spanish Civil War that assassinated anyone fingered by the commissars, the PCF had set up the *Valmy* assassination squad to kill not only traitors who betrayed their comrades, but also members who defied instructions of the Party or disagreed with its policies – particularly the attacks on German personnel that brought death to so many hostages.

The name *Valmy* had been previously used by a group of Parisian students using a child's printing set to print flyers and who chalked slogans on walls like *We have one enemy: the invader* and *Hitler's Hoover is emptying our country faster than you know.* They had chosen the name of the town in the Champagne region where an unexpected victory over a Prussian army during the French Revolution had raised the morale of French people fighting the invaders 150 years earlier. The *Valmy* assassination gang was of another ilk.

This particular victim was Mathilde Dardant, secretary of a political rival of Duclos. The motive for killing her? She had just been rejected by her PCF lover and it was suspected that she *might* divulge information out of a desire to revenge herself on him and the Party. The murderous excesses and torture sessions committed by 'special group No 1' of *Valmy* apparently eliminated as many as 250 suspects without any real proof against most of them. Eventually sickened by their work despite the relatively high money they were paid, compared with FTP rank-and-file *résistants*, the killers rebelled after learning that they had murdered the wrong people time after time, or killed the designated targets, whose only fault was to have disagreed on some political point with the leadership of the Party. Tracked down by the *brigades spéciales*, the *Valmy* teams were dismantled by the French police at the end of 1942, to no one's great regret.[13]

By now, most French people had come to terms with being occupied, with less than one in a hundred involved in the various Resistance movements. Everything changed on 8 November 1942, when Anglo-American forces under the command of General Dwight D. Eisenhower landed at eight places on the coasts of Morocco and Algeria as a vital stepping-stone to a European invasion.

Pétain's reaction to the Anglo-American landings in North Africa was to order the French forces there to resist at all costs this incursion into

Allied Supreme Commander
General Dwight Eisenhower.

French territory. Resistance, however, lasted in most places for only a matter of hours. The reactions of the Germans was more forceful. For strategic reasons Hitler could not leave the French Mediterranean littoral vulnerable to a swift Allied move across the inland sea. On 11 November, exactly twenty-four years after the end of the First World War, the *Wehrmacht* marched and rode across the Demarcation Line and ended the last pretence of Vichy's autonomy. Henceforth, what had been the Free Zone was re-designated 'the southern zone' and the Occupied Zone became 'the northern zone'.

For protesting against this violation of the Armistice agreement and disagreeing with Pétain's decision that no resistance should be offered, a senior Vichy figure (General De Lattre De Tassigny), was court-martialled on 9 January 1943 and given a 10-year prison sentence for 'attempted treason'. After six months in Riom prison he mysteriously managed to escape and make his way to London.

Now, not even Laval could hope for a favourable outcome of an eventual peace conference. Support for Pétain dwindled overnight to a diehard one-third of people, most of whom only continued to believe in him *because there was no one else*. Pétain was now a tired old man in the habit of falling asleep during afternoon meetings and waking up with a start to agree with the last speaker – the only one he had heard. The habit was exploited by Laval to bulldoze through projects the Marshal might have resisted, if awake.

Judging by his reaction to two followers announcing their political reorientation after the German occupation of the southern zone, even Pétain was having doubts. On 12 November Guillaume de Tournemire, head of the Pétainist youth organisation, told the Marshal that he was going underground with the Resistance. Pétain replied, 'I've decided that my duty is to stay here. I'm aware that I have lost my prestige, but by doing this I shall protect France from some of the misfortunes she would suffer without me.' De Tournemire protested his personal loyalty to the Marshal, adding that this would not stop him working against the occupiers. Pétain replied, 'Do all you can, but be prudent for the sake of your young members. I shall do what I can to help. Good luck!' Three days later, Pétain received his former *chef de cabinet* Roger De Saivre, who told the Marshal that he intended making clandestinely for North Africa to get back into the fight. Pétain embraced him, saying, 'If I were your age, I'd do the same. But, as it is, my place is here. Good luck, my son.'

On 12 October 1942 an FAFL pilot who had learned to fly at the airfield of Octeville flew a solo reconnaissance mission over Le Havre, where his family still lived. In full daylight, Jean Maridor chicaned through the flak coming up at him and zoomed over streets and houses where he had grown up, the sickly son of a baker who was destined to become apprenticed to a men's hairdresser, had not his father found the money for him to join the local flying club, where all the boy's pocket money was spent on extra flying lessons. In December 1936, aged just sixteen, he became the youngest pilot to pass a flying test in France, but had to wait six months for the minimum age to be given a pilot's licence. Joining the French Air Force on 30 August 1939, he passed out first in his *promotion* and escaped after the defeat with four comrades on a ship from St Jean de Luz. With Britain desperately short of qualified pilots, he joined De Gaulle's FAFL, writing to a friend:

> When you attack (an anti-aircraft position), you feel you are entering a hell from which you can never come out alive.

Worse, those bastard Messers (Bf 109s) come at you from above with their machine guns. You come home at wave-top level with them on your tail all the way. It's fantastic.

In the letter, he could have been referring to his successful raid on eight anti-aircraft barges defending Dieppe on 1 October 1941, all destroyed. Over St Omer on 31 October his aircraft was seriously damaged, after which he wrote to a friend:

I don't know whether I'll get to the French squadron[14] because the CO doesn't want to let me go. I'm the only Frenchman left here (in 615 Squadron) and he has made a special request to the Air Ministry, to keep me. I don't know what will happen about that, but I don't care. The only thing that matters is to fight.

On 15 December 1941, his numerous victories having earned him a commission as Flight Lieutenant in the RAF, Maridor wrote to his family via the Resistance. It was a brief and carefully worded note: 'At the moment, I have a very interesting job which, as you know, is my passion.'[15]

On a mission over Le Havre on 12 October, he recognised the restaurant next door to his parents' house and dropped even lower, skimming the roof. In the street below was a single male figure who seemed to be waving, but before he could be certain that it was his father, Maridor was well past him and taking evading action from the anti-aircraft fire. The man in the street was indeed his father. For waving a greeting at an RAF plane, he was denounced to the Germans, who took no action. The only consequence of the denunciation was an inter-zonal letter from the French Air Force records office at Orange-Caritat that Maridor *père* received a few days later: 'I should be grateful for any information you have on the present whereabouts of Sgt Maridor, Jean-Pierre-Edmond, demobilised at …'

Monsieur Maridor did not reply.[16]

Chapter 9

Milice v. *Maquis* – a war to the death

If the motivation of pilots like Jean Maridor seem clear enough, less clear is what motivated and gave the courage required for ordinary people to risk death by saving Allied fliers whose aircraft were shot down over the heavily patrolled forbidden zones while they were dropping bombs that killed French civilians. Gaston Brogniart was a trucker who picked up a downed Canadian pilot in a gesture of spontaneous humanity while driving home to Le Touquet during Autumn 1942. Hiding the Canadian in the home of Madame Illidge, a friend who was married to a British POW held in a camp near Breslau, he mobilised several other friends to procure false identity papers and food. Before the group of friends could contact an escape line for Allied servicemen, they were betrayed. Their Canadian protégé was protected by his status as a POW, but they were not. At first locked up in the Hotel Westminster in Le Touquet, then in Loos-lès-Lille prison, Brogniart and two others were shot on 20 July 1943; another friend and Madame Illidge were deported to concentration camps in Germany.[1]

Meeting with Pétain on 19 December 1942, Hitler demanded the creation of a paramilitary police force to repress dissidence in France and hunt down the mainly Communist activists who were assassinating members of the occupation forces. What the Marshal thought about this is not on record, but Laval solved the problem – something he so often did for Pétain – by enlisting SOL extremists in an armed militia entitled *La Milice*, commanded by Aimé-Joseph Darnand. 'Goebbels' Henriot proclaimed on Radio Paris that recruitment into the *Milice* was open to physically fit men 'of good will who wish to serve their country'.

La Milice thus formed by the law of 30 January 1943 'to correct the political, social, economic and moral' transgressions of their fellow-citizens,

Milice on parade.

was composed of some convinced right-wing sympathisers with the German cause, but mostly of misfits delighting in their new-found power over Jews, escaped POWs, *résistants* of all political hues and any other 'enemy of the regime'. Not everyone in the Vichy administration approved. In a letter to Laval the energetically collaborationist police secretary-general René Bousquet wrote, 'I remain convinced that the transformation of the SOL into the *Milice* is a gross mistake.' His objection had little to do with the spate of excesses by *miliciens* but was made on the grounds that they were not disciplined police officers under his control.

In the eyes of historian Robert Paxton, among the first to document the Vichy years, the creation of the *Milice* was the final step in the evolution of the Pétainist fascist state. The Germans were understandably uneasy about arming the riff-raff who made up the rank-and-file of the *Milice*, but within a year its members had so compromised themselves by brutality, torture and murder of fellow Frenchmen and Frenchwomen that they were accepted in the northern zone as well after March 1944. The *Milice* was to become the most widely hated of the several French 'police' organisations working hand-in-glove with the *Gestapo*, and thousands of *miliciens* were killed out of hand at the Liberation.

Their easiest targets were young men on the run from the increasingly draconian labour conscription laws. The law of 4 September 1942 required every male person between 18 and 50 and every female between 21 and 35 to accept whatever work the government considered of national interest.[2] A week later, all adults in these age brackets who worked fewer than thirty hours per week were made liable for compulsory re-assignment. This ill-considered legislation caused severe rifts between the business community and Pétain's government because the only firms allowed to keep their labour force intact were those fulfilling German orders. The laws also drove a wedge between the general population and all but the staunchest supporters of the Marshal.

In October 1942 the second round-up of Jews in Le Havre had netted just seven victims – seven individual tragedies, despatched to Rouen and thence to Drancy concentration camp and Auschwitz by the French *gendarmes* who had arrested them. Eager to demonstrate his keenness to his bosses in Paris, Rouen's *Préfet* André Parmentier ordered a third *rafle* of Jews in the *département* on 15 and 16 January 1943 after an attack on a German officer in Rouen. Given the travel restrictions, it was virtually impossible for any of those arrested in Le Havre to have been involved. In any case, one was a veteran of the first war, whose service should have exempted him, the eldest was 80-year-old Eugénie Mayer and the youngest person arrested was 5-year-old Charles Klein, whose mother was in the last days of another pregnancy. Giving birth to a second son in the filth of the camp at Drancy, she was shipped off with both children on Convoy No 57 of 18 July 1943 to the gas chambers of Auschwitz.[3]

Few people not directly involved concerned themselves with the fate of these unfortunates because everyone had problems. In all the Channel ports, the Germans requisitioned buildings partly to house their troops or to convert into blockhouses and partly to drive out 'useless mouths' who might contribute to the security problems in the event of invasion. At Le Havre, by February 1943 they had thus requisitioned sixty hotels and large houses and 900 ordinary homes, whose inhabitants joined those made homeless by British and American bombs, but the occupiers' expectation of precipitating a mass evacuation was not achieved. Despite the undoubted dangers, the inconvenience, the constant identity checks within these high-security areas and the liability to arrest for minor infringements of local regulations, people clung all the more strongly to what remained of their homes and, if those no longer existed, to streets and places that were familiar and the comfort of friends and neighbours, or even just the cemetery where their loved ones were buried, rather than take their chances among strangers.[4]

One essential of modern life could not be bought on the black market: electricity production in France was inexorably declining, with most of the country's coal being requisitioned for the *Reich*. In January 1943 theatres and cinemas were ordered to close one day each week to save on heating costs, and it became a crime to heat one's apartment by electricity. But even in large towns the sick, very young and elderly were dying of hypothermia. In schools, children kept their overcoats on and covered themselves in old blankets to try and keep warm. Restaurants had no candles for emergency lighting during power cuts, so the clientele had to put up with the acrid fumes of acetylene lamps placed on the tables.

For the majority who had no money to eat out, the cards issued by the *Ravitaillement Générale* entitled an adult to a daily bread allowance of 275–350 grams, depending on category of work. In April this was reduced to 120 grams a day and the nutritional value can be judged from the requirement that bakers produce 134kg of bread from each 100kg sack of flour, additives including sawdust. The cheese ration was dropped to 50g per person per week, with 120g of meat and 300g of fats – and 500g of sugar per month. Even these quantities were more theoretical than actual because erratic food deliveries sometimes saw only half the required quantity delivered to Le Havre and other cities. Even milk for young children was scarce. The so-called 'national coffee' contained only one-tenth real coffee grains.

Wine, traditional on French tables at lunch and dinner, was restricted to four litres a month per adult. Even vegetables were rationed, with the exception of turnips and swedes. Some foods were simply priced out of the open market and disappeared into the black sector, where the poor had no chance of buying them. Due also to the possibility of selling produce to the black market, many foods that were officially cheap were only available in very limited supplies. The expression 'black market' was defined for the first time in the *Petit Larousse* dictionary after a law of 15 March 1943 detailed severe penalties for illicit trafficking.

The tax on a bicycle was raised to forty francs, but they were essential, not just for travelling to work. Each weekend people in the towns cycled out into the countryside where peasants could be persuaded to part with an egg or some home-made butter in what was called 'the grey market'.

A few eggs in one's pockets was one thing, but cycling home with a knapsack of food for the children meant almost certainly being stopped at a German checkpoint for an identity check and the contents examined, in case they were explosives or weapons. Once the illicit food had been revealed, summary justice saw the imprudent grey marketeer thrown into prison and there treated as a hostage to be shot in reprisal for an attack on German personnel or sabotage. One woman, whose family is known to the author, was sent to a concentration camp after being caught in a routine identity check at a railway station with a whole ham in her suitcase.

After Sauckel upped his demands to 250,000 workers, including 150,000 skilled workers, on 15 February 1943 Laval created *Le Service Obligatoire du Travail*, abbreviated to SOT. Unfortunately *sot* means 'stupid', so the title was swiftly changed to *Service du Travail Obligatoire* (STO) in order to 'end the shocking inequality which burdened French workers with the obligation that should rest fairly on all French citizens, whatever their social status or work'. Some 240,386 workers were conscripted between June and December 1942, plus 456,000 in 1943. Major German companies that profited from this cheap labour include names famous today, like Volkswagen, Daimler-Benz, Messerschmitt,

The caption reads: 'Young people of France, make the right choice (between being killed for the Jewish-British-American bankers and working in a German factory).'

Siemens, BMW, Telefunken, BASF and IG Farben, the dyestuffs and pesticides conglomerate that made *Zyklon B* gas for the death factories at Auschwitz and elsewhere.[5]

Published as the law of 16 February 1943, the new legislation conscripted all men born between 1 January 1920 and 31 December 1922. The summons arrived couched in elegant officialese:

> I have the honour to inform you that the joint Franco-German Commission … has selected you for work with the *Todt* Organisation / to work in Germany. I invite you to present yourself at the German Labour Office on … to learn the date and time of your departure. Failure to comply with this posting is punishable under the provisions of the law.[6]

Penalties for non-compliance ranged from imprisonment for a minimum of three months to a maximum sentence of five years and fines from 200 francs upwards. In the southern zone, one third of this age group was serving in Pétain's *Chantiers de Jeunesse* – youth labour camps – where they were given fifteen-day leave passes and a written instruction to report for STO at the end of their leave. Roughly half of them interpreted this as tacit permission to desert.

Resistance tracts warned that going to work in Germany meant living under Allied bombs and that leaving France was treason. For once the Communists and the Church were on the same side. On 21 March Cardinal Liénart announced in Lyon that reporting for the STO was not a duty of conscience, while in every town posters of the local *Feldkommandantur* threatened 'pitiless sanctions' for those who did not present themselves at the recruitment centres and railway stations to catch their trains. Women were also liable to labour conscription in theory, but Vichy dared not defy the Church's disapproval of the moral risks they ran in being separated from their families. Although thousands of women volunteered for the money, not one was forced to go to Germany.

Some neighbours of the author set out for their STO train in a *gazogène* car that conveniently 'broke down' in front of the village *gendarme*, who obligingly issued a *procès verbal* confirming that their late arrival was due to the 'breakdown'. They continued their journey to the railway station, taking care to arrive well after the departure of their train. The *procès verbal* stamped a second time, they returned home. A second summons never arrived, presumably because their files had been lost somewhere in the administrative machine. At Vesoul in Franche-Comté only three of 400 STO conscripts reported for duty; in the Jura twenty-five out of 850; in Seine-et-Loire only thirty-one from 3,700.[7] The attitude of many police officers towards arresting defaulters was summed up by Lt Theret, head of the detachment at Paris Gare d'Orsay, who warned his men on 9 March 1943 that he 'would not find a single *réfractaire* – or STO dodger – and counted on them to do likewise as good Frenchmen'.[8]

The intensely farmed landscape of Normandy presented little cover for the large bands of *maquisards* to be found by now in central and southern France, but there was sufficient woodland to harbour small groups of STO no-shows. Albert Lacour was a metal-worker who built a hideout in an abandoned marlpit near Bourg-Achard to the west of Rouen in 1943. Around him, he gathered fourteen other young men on the run. It is hard to say how many were STO no-shows because afterwards the PCF claimed them as FTP martyrs. Of one member of Lacour's gang, there was no doubt, because he was an Austrian deserter from the *Wehrmacht*. Driven by whatever complex of motives, the gang claimed about fifty sabotage operations before the marlpit was surrounded by 200 German soldiers and 100 French *miliciens* on 22 August 1943. Seven of Lacour's men were killed, six others deported to the camps in Germany. Of the fate of the Austrian deserter, nothing is known. Was he a double agent who gave them all away, or was he simply given short shrift as a traitor when captured?

A number of French organisations experienced a rush of recruits because they offered shelter from STO. These included the police, *gendarmerie*, fire services, railways and Civil Defence – and, of course, the *Milice*. If none of those had local openings, working as a civilian employee of the German occupation forces was another option for 2,000 men who joined the *Kriegsmarine* as fitters and civilian guards; 1,982 others donned the uniform of drivers in NSKK *Motorgruppe*, freeing German personnel for more military tasks. In addition to its hundreds of thousands of *requis*, Organisation *Todt* employed 3,000 Frenchmen in uniform as armed guards for construction sites. At its peak in 1944, Organisation *Todt* was the biggest employer in Europe, with 336,000 German staff controlling over a million foreign workers, including 165,000 POWs and 120,000 concentration camp prisoners.

Some in the Catholic hierarchy still supported Pétain, if less enthusiastically than in 1940, but one priest who followed his conscience to plough a lonely and dangerous furrow was commemorated on 15 April 1943 when a huge crowd of people from all walks of life defied German bans on public meetings to gather at the church of St Martin in Dunkirk for a silent demonstration of loyalty to René Bonpain, vicar of the parish of Notre-Dame de l'Assomption in the suburb of Rosendaël, who had been shot at Bondues on 30 March. Bonpain had repeatedly been accused by the occupation authorities of encouraging anti-German feelings among his young parishioners, but was arrested in November 1942 for espionage on behalf of London. Grievously tortured at the Gestapo HQ in the Villa Duflos in his native Malo-les-Bains, the courageous priest's last letter was a plea that no one should seek vengeance for his death, and was signed 'René Bonpain, on his way to Heaven'.[9]

In a radio broadcast of 30 March Philippe Henriot announced that the *Milice* was an order of knighthood charged with implementing the Marshal's national revolutionary mission to give France back her soul. Defying the open disapproval of cardinals Gerlier and Suhard, the *Abbé* Bouillon appointed himself national chaplain of the *Milice*, which numbered in a few months 10,000 men and women with their own training school and newspaper called *Combats*. Honoured with the rank of *SS-Obersturmführer*, Darnand now effectively commanded his own small army equipped by the Germans and afforded training facilities alongside the *Légion des Volontaires Français*, composed of men with nothing to lose who had volunteered to fight on the eastern front with the *Wehrmacht* and *Waffen-SS*.

Between 1 May and 31 August 1943 no fewer than 48,356 men conscripted for work in Germany went missing while on leave in France. From then onwards, home leave was abolished, making STO even less attractive. Understandably, thousands of young men decided not to report after receiving a summons. Some simply stayed at home, where they ran the risk of being betrayed by a neighbour; others sought work as labourers on remote farms where the peasants only too glad to have an extra pair of hands to ask awkward questions. Later, by the law of 11 June 1943, anyone helping a runaway from STO was liable to a fine between 10,000 and 100,000 francs. Nevertheless, in the heavily controlled north-east of France, 37,000 steelworkers went missing.

A consequence of STO which the Vichy government had not foreseen was that thousands of these *réfractaires* who refused to comply with the conscription laws went on the run and hid out in the wilder upland and

Three *maquisards* with parachuted weapons.

forested regions of France, living rough in small gangs, some of whom robbed country post offices for money and tobacco and demanded food and clothing from remote households in the middle of the night, often at gunpoint. One *gendarmerie* report dated 22 March 1943 read, 'No-shows for STO are so numerous that only fifty of 340 reported in. Many men have abandoned their homes, their work and their family to take to the *maquis* instead.'[10]

The word *maquis* meant simply 'scrubland'. From there, it came to be used as a collective noun for 'those hiding in rough country' and *maquisard* was coined to mean 'a man hiding in remote country'. Without any original political motivation except antipathy towards the government by whom they felt betrayed, the *réfractaires* became the core of the eventual *Maquis* movement. It was not only farmers on remote properties seeking cheap labour who protected them. Many public officials turned a blind eye. Mayor Jean Puech of Neuville-lès-Dieppe went a step further.

Arrested on 10 October 1943 for non-implementation of the STO laws, he courageously informed his judges, 'Our role is to protect those who elected us, not to hand them over to the Germans.' He died in Dachau concentration camp on 14 January 1945.

If some functionaries refused to apply the sanctions against *réfractaires* and those who protected them, this was not the case with the *Milice*, who made it a crusade to hunt them down – on occasion in pitched battles. This in turn obliged the *maquisards* to band together in more organised groups capable of supporting each other in the hour of need, so that Laval's new laws created a civil war within France, in which eventually tens of thousands of young men with no initial political motivation fought a dirty war with no holds barred against the *Milice*.

A second agreement was signed between Bousquet and Oberg in Paris on 16 April 1943, of which Article 5 stipulated that the *Feldgendarmerie* would henceforward deal only with discipline and protection of German personnel, while the various French police services took over responsibility for tracking down *résistants* and anyone contravening Vichy legislation. With the *Maquis* building up into an admittedly ill-organised army – but still an army – of outlaws, this new accord polarised millions of previous 'don't knows' into open disaffection from Pétain and Laval and all they stood for.

Chapter 10

Hell-on-Sea

As the scale and pace of Allied air raids on Germany and occupied Europe rose rapidly, concern was expressed at the large numbers of civilians bound to be killed, even when residential areas were not the specified target. When such deaths were of German civilians, the logic was that they had it coming to them for supporting in whatever way the war effort of the Nazi government that had dragged half the world into the conflict it had launched. But what about raids on targets in occupied countries, where the civilians incidentally killed – dubbed 'collateral damage' in the euphemism coined in the US war in Vietnam to avoid the unpleasant phrase 'civilian deaths' when these were counted in tens of thousands – had been, and would one day again be, allies and neighbours?

Grappling with these issues, on 29 October 1942 the Assistant Chief of Air Staff (Policy) drew up a four-page document which laid down the RAF's policy on bombing targets in the vicinity of civilian areas:

> Intentional bombardment of civilian populations, as such, (is) forbidden. (It) must be possible to identify the objective (and the) attack must be made with reasonable care to avoid undue loss of civilian life in the vicinity of the target. (If) any doubt exists as to the possibility of accurate bombing and if a large error would involve the risk of serious damage to a populated area, no attack (is) to be made; and provisions of Red Cross conventions (are) to be observed.[1]

Whether inspired by the hostile propaganda put out by the Vichy regime and the German *Propagandastaffel* after raids on French targets, or by morality, these were noble intentions in the middle of a total war. However,

125

with the build-up in Britain of American troops and equipment, especially the new bomber squadrons with the larger, long-range and heavily armed Flying Fortresses of Lieutenant-General Ira C. Eaker's Eighth Air Force, noble intentions were bested by the argument that the Allies had to be as ruthless as the enemy and that, wherever there was a chance of hitting that enemy in occupied territory, deaths by 'friendly bombs' falling on the neutral civilian population were not only inevitable but, as De Gaulle said, part of the price their countries had to pay for liberation by the Allies.

The year 1943 began relatively quietly as far as air raids on France were concerned because the priority of the Allied air forces in Britain was for massive raids on targets and towns inside the *Reich*. Yet, in the month of May, there were 1,284 Allied raids against 793 different French towns, with Cambrai bombed eleven times and Douai nine times – plus another 2,307 raids in June. By the end of August an estimated half-million high-explosive and 35,317 incendiary bombs had dropped on French urban areas – many to be unearthed decades later, to the incomprehension of the modern generation. In Le Havre all the water mains had burst, forcing the fire service to pump water from canals and the sea, until they ran out of diesel fuel and had to beg some from German units nearby. It was not just fuel that was lacking: equipment was by then so worn out that rescue services regularly borrowed car batteries from garage-owners to have some emergency lighting at night.

The infrastructure of France was crumbling, its political leaders discredited, its economy in ruins. Yet, in the midst of the social chaos, individual civil servants, local government officers and volunteers wrought miracles. After each raid, trucks of the *Secours National* toured the devastated areas with food, clean drinking water, clothing and fuel for heating and cooking. The Red Cross and the Refugee Service also did what they could and central government cut through the red tape by setting up *Le Service Interministériel de Protection contre les Evénements de Guerre* (SIPEG), which fitted out two trains as mobile emergency task forces that could be immediately despatched to hard-hit areas. Each train had an operating theatre, a thirty-bed emergency ward, a maternity ward and an industrial-scale kitchen able to provide 14,000 meals a day – as well as supplies of clothing, bedding and basic cooking utensils for *les sinistrés* – those made homeless by Allied bombs.

Some RAF sorties dropped very different loads far from the towns. In the strictly controlled northern zones very little stockpiling of arms by the

'Cowards! France will not forget this.'

Resistance had been possible. There was a desperate need for weapons, explosives and ammunition, which the RAF delivered in daring low-level *parachutages* to individual groups, all of whose members risked death for themselves and their friends and families each time they assembled at a dropping zone, or took delivery of arms and hid them until needed. Weighing 2.5 tonnes, a typical consignment dropped in quick-opening man-size metal containers included six Brens, twenty-seven Stens, thirty-six .303 rifles, five automatic pistols, 18,000 rounds of ammunition, Mills grenades and 8 kg of plastic explosive with detonators, plus medical kits. Sometimes chocolate, money and cigarettes were stuffed into empty spaces, to make up the load.

In all the hecatomb, perhaps the most moving testimony to the violence and harshness of the occupation of the Nord / Pas de Calais region is the crypt at Vitry-en-Artois dedicated to the nine *résistants* of the OCM, *Voix du Nord* and *Centurie* networks arrested by the Germans in September 1943 after being caught receiving a *parachutage* of arms from a British aircraft. Deported without trial, they were sentenced by a Nazi People's Court in Munich on 16 September 1944 to death by beheading. The barbaric medieval sentence was carried out by a man using an axe on 28 November. These were not Communist activists, striking miners or youths 'avid for some great glory'. They were husbands and fathers, respected members of their community. Léon Javelot was a 33-year-old office manager; 24-year-old René Vaze worked in a rolling mill; 42-year-old Emile Delfosse was a *gendarme*, as were 39-year-old Pierre Seneuze and 40-year-old Louis Defontaine; 38-year-old Eugène Dumont was a self-employed craftsman; 42-year-old René Grodecoeur was a labourer; 46-year-old Jules Lambart was a junior school teacher and 40-year-old André Serrure was a tax inspector.

The drops to the Resistance were coordinated by coded messages passed over the BBC French Service, listening to which was not easy, thanks to the German jamming stations. It was also punishable by imprisonment. An instant hit from its first broadcast was *The Partisans' Song*, which listeners thought had been written by a few *maquisards* around a hidden campfire, the chords being plucked out on a guitar. The truth is more prosaic. The BBC wanted a pompous signature tune for the programme *Honneur et Patrie*, but several Free French journalists disagreed and three singer-songwriters, who had escaped together from France at Christmas 1942, sat down in the London suburbs in the afternoon of 30 May to write the song. The words were a call to arms: *Come up from the mines, comrades. Come down from the hills.* There was no ambiguity about its message: *We break the bars of our brothers' prisons... If you fall, a friend will take your place.*

The war in the shadows was now in full spate, as German counter-intelligence services and the *brigades spéciales* stepped up the pace and brutality of their struggle to track down and crush the Resistance networks that were busily feeding the latest troop movements and other military information to London, and stockpiling arms and ammunition with which to attack the occupation forces behind the battle lines, once the Allied armies had landed. Because the poor coordination due to the proliferation of networks with different agenda often led to fatal results, a *Comité D*épartemental de Libération Nationale (CDL) was set up in each *département* to lay a political foundation for assumption of administrative powers after the Liberation and to co-ordinate the various networks' activities meanwhile so that they did not inadvertently give each other away. Sometimes this achieved the reverse of what was intended, by bringing together too many Resistance leaders in one place at their meetings.

On the very day *The Partisans' Song* was composed, the words were proven tragically prophetic in Rouen. Césaire Levillain, director of the business school, was arrested after working for the Allies since 1940 in the *Libération Nord* network with a group of other ex-POWs he trusted. His detention and interrogation was to last for a long, cruel year until he was shot on 4 May 1944 at the firing range of Le Madrillet in Rouen – one of the last to be executed there. Immediately after his arrest, his deputy Raoul Leprettre, a printer, took over the network until he too was arrested and deported to Dachau on 2 July 1944 in the same transport as another of Levillain's small band of ex-POWs. Neither man survived. In the heat of midsummer, of the 2,500 prisoners packed like sardines into the cattle trucks marked *for 8 horses or 40 men*, 984 men died of suffocation or heat exhaustion on the three-day journey. Among them were the commander of the Communist FTP underground army on the left bank of the Seine and other Resistance leaders, betrayed and captured while at a meeting of the CDLN in Rouen on 3 June. To have nine out of the twelve senior Resistance commanders on that train – only three of them ever came home – was a major triumph for the *Gestapo* and their French henchmen, but it came too late to change the course of the war.

As month succeeded month, every aspect of life in France became more complicated because the whole economy was crippled by the requisitions and the labour conscription laws. There was, for example, an abundance of seeds to be crushed for cooking oil that year but the trucks necessary to transport them to the factories had disappeared eastwards long since. So, apart from small quantities produced by peasants on ancient manual presses, no oil was made that year.

On 5 June Laval tightened the screw again, calling up for labour service all those becoming eligible in 1942 without any exceptions, with the families of those failing to report subject to rigorous penalties. After a concerted drive by mayors, police and *gendarmerie*, by the end of the month 400,000 young Frenchmen had been sent off to Germany, the *département* of Gironde being one of the first to fulfil its quota, under the energetic *Préfet* Maurice Sabatier and his equally enthusiastic secretary-general Maurice Papon.[2] Giving the lie to the speeches pretending there was any merit in this forced deportation, some of the trains departed covered with daubed graffiti like *Vive la France! Laval should be shot!* and railway workers showed solidarity by delaying the departure of STO trains until forced by armed French police and *gendarmes* to despatch them.

More misery was on the way for people whose lives were still outwardly normal – especially those living along the Channel coast. The Casablanca conference of Allied leaders in January 1943 had decided to appoint a planning staff to coordinate preparations for an invasion of the Continent in the following year. Designated Chief of Staff to Supreme Allied Commander (COSSAC) on 12 March 1943, Lieutenant-General F.E. Morgan set immediately to work on the logistics of the most complicated military operation of the war. He was a brilliant planner, kept in office as deputy to Gen Walter Bedell Smith when Eisenhower was subsequently appointed Supreme Commander, but he was also a complicated person, highly anti-Semitic and prone to asking casual acquaintances in bars, providing they were not obviously Jewish, what they thought should be the future direction of the war effort.[3]

With the build-up in Britain of hundreds of thousands of US servicemen and thousands of aircraft, ships and military vehicles, the intention to invade the Continent was impossible to conceal from *Luftwaffe* photo-reconnaissance over-flights or from neutral diplomats and others who passed information on to German contacts. British newspapers printed cartoons poking fun at the imminent invasion. The only problem for OKW was guessing when and where it would happen. To render this more difficult, a programme of deception operations code-named *Cockade* was built into Morgan's Appreciation for Outline Plan of 26 May 1943.

One of the sub–plots intended to reinforce Hitler's belief that invading forces must swiftly capture a major port through which to reinforce the bridgehead was a mock invasion labelled Operation *Starkey*.

Hitler adored looking at maps, and on a map, the most likely place for an Allied invasion appeared to be at the Straits of Dover, in the area of Boulogne and Calais, where the crossing was shortest. Operation *Starkey* was planned with that in mind, and also aimed at placating Stalin by deterring OKW from moving occupation troops to the eastern front and possibly even drawing Axis ground forces away from the Italian front. On 8 June the idea of using two nearly obsolete R Class battleships in the mock invasion was quietly scuttled by Admiral of the Fleet Sir Dudley Pound at a meeting of the Chiefs of Staff Committee, which minuted that 'this proposal would require very careful consideration before the employment of battleships in the Channel could be sanctioned'.[4] Obsolete the ships might be, but the Royal Navy did not intend to place two of its capital ships within range of both the *Luftwaffe* and German long-range batteries on the French coast – this in the knowledge that, should one of them be put out of action or sunk, the news would be proclaimed in Berlin as a great victory against Britain.

The following week, the Joint Planning Staff defined the object of *Starkey* as to, 'convince the enemy that a large-scale landing in the Pas de Calais area is imminent and to bring the German Air Force to battle. There is no intention of converting *Starkey* into an actual landing. The planning of *Starkey* is therefore limited to purely deceptive measures.'[5]

Confusingly, at the first detailed planning meeting for *Starkey* on 7 July 1943, Air Marshal Sir Trafford Leigh-Mallory, in his capacity as Eisenhower's deputy for all Allied air operations in the European theatre, made the point that the operation was not (this was underlined in the minutes) a deception operation, but a rehearsal for invasion with the definite object of (1) deceiving the enemy into thinking that an invasion was imminent, and (2) inflicting the greatest possible damage on the German Air Force. Reference to *Starkey* as a deception plan 'was therefore to be assiduously avoided'.[6] Possibly, Leigh-Mallory was worried that such reference, if leaked to the enemy, would cause *Starkey* to fizzle out like a damp squib. Yet, the intrinsic contradiction and the re-branding of the operation as 'not a deception operation' confused many people as to its objective – always a dangerous thing in military operations, where the objective should be the first thing clearly established in the planning phase.

On the same date, a combined US–UK planning statement recognised that the air raids should be not 'on such a scale as to neutralise the enemy defences but rather to persuade the enemy of our intention to assault'.[7]

On 22 July a conference at COSSAC HQ in London drafted a document defining the object of *Starkey* as 'a major amphibious operation against the Pas de Calais ... to convince the enemy that a large-scale landing is imminent ... and to compel the German Fighter Force to engage in air battles of attrition at times and places advantageous to us.'[8]

By 26 August 'Bomber' Harris was on record as stating that the targets designated for Bomber Command in *Starkey* were unsuitable for heavy bombers according to the RAF's Operational Research Section, which took into account that the *average* bombing error spread impact points over a rough circle a radius of between half a mile and a mile from the target. Such a margin of error in the case of two particular *Starkey* targets would place an entire town as much at risk as the German coastal batteries closely adjacent on either side of it. The name of that town was Le Portel, meaning 'little port', as compared with neighbouring Boulogne.

Harris made it plain that he resented being required to keep a sizeable Bomber Command force available for what he categorised as 'a harmless piece of play-acting'. On that day the Chiefs of Staff Committee accommodated him by agreeing that the British air raids built into *Starkey* should be made by Operational Training Units (OTUs).[9] This seemed to make sense, since it was preferable to 'blood' crews in training against less heavily defended targets in France, Belgium and Holland before sending them over the Ruhr, with its heavy concentrations of anti-aircraft defences and well-organised night fighter network. Like Harris, General James H. Doolittle, now commanding the US Eighth Air Force in Britain, thought the whole operation a waste of resources and a distraction from the main business of the war, which both commanders considered to be the massed bombing raids on strategic targets inside the *Reich*.

A sizeable radio deception operation broadcast fake messages from transmitters in southern England which were supposed to hoodwink German listening stations into believing that an invasion was in the offing. Twice during August the BBC broadcast coded messages to France alerting Resistance groups to a fictitious imminent invasion in the hope that, whether by double agents, carelessness or capture and torture of *résistants*, this would reach the Germans.[10] Greater verisimilitude was to be conferred by intensive softening-up bombing of selected targets in the Pas de Calais. However, high winds and cloud cover not only reduced the number of these raids but also prevented *Luftwaffe* photo-reconnaissance over-flights that would have revealed the build-up of the mock invasion fleet in ports along the south coast and large-scale movement of troops to these ports for embarkation. When intelligence reports from occupied France brought no indication that the Germans had been taken in by the preparations, and that the *Luftwaffe* was not especially concentrating its forces in northern France, even General Morgan expressed doubts as to whether there was any point in *Starkey* going ahead.[11]

On the assumption that it nevertheless was – and by this stage so large an operation had acquired a momentum of its own – suitable beaches were selected to the north and south of Boulogne for the mock invasion landing area. The port of Boulogne itself was too heavily defended to seaward for a landing there to be practicable and the whole 'fortress area' was defended by some 7,000 German troops. The suburb known as Le Portel was therefore selected as the ideal place for a notional bridgehead from which troops could move swiftly overland into Boulogne itself and prevent last-minute demolition of the port facilities there by the German occupation forces.

Le Portel was a picturesque fishing village and holiday resort at the seaward end of the valley of the Tihen stream. A century and a half before the Germans installed two long-range coastal defence batteries on either side of the village, Napoleon appreciated its strategic position and changed the sea view permanently by the construction of three massive offshore forts to interdict a British invasion. Later in the nineteenth century, when the railway from Paris arrived at Boulogne, Le Portel became an artists' colony. Narrow streets of picturesque fishermen's cottages wound their way down to the small harbour redolent of tar and seaweed, where fishing boats were hauled up the beach of fine sand between windbreaks and bathing tents in prewar summers. A few hotels with names like 'Hôtel des Bains et Belle Vue' accommodated the peacetime visitors, many of whom arrived by the tramway that connected the village with the main railway station in Boulogne. Fishing was the only all-year-round activity for the Portelois men, whose women were equally tough, and noted for gathering up their skirts and wading barefoot into the sea with huge shrimping nets when not engaged in mending the nets.

Le Portel before the Second World War.

The first four years of the war seemed largely to have passed Le Portel by, except for a handful of people killed on shore and at sea and when bodies of Canadians killed at Dieppe were washed ashore in August 1942. But life was far from easy in this ultra-high-security zone, where people were prohibited from travelling more than 4km from their homes; even within that radius there were forbidden areas, the penalties for transgressing which could mean deportation or death.

London passed prior notice of *Starkey* to Moscow, so that Stalin would not be taken in by subsequent German propaganda claiming that an Allied invasion had been defeated, but the softening-up phase between 16 and 24 August was real enough: 680 USAAF and 156 RAF aircraft bombed airfields and other strategic targets in the area. From 25 August to 8 September, the bomber force grew to 2,394 aircraft targeting also fuel and ammunition dumps hidden in forests near Boulogne. Because the distance from base to target was so much shorter than for raids into the Reich, fuel loads were reduced, enabling bomb loads to be increased accordingly.

To reinforce the idea of Le Portel as the location selected for the initial bridgehead, two of the coastal batteries were to be given special attention. They were at Fort de Couppes to the north and Cap d'Alprech to the south of the town, code-named *Religion* and *Andante*. Because they were extremely close to the town, reference was made at the Air Ministry and

134

COSSAC to the policy laid down by the Assistant Chief of Air Staff (Policy) in the previous October.

Preparatory raids on the Boulogne area took place on 4, 6 and 8 September. The daylight raid of 4 September saw a force of RAF medium bombers also hit Le Portel, doubling the previous casualties with seven more civilian deaths, six badly injured and damage to property in a community that was inured to losses of its menfolk at sea, but not of women and children in what was thought of as the safety of their homes.

The weather forecast for 8 September was so bad that the sailing of the mock invasion fleet was postponed by twenty-four hours – as were most of the air raids planned in conjunction with it for the fake D-Day, which included heavy bombing to neutralise the batteries adjacent to Le Portel. On the ground in Le Portel, however, it was a balmy summer day under a blue sky – until, towards dusk, the siren on the town hall wailed its warning as American twin-engined Marauder medium bombers arrived directly over the town, bomb bays open to scatter their loads all over the town. The raid was swiftly over, leaving the shocked population looking at houses levelled, homes ablaze and bodies being hauled out of the debris by the rescue teams, who had to requisition private cars to get so many victims to hospital in Boulogne. Without any instructions being given, several hundred people packed up basic necessities and headed out of town, intending to spend the night in the fields for safety. But most survivors of the afternoon raid stayed where they were, in the belief that nothing worse could happen. Surely, they reasoned, the raid had been a ghastly mistake?

Rescue teams did not wait for the end of the bombardment, but arrived several hundred strong with the first fire team from Boulogne and the local ambulance service operating a shuttle service for the wounded between Le Portel and the St Louis hospital in Boulogne. Before dusk two RAF photo-reconnaissance aircraft flew over the stricken area, clearly recording that the German batteries had taken little punishment and were still serviceable. As night made their work more difficult, the rescue teams continued their work by pocket torches and acetylene lamps taken from the fishing boats, unearthing roughly equal numbers of corpses and traumatised and wounded survivors. Then, at 22.00hrs local time, flight after flight of Allied bombers returned to pummel Le Portel afresh, trapping the rescuers in the cellars beneath the rubble. This went on for three hours. For the night of 8–9 September, the Bomber Command campaign diary recorded:

> (Target) Boulogne gun positions: 257 aircraft – 119 Wellingtons, 112 Stirlings, 16 Mosquitos, 10 Halifaxes. OTU aircraft formed part of this force and 5 B-17s (Flying Fortresses) also flew the first American night-bombing sorties of the war with Bomber Command. No 4 and No 5 Groups did not take part in the raid. The target was the site of a German long-range gun battery and the marking was mainly provided by *Oboe*-guided Mosquitos, some of whom were experimenting with a new technique. But the raid was not successful; the marking and the bombing were not accurate and the battery does not appear to have been damaged. No aircraft lost. [12]

At this stage of the war, bad weather conditions and cloud cover over German targets were being combated by radio guidance systems – the *Oboe* and *Baillie* beams – indicating exactly the course to be followed from base to target and cueing the release of the target indicators (TIs), to show where the main bomber force should drop its loads. For targets in northern France, the *Oboe* system was by no means foolproof because of the reduced 'angle of cut' between the transmitters and the target, compared with targets hundreds of miles to the east in Germany, for which the system was designed. Since the raid on Le Portel was partly for training inexperienced crews and to explore whether mixing USAAF and RAF aircraft in the same raid was a good idea – it proved not to be – it is the more ironic that a tragedy was about to unfold on a night when there was no cloud cover and bright moonlight.

As it happened, personnel at the *Oboe* transmitter station designated Hawkshill Down 1 were able to witness things going wrong across the Channel, since the TIs floated down after release at altitude in full view for them, burning brilliantly. In Phase One, the experienced Pathfinder crew did not drop the first, red, marker, due to the *Oboe* signal failing at the crucial moment. The secondary greens were seen two minutes behind schedule, one landing inside the town, where most residents were cowering in their cellars, which were no protection against a direct, or even close, hit. In the streets, the rescue workers were falling victim not only to explosions of Allied bombs and flying fragments, but also to the shards of red-hot shrapnel from the sustained anti-aircraft fire. Aiming at the visible TIs, the aircraft in the first phase dropped 340 tons of bombs, most of which landed in the town. In Phase Two, one of the TIs broke into three segments that landed half a mile apart in a neat line, straddling Le Portel. Taking these as the aiming points, the 234 aircraft in this phase dropped three-quarters

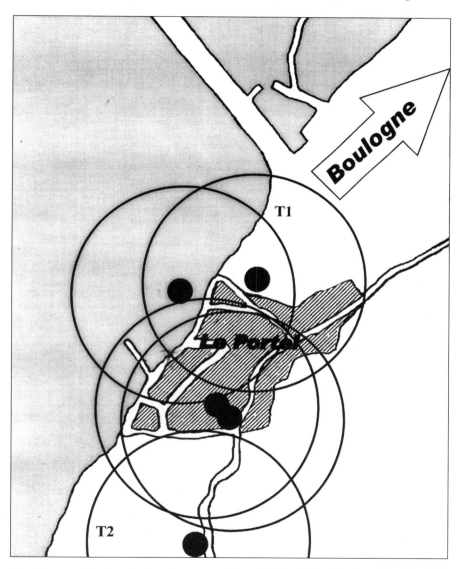

Sketch map of Le Portel, showing targets T1 and T2 and distribution of the five fatal target indicators with circles showing total destruction in radius of approximately one half-mile.

of the 337.5 tons of high-explosive and 5.9 tons of incendiaries they were carrying on the town itself.[13] The grand total for the raid of 684 tons of high explosive and incendiaries literally blew the buildings and the people of Le Portel, and their would-be rescuers, into dust and ashes.

As dawn came, the teams still labouring in Le Portel were beset on all sides by the groans and pleas for help coming from beneath the heaps of smoking rubble, many people being asphyxiated or burned to death before anyone could reach them, despite heroic efforts. Many uninjured Portellois, who could have helped, were so traumatised that they fled into the fields as soon as they were released. Some were in nightclothes, others half-dressed, but all had only one thought in their heads – to put as much distance as possible between themselves and the carnage.

In the cellars of a house in the rue Victor Hugo, a six-man fire crew from Boulogne and two local men were killed when the building fell in on them after they had laboured for twelve hours to free victims of the first raid. Elsewhere, a doctor had to be called to cut through a corpse in order to release a woman trapped beneath it. A mother who had been breast-feeding her baby was found dead, with the baby alive on her lap. The horrors went on and on.

The scale of the damage and the heavy casualties to the original rescue teams had brought more helpers from Calais, Lille and much further away. The noise of the bombardment, and the smoke and ash from Le Portel that was landing in Boulogne like a coating of volcanic ash, sparked rumours among the civilian population there that had many of them heading for the shelters and down into their cellars with a supply of food and water, prepared to wait out the further raids and street fighting of the invasion that they thought must be imminent. With no mortuary at Le Portel, nor transport to take them away, the dead were laid in long lines on the ground where Le Portel's town hall had stood. They eventually numbered approximately 500, many body parts being difficult to identify, and took their place among the 2,787 French civilians killed and 4,292 wounded by Allied air raids in September 1943.[14] The northern SIPEG train arrived next morning to succour the survivors, but even its resources were inadequate for devastation and death on this scale.

As if the catastrophe of the night raid was in any way wanting, at 07.45hrs, 202-plus aircraft of US VIII Air Support Command attacked Le Portel during two hours. The Photographic Interpretation Report SA 555, headed, *Attack on targets in the Boulogne area on 9.9.43'* noted that, 'The heaviest concentration of bursts is noted on and near the town of Le Portel.'[15] These groups of USAAF B26 Marauder medium bombers were accompanied by a heavy fighter escort that was supposed to pulverise the *Luftwaffe*. A few night-fighters had been observed by RAF crews during the night, without causing much damage, and the expected *Luftwaffe* mass attack did not materialise, even when the decoy invasion fleet of 355 vessels emerged as planned from south coast ports at dawn and spread out across a mile of sea, protected by Royal Navy destroyers, so as to be clearly visible from the French coast. At 09.00hrs the code-word *Backchat* transmitted from HMS *Albrighton* saw every vessel executing a 180-degree turn behind a smoke screen, to return to port while the Marauders were still attacking Le Portel.

The German garrison not having been taken in by the deception operation, when the Free French destroyer *La Combattante* steamed towards Boulogne, Sub-Lieutenant Bernard Leglise recorded that there came not a single salvo from the coastal batteries and no German aircraft appeared overhead, even when *La Combattante* was close enough to the coast for him to see clearly Napoleon's column in the town.[16]

Eight weeks after the raids on Le Portel the official tally was that ninety-three per cent of homes were destroyed; only 367 of the 500-odd dead had been positively identified because so many bodies were unidentifiable; of the 1,200 injured, 400 were severely so. Some 200 stubborn people with nowhere else to go were camping in the ruins of their homes despite the trauma and the health hazard from decomposing human remains that had not been found. Among German personnel, casualties were just two dead and five injured.

Having failed to prevent the transfer of ten divisions from France and to draw the *Luftwaffe* into a confrontation, the question remains whether *Starkey* was a total failure, or whether all the civilians killed, and the razing of Le Portel,had some value in keeping the Germans waiting for a landing at Boulogne or Calais on 6 June 1944.[17] US Army historian Forrest C. Pogue summed up by saying that it was impossible to determine to what extent the three deception operations of *Cockade* caused problems for the Germans.[18]

In the midst of all their agony, some Portellois saw the people killing them as allies and protested at German troops machine-gunning a bomber crew that was parachuting down after their aircraft had been hit. Yet, this was not a solitary instance of solidarity with men who brought death from the sky. The previous February, several Allied aircrew managed to parachute from their stricken aircraft and landed in the Dunkirk suburb of Malo-les-Bains. A large crowd of French civilians gathered to prevent German soldiers arresting the airmen, giving way only after shots had been fired into the air. French police at the scene did not intervene, which led to their subsequent arrest. In March all the *mairies* in the Nord and Pas de Calais *départements* received from their *Préfectures* copies of a note of protest from Dr Menglowski of the 670th *Feldkommandantur*, warning of stronger measures that would be taken in future events of this kind.[19]

Two months after Le Portel was wiped off the map, one of the most daring exploits of the French Resistance came on the symbolic date of 11 November 1943 in the little village of Audinghen, just 15km to the north. In August 1940 all the inhabitants had been forcibly evacuated by the German army and the village taken over as headquarters of Organisation *Todt* for the construction of the Atlantic Wall from the Franco–Belgian border to the border with Spain and the construction of the V1 and V2 launching sites. After a radio message to London from the *Centurie* network, units of the US 2nd Tactical Air Force effected two carefully timed raids on that day. The first, between 14.30hrs and 14.50hrs, destroyed the village completely, its purpose being to frighten the German bosses, engineers and supervisors away from their offices and permit an agent named Michel Blot to enter those offices, photograph plans of 102 V1 sites and steal 5kg of top secret papers covering the coast around Boulogne, which reached London a few days later. The second raid 17.30hrs – 18.30hrs was intended to cause so much damage and confusion in the headquarters building that the theft would not be noticed.[20]

PART 3

PREPARATION AND PAIN

Chapter 11

Spies, spy-hunters and bishops

It is difficult to distinguish between behaviour during the occupation that was open or concealed collaboration and what was necessary 'to get by'. On 7 October 1943, to keep Sauckel at arm's length for a while, Pétain's Secretary of State for Industrial Production Jean Bichelonne did a deal with Hitler's Armaments Minister Albert Speer under which 10,000 French factories, working full-time for Germany, were designated 'S' and their work-force exempted from the STO. Obviously the workers and their families preferred that to being shipped off for work in the Reich. For the factory owners, there was no choice, since the occupation authorities controlled the allocation of raw materials, and refusing their orders would have meant closing down and laying off the work-force, making all the male workers immediately liable for STO.

On 11 November 1943 a resident of Cherbourg named René Sallé noted in his diary more than 200 aircraft over-flying towards the Organisation *Todt* construction site at Couville, ten kilometers outside town. Code-named *Wasserwerk Cherbourg Bauwerk* 8 - B 8, this vast complex of reinforced concrete bunkers was designed to store 150 V1s – nicknamed 'flying bombs' or 'doodle-bugs' – with magnetically shielded workshops for setting the compasses and all the logistics necessary to keep firing them at regular intervals for five days, including vast storage tanks of aviation fuel, hydrogen peroxide and potassium permanganate. It was one of a network of sixty-four launching sites on the Cotentin peninsula for V1s, V2s and the ultimate V3 weapon, all oriented towards southern Britain. Sallé wrote:

> For two solid hours windows shook with the vibrations from
> the explosions. According to *requis* who got away, the whole
> site was turned into a hellish lunar landscape with hundreds

of slave labourers crushed beneath the five-metre-thick reinforced concrete roofs. Officially, the slave workers did not exist, so only twenty-five dead (French) workers had been injured or killed. The whole construction site was cratered and roofs blown off farms in the neighbourhood. In Couville itself most of the houses are damaged. At the funeral service, there were twenty-five coffins of *requis* draped with the tricolor and those of the German soldiers with Nazi flags, but we knew that some coffins contained what was left of ten or more workers.[1]

Once it was obvious to everyone in France that an Allied invasion was imminent, the Vichy-controlled police and *gendarmerie* tended to become less enthusiastic in their collaboration with the German authorities. To compensate for this, from the beginning of 1944 the *Gestapo* did not bother with accusations or trials, simply arresting people on suspicion under *Schutzhaft* or preventive detention and despatching them, usually after torture, to concentration camps. The *Milice* worked hand in hand with the *Gestapo*. Despised and hated by the general population, they knew that they would have to pay for their conduct after the Liberation and therefore had nothing to lose by tracking down and maltreating *résistants* right up to the very last day they had the power to do so.

One man who had nothing to fear from them, or anyone else of whatever political persuasion, was Pierre Courant. On 17 January he told the town council of Le Havre of his efforts to obtain financial aid from Vichy:

In vain, I told them of the ninety raids we have suffered, of our 350 dead, of the daily air raid alerts wearing down everyone's nerves – like on 16 August last, when the sirens wailed seven or eight times in twenty-four hours. Nobody would listen.

Nobody in central government would listen because the machinery of the Vichy state was disintegrating as a result of all the German exactions of resources and labour. Among minor problems discussed at the meeting in Le Havre town hall was the lack of wood to make coffins, so that corpses had to be interred wrapped in a sheet. The scant funds of the

Treasurer's Department had to cover the funeral expenses of air raid victims. More than 50,000 people had fled greater Le Havre, yet for those who remained unemployment was a problem, with the big employers like Schneider, Bertrand and Les Huileries Desmarrais having laid off their labour forces after the factories were bombed out of production. Each day, the municipal restaurants served 4,000 meals to needy families, the unemployed and the homeless.[2]

The various Resistance factions that were politically grouped under the label *Forces Françaises de l'Intérieur,* thanks to astute manoeuvring and bribery by De Gaulle's emissary Jean Moulin, stepped up their activities – as did the forces, both French and German, arrayed against them. The grim, black-edged posters announcing the execution of activists became more and more familiar, epecially in the Nord and Pas de Calais regions.

Yet, the sabotage continued. Roger Speybroeck was a 24-year-old member of the *Alliance* network that put out of action eleven locomotives and all the repair facilities at Tourcoing, near Dunkirk, on 28 December 1943. Shot at Bondues on 19 January 1944 he wrote what was perhaps the most dispassionate last letter of all, with no patriotic slogans, no political aspirations and no religious references. Echoing Christina Rosetti's lines *Better by far you should forget and smile, than that you should remember and be sad,* he wrote to his family: 'I love you so much that I should like to be forgotten by you, if thinking about me makes you sad. Do not utter my name and let your love fade with my life.'[3]

In the eyes of both Gaullist and British spymasters in London, their agents in occupied France were all expendable in the insanely dangerous game of active resistance, in which every act of sabotage and every radio message transmitted to Britain was a challenge to the dedicated *Gestapo*, German army and French units which held all the aces in the game, from double agents to confessions given under torture to direction-finding vans able to pinpoint the location of Resistance transmitters. Earlier in the war, after being flown clandestinely to London to meet De Gaulle, Christian Pineau – founder of *Libération Nord* network and publisher of the clandestine weekly *Libération* – wrote:

> I found De Gaulle's thinking entirely military. When I explained that Pétain had substantial support, and that we were also up against the Communists playing their own game, he was unmoved by the dangers we were running.

For him, (it was normal for) every combatant to risk his life whether in a tank in North Africa or posting handbills on walls in France.[4]

Two weeks after Speybroeck was shot, André Wannin took one risk too many. In civilian life a plumbing and heating engineer, he had been evacuated from Dunkirk in May 1940, returned to France via Brest and took up arms again, winning the *Croix de Guerre*. After the surrender, Wannin operated a transmitter which sent back to London copious intelligence on airfields and other military objectives. Wanting to do more, he joined an FTP sabotage team and was arrested on 4 February 1944, together with three other members of the group. He was thirty years old, mechanic Adolphe Hugé was thirty-two, builder's labourer Lucien Desjardin was twenty-four and his brother Edouard was a 22-year-old butcher's apprentice. Condemned by a German court martial on 6 February, they were shot with twenty-three others at St Quentin on 8 April. Although their group was Communist-led, Wannin at least was devout, mentioning in his last letter that he was completing his second novena to St Theresa asking that she give his wife and parents strength to cope with their imminent bereavement and that he was also about to make his confession to a German Catholic chaplain. Like many others awaiting execution, he also begged their forgiveness for the pain he had caused and – envisaging that his decomposed corpse would need to be identified after the war when disinterred from an anonymous mass grave to be reburied nearer home – confided that he was keeping on him a comb and a toothbrush handle, on which his name was carved.[5]

Sauckel's demands for French labour still being unsatisfied, on 1 February 1944 yet another conscription law was passed, with the intention of weeding out those 'unnecessarily' employed in France, or not employed. This was followed up at the beginning of March by a circular to all local authorities in the northern zone ordering that, 'all men aged eighteen to forty-five should be presumed suspect and sent to an investigation centre.'[6] Laval was now scraping the bottom of the barrel and found only another 32,244 before the system broke down at the end of May 1944.

To these figures, one has to add the many thousands of French workers employed in France by Organisation *Todt*. The *Wehrmacht* also had 65,000 French auxiliaries and the *Luftwaffe* a further 137,000. To these figures can be added 2 million working in the mines and the S factories, where most, if not all, of their work benefited the *Reich*.[7]

Dubbed 'the man who saved London' by General Sir Brian Horrocks, one of the most important agents working in France for the Allied cause was Colonel Michel Hollard. He was also among the luckiest, if one can put it like that. A 44-year-old father of three, Hollard founded the *Agir*[8] network in 1941 and recruited some 100 sub-agents – far too many for good security. He personally delivered to the British Embassy in Berne much information on German troop movements, crossing the closely guarded Franco–Swiss frontier ninety-eight times. In 1943 he pulled off his greatest coup, mapping the locations of 103 launch sites being constructed in northern France for the V1 flying bombs. With the help of railway workers, he also succeeded in penetrating a high-security munitions warehouse in Auffay, near Dieppe, and removing the detailed plans of an 8-metre long V2 rocket, able to deliver a warhead of 850kg at a range of 250km from the launch pad.

After forwarding these to London, in February 1944 Hollard was arrested in Paris with two of his sub-agents. They were all tortured in the prison at Fresnes, condemned to death and sent to Germany. When the Neuengamme concentration camp was over-run on 4 May 1945, it was found to be empty, the last commandant having force-marched the prisoners to Hamburg harbour, where they were packed into several requisitioned ships without life-jackets or life-rafts, his intention being to have U-boats torpedo the vessels and drown all aboard. Sighted by Allied reconnaissance aircraft, the ships were also designated a target for an RAF bombing mission. With a small number of other prisoners, Hollard was saved at the last minute from embarkation on the fatal convoy by the personal intervention of Count Bernadotte of the Swedish Red Cross – and lived to die naturally in 1993, aged ninety-five years old.

On 15 February 1944 René Sallé was travelling between Cherbourg and Valognes when he saw:

> ... a group of twenty-seven aircraft at 10.45hrs, followed by three groups of eighteen and a last group of twenty-two: (They) made three circuits above Sottevast. Each time, a wall of anti-aircraft fire rained shrapnel all over the countryside. I took refuge in a house and watched a plane in flames apparently heading straight towards me for several

seconds before straightening out and crashing near Ruffosses or Le Theil. Another plane came down in flames near Querqueville. Bombs were falling on Négreville near a German site, killing five civilians and two of the *requis*.[9]

There were several other raids on German rocket sites that day. As always, civilians paid the price for the bomb-aimers' inaccuracy – a few here and many there, all adding up to a terrible toll of deaths among men and women who were not enemies of those who killed them. Just six days prior to the raid on Sottevast, Bishop George Bell of Chichester rose to speak in the House of Lords. Although a loyal supporter of the war effort and accepting of tactical air raids, he had previously deplored publicly the civilian deaths from area bombing. Not all the Lords Spiritual agreed with him: Archbishop Temple of Canterbury and Dr Garbett, Bishop of York, supported the bombing campaign as the lesser of two evils, necessary to deliver millions from German slavery.

In a 1941 letter to *The Times*, Bishop Bell had called the bombing of women and children a barbarian act that would destroy the just,

Bishop George Bell.

147

i.e. Allied, cause. On several occasions he spoke out against the War Cabinet's decision to authorise area bombing. On 9 February 1944, Bell asked again:

> Does the Government understand the full force of what area bombardment is doing and is destroying now? Are they alive not only to the vastness of the material damage, much of which is irreparable, but also to the harvest they are laying up for the future relationships of the peoples of Europe, as well as to its moral implications? I recognize the legitimacy of concentrated attack on industrial and military objectives, on airfields and air bases. I fully realize that in attacks on centres of war industry and transport, the killing of civilians (is the) inevitable result of bona fide military activity.

On another occasion in the House of Lords, he demanded, 'How can the War Cabinet fail to see that this progressive devastation of cities is threatening the roots of civilization?'[10]

The bishop's pleas fell on deaf ears in the Chamber, but were reported to the prime minister, who disapproved of his stand. It was said by his many supporters that George Bell's unflinching morality twice cost him the see of Canterbury in the period when it was in the giving of Winston Churchill.

The alternative to the massive civilian casualties was sabotage by *résistants*. The reaction of local occupation troops was always unpredictable, the German military code usually ensuring honourable treatment of captured enemy soldiers in uniform, but permitting brutal repression of 'partisan' activities. On the night of 1–2 April 1944 a German military train was derailed at Ascq, outside Lille. Unfortunately for local residents, the nearest German troops were from the fanatical *SS-Panzerdivision Hitlerjugend*, who rounded up and shot eighty-six civilians living nearby, few of whom had even known of the sabotage operation. The news provoked horror across France, which decided the Lille *Feldkommandantur* to 'justify' the reprisals by tracking down and putting on trial the railway staff who had carried out the sabotage. Henri Gallois and seven other *cheminots* belonging to the *Alliance* network were convicted and condemned to death, making a total of ninety-four deaths in reprisal for this one operation.[11]

Cinema films and television dramas and documentaries have portrayed the risks run by Resistance men and women collecting intelligence in France as a heroic adrenalin trip, but at the time survival depended on discipline and paranoid precautions, the price for not observing which was death – and not a grand heroic death, but as a result of, or release from, intolerable torture.

One of those who took the risks from June 1940 to the end of the occupation was a farmer and father of nine children from the sleepy Dordogne village of Le Breuilh. Louis de la Bardonnie was initially a supporter of Pétain until he realised shortly after the surrender where the Marshal and Laval were taking France. He then enlisted Bordeaux river pilots to provide details of U-boat movements in the River Gironde between Bordeaux and the sea, eventually claiming eleven U-boats destroyed by Allied aircraft shortly after leaving the estuary. By late 1943 Bardonnie's clandestine activities for the *Confrèrie Notre Dame* network in all the high-security coastal zones, disguised as a railway inspector and under other aliases that allowed him to travel all over France, were attracting increasing attention. On one mission in his four-year clandestine career he was disguised as a priest, using a Minox miniature camera supplied from London to take 1,250 photographs of documents and scenes in the port of Cherbourg. There, he was unmasked, fortunately not by the Gestapo, but by devout co-religionists who saw through him when he attempted to confess them!

His *Gestapo* Paris file AT/87.878/FR 1943/44 recorded him as an exceptionally dangerous agent, to be eliminated at all costs – if possible, to be taken alive, with 1 million francs reward for his arrest or betrayal.[12]

Humint – the information collected by agents on the ground like Bardonnie – depends on having access to high-security sites or special knowledge about them. If it was difficult for the FAFL pilots to think of their countrymen they had killed and wounded at a distance, it was far more harrowing for those local agents when death from the sky killed people they knew and worked with. There was also an element of selecting which of them should be the victims when raids were timed to occur with the minimum number of workers inside a targeted factory.

Happily for Bardonnie, the many divisions of German counter-intelligence competed more often than they cooperated, but his long run as a highly productive agent was due to him using the *need-to-know* principle with his sub-agents and organising them in cells, with cut-outs so that no one could betray more than his or her immediate contacts.

Chapter 12

The ravaging of Rouen

Henri Tafforeau was fifteen in 1944, a lonely boy evacuated from Paris to stay with his grandparents in a town that was thought to be a safe haven. Whereas other adolescents fill their diaries with notes of sports events, outings with friends and meetings with boy- or girlfriends, young Henri used his to document the events that might easily have ended his young life. Fortunately, his son found the notebooks many years later and had them published.[1]

On 21 January 1944 Henri was listening to the radio when he heard 'the shriek of a stick of bombs growing louder and louder, followed by an enormous explosion that rattled all the windows and doors'. These were not Allied bombs. In November 1943 Goering had ordered the *Luftwaffe* to resume mass bombing raids against southern England. Like most of his ideas during the war, the idea was a pipe dream which cost so many vitally needed aircraft and aircrew that by 1 July 1944 there were only ninety bombers and seventy other aircraft left for the defence of occupied France.

Even with the *Reichsmarschal's* personal backing, it took two months to assemble on northern French airfields a heterogeneous force of 515 Junkers, Dornier, Messerschmitt and Heinkel bombers, whose raid of 21 January 1944 was the first mass raid on Britain since 1941. With the aircrew inexperienced in night navigation, only thirty-two bombs actually fell on London that night – which was scant consolation for those killed and maimed in Rouen. The following day's German-sponsored *Journal de Rouen* printed an apology from the *Kommandantur* expressing regret that a *Luftwaffe* aircraft bombed up for the raid on Britain had got into difficulties after take-off and had to jettison its bombs.

Sleep patterns in Rouen were disturbed by twenty-nine air raid alerts in January and thirty-four in February, but most signalled the over-flight of Allied bombers heading for targets elsewhere, so that the Rouennais became accustomed to the roar of bomber formations passing overhead and the crack of the German ack-ack batteries sited in and around the town. In preparation for an Allied invasion, German troops erected concrete anti-tank barriers in Rouen and put in hand, down by the docks, construction of a new *Kommandantur* building in 4-metre-thick reinforced concrete. On 21 March the Germans ordered all radio receivers to be handed in, so that the coded messages to the Resistance from London could no longer be heard. On pain of severe penalties for non-compliance, 45,000 sets were handed in, in greater Rouen alone. As Henri Tafforeau commented in his diary, the town was now cut off from all news from across the Channel, so that rumours became wilder and wilder – as testified by Pétain's radio talk to the nation on 28 April, when he said:

> The possibility of liberation is the most dangerous of the mirages to which you may succumb. Thanks to German defence of the Continent our civilisation will be permanently protected from the menace of Bolshevism.[2]

However, it was not the menace of Bolshevism that brought terror to Rouen on the night of 18–19 April. The principal strategic targets were the bridges across the Seine, the riverine port installations and the large railway marshalling yards of the lower town, called Sotteville. In this one raid, 6,000 bombs were dropped. It was described thus in the RAF Bomber Command campaign diary:

> 273 Lancasters and 16 Mosquitos of Nos 1, 3 and 8 Groups to Rouen. No aircraft lost (in) a concentrated attack on the railway yards, with much destruction.

On the same night Mosquitos of Nos 6 and 8 Groups raided railway yards at Tergnier, 160km east of Dieppe, where local intelligence afterwards reported that most of the bombs fell on residential areas in a zone 6km long and 3km wide, with 750 dwellings destroyed, 464 French civilians killed and 370 injured. The campaign diary sums up the night's work as:

1,125 sorties, 14 aircraft (1.2 per cent) lost. The total number of sorties on this night was a new Bomber Command record.[3]

Henri Tafforeau noted in his diary that school resumed early that year after the Easter holiday because it was expected that the summer term would be interrupted by an Allied invasion. On Wednesday 18 April he finished his maths homework and went to bed around 22.00hrs. As in wartime Britain, entertainments attracted full houses of people desperate for any escape. The grande dame of French theatre, Cécile Sorel, was playing the title role in *Le Roi Christine* to a full house at the *Théatre Français*. Hardly had she reached her hotel in the town centre after the performance than a distant murmur grew to a roar overhead. The clear night sky with its twinkling stars was obliterated by an artificial sun made by what seemed like hundreds of parachute flares as sixteen Pathfinder Force Mosquitoes released their green and red target indicators.

People still in the streets hurried home as a series of huge explosions in the direction of the port and marshalling yards rattled windows all over the town, waking up the sleepers. Only then did the sirens wail. People fled to the shelters or took refuge in their cellars. In the town centre local poet Francis Yard described watching the parachute flares fall, one in his neighbour's garden, making everything as bright as day. After ten minutes it seemed that the raid was over. Then the town was bathed in light again.[4] Shortly after that, came the noise of a hail of 350kg and 300kg bombs targeting the port and marshalling yards, but landing in residential districts on the right bank of the Seine, smashing the medieval heart of Rouen into a field of blazing ruins, where at least 900 people died. The theatre was destroyed, the medieval cathedral badly damaged, as were the ancient law courts. The ancient timber-framed houses in the town centre were ablaze. So were the elegant seventeenth- and eighteenth-century houses of the rich.

Henri Tafforeau's diary recorded it blow by blow:

> 00.15hrs – I woke up again with a start. The whole house was shaking. Explosions everywhere. The alert sounded.

> 00.17hrs – We hurried down to the cellar in our pyjamas. The noise of bombers was terribly loud. The ack–ack was firing without stop and we could hear sticks of bombs falling in the lower town.

> 00.30 – The raid seemed to be over, so I went upstairs with a neighbour, to look outside. The sky was clear with stars shining. Guns were firing in the distance. Suddenly we heard an aircraft

overhead and the nearby ack-ack opened up again. With a long whistling scream and a yellow lightning flash, marker bombs were falling. We went back down to the cellar, but said nothing to the women there, who would learn soon enough what was happening. The ground was shaking and blast waves buffeted us even in the cellar. We heard a noise on the stairs. It was my grandfather, who had always refused to come down in previous raids. The lights flickered and went out completely. Huddled against the walls, we listened to the scream of bombs and the explosions getting louder and closer. One colossal explosion shook the cellar walls of solid stone. I realised how fragile life was, and prayed. This went on and on for half an hour.

In the strange silence that followed, there was no 'all clear' siren because the town was without electricity. We were all too exhausted to go upstairs, and also we were afraid there would be a third wave of bombers. When my grandfather and a neighbour went up to have a look around, they came back to announce that houses were burning nearby. When I went up to street level, I was horrified to see houses on fire only 200 metres away, at the end of our street. Huge flames shot up, lighting up the sky.

At this moment, a classmate arrived, whose house was surrounded by others destroyed and on fire. With all the water mains cut, nothing could be done to fight the fires. So, he came to ask for help in removing the family's precious possessions before the fires made this impossible. The diary continues:

I helped Serge by the light of the burning houses to carry the hastily filled suitcases back to my house. There were a lot of people running about. At 04.00hrs the police patrolling the damaged streets came round with a warning that a new raid was expected. That kept us awake even after we ate breakfast about 05.00hrs. There was no gas, no electricity and no water in the taps. Rouen burned all night long. In the morning a thick veil of smoke hid the sun. In a house next to Serge's a bomb had failed to explode. We wondered whether it would go off as we walked past.

Journalist and historian R–G. Nobécourt recorded:

> When the 'all clear' was sounded at 01.40hrs those of us
> who had not been driven out of our shelters by the fires or
> crushed beneath the ruins emerged into a scene of horror.
> The centre of the town was one huge inferno, threatening to
> spread even further.[5]

Numbering just twenty-seven men and with their commanding officer
absent on a training course in Paris, the town's fire service had no hope of
extinguishing such a blaze. The water mains were all ruptured, so water
had to be pumped uphill from the river. With neighbouring towns also
raided that night, no outside help arrived before 02.25hrs, when fire teams
and rescue workers arrived, bringing pumps to raise the water from the
river to holding pools, from which it could be pumped higher to where
the fires were worst.

One of the worst horrors was at the law courts, where captured
résistants and hostages locked in the basement cells were trapped beneath
the blazing ruins overhead. Fortunately the floor did not cave in on them
when the roof fell in, but they could hear the roar of the flames and feel the
heat getting steadily worse until some German guards managed to break
through to them about 04.00hrs. Induced by promises that cooperation
would be rewarded by reduced sentences, some of the prisoners helped
to find and deal with unexploded bombs. The promises were never
honoured. Nobécourt again:

> When daybreak came, the full scope and cruelty of the
> disaster was clear. Many of our famous monuments were
> burned, destroyed or damaged. Eighty-five house facades
> in the famous centre of old Rouen were destroyed and
> another sixteen badly damaged, with 588 houses destroyed
> or rendered uninhabitable.[6]

By 08.00hrs three emergency trucks had already arrived from Paris and
were distributing food, blankets – and shoes to those who had none. Henri
Taffoureau walked to school through streets foul with smoke and ashes
and stinking with the smell of charred flesh, stepping over fire hoses and
avoiding the worst fires, to find that only nine other boys turned up that

day. The good news was that none of his friends had been killed, although several were homeless. His diary reads:

> After two hours of lessons, they sent us home for the afternoon. I took a walk with my grandfather and saw the damaged cathedral and a huge crater in front of the main entrance made by a high-explosive bomb. It was a sad half-day holiday. People scurried around with a few saved possessions in a wheelbarrow or a pram. In front of the cathedral, a pile of mattresses, some chairs, bundles of clothes and bed linen. A man on a ladder, trying to get into a first-floor window of his bombed house. People started saying that leaflets had been dropped announcing that THEY (the RAF) would be back that evening. Still in shock and feeling as though I had been physically beaten up, I watched it get dark with a mounting terror, but then the sky clouded over, which was a great relief for us all.
>
> Next day, I went back to school. Houses were still burning, thirty-six hours after the raid. We had that afternoon off, so I went home, just as terrified as the previous day. We had four alerts that day, two more in the night and three on the Friday. We didn't know what to do with ourselves because we thought it was all going to start again.[7]

Henri's account was only that of one terrified young eyewitness, who did not see the full extent of the damage that left the centre of Normandy's ancient capital looking like Berlin in May 1945. Nor did he then know that this one raid left more than 722 corpses in the ruins. Vagueness in the body count was partly due to the number of bodies so consumed by fire that, in one house of the rue du Vieux Palais, remains identified as those of a woman were later found to be of a man and his son; a few metres away human remains carefully separated into two 'bodies' proved to belong to one 30-year-old man.[8] The final body count was 816 dead in Rouen and 20,000 people were left homeless.[9]

At the funeral service in the abbey church of St-Ouen grieving relatives gazed on 300 sealed coffins containing parts of at least 367 corpses, the extent of the tragedy sparking a rumour that the English were intent on burning Rouen's heroine Joan of Arc all over again.[10] So deep was the

155

groundswell of anti-British feeling that a local resistance group radioed London in protest at all the senseless deaths.

Yet one group of people had something for which to be temporarily grateful to the bomb-aimers who so nearly killed them. Instead of being shot within the next few days, the prisoners beneath the law courts were transferred *en masse* to concentration camps, where some survived. Raoul Boulanger and his brother Henri were joint heads of a Resistance group working for Major Maurice Buckmaster's French section of Special Operations Executive, and had been betrayed to Inspector Alie of the *brigades spéciales* anti-terrorist police in Rouen. Arrested on 14 March, neither man had given anything away, despite being atrociously tortured by Alie's thugs and *Gestapo* men for more than four weeks, during which their fingers had been crushed and nails torn out. Henri's skull had also been fractured.

With the files and records of the *Gestapo*'s interrogations destroyed by fire, the simplest way to deal with all the prisoners was to deport them all – guilty and innocent alike – to concentration and death camps in Germany. A few days after the raid, at 04.00hrs, all the prisoners were taken out of their cells and handcuffed in pairs. From all the beatings, Henri's face and body were unrecognisable. Raoul only identified him by the sweater, matted with blood, that he had been wearing when they were arrested. They were sent to Flossenburg, where Henri died from his injuries and malnutrition a few weeks later. Frustrated by the brothers' refusal to speak, Alie also had their wives arrested and despatched to the women's concentration camp at Ravensbrück, and from there to Bergen-Belsen, where Henri's wife succumbed to disease and starvation. Raoul Boulanger was liberated on 1 May 1945 after fourteen months of torture, suffering and starvation. When Belsen was liberated by British troops on 15 April 1945, his wife was one of the walking skeletons they found among the thousands of corpses. After six weeks of convalescence, she returned to the family home and tried to pick up the pieces of her family life.[11]

At midday on 29 May 1944 Rouen was on alert for three hours while nearby Orival, whose name comes from the latin *aurea vallis*, meaning 'golden valley', was being turned into a vale of death and destruction. The target was the railway viaduct across the Seine, unsuccessfully attacked on 7, 9 and 18 May. This time, many Orivalais cowered in the limestone caves nearby, but others felt themselves safe in the village, which was of no strategic or tactical importance. The first wave of Allied bombers at last brought down the imposing structure of the viaduct, producing a dust cloud that completely obscured the target area from the second wave which, in consequence, dropped its bombs on the village instead, destroying eighty per cent of the houses.

The following day, Rouen itself was again the target. More precisely, the aim was to destroy the two road bridges across the Seine within the town and the Eauplet viaduct some distance upstream. At 09.40hrs Rouennais looked up into the perfect blue sky, relieved that the stream of twin-engined American aircraft was over-flying the town en route to another viaduct, upstream at Elbeuf. The 'all clear' for that raid sounded at 10.25hrs. Half an hour later came another alert, just before three waves of bombers dive-bombed the town bridges in a raid that spread a belt of devastation through adjacent residential areas one kilometre long. By 12.09hrs, according to the Civil Defence log, all was calm again, but not in the cellars beneath the Customs House, where 140 people had taken shelter and were buried beneath a mountain of shattered masonry that had been the upper floors of the building. When rescuers realised that water was pouring into the cellars, fire pumps were brought in, but the water won that race, drowning the trapped people. It took ten days for miners to tunnel through the debris, where the stench was so strong that they had to wear breathing apparatus and could only cover the decomposing corpses with quicklime.

In another raid on 31 May, sixty people were crushed, suffocated or drowned in the ruins of a school. Fires raged out of control. On 1 June – the fourth consecutive day of bombardment – the town was without electricity, so police cycled through the streets, blowing whistles to signal the alert. People ran, scrambled and hauled themselves up the hill, away from the town centre. A false alarm, but at 15.30hrs came another alert without sirens. The electricity being restored, the third alert was given by siren at 17.30hrs. No bombs fell, but the people watching from the upper town gasped as smouldering embers from the previous day, fanned by the wind, set the cathedral on fire again. About 19.30hrs part of the roof fell in, sending up a cloud of burning fragments that set on fire all the nearby houses not already destroyed. The blaze could be seen 30km distant. So intense was the heat that, twenty minutes later, the huge bronze bells in the tower – the one called Jeanne d'Arc weighing 20 tonnes – melted and dripped to the floor in a molten mass. At 23.30hrs the wooden floor at the base of the spire caught fire too and a bucket chain of teenage boys carried water up ninety metres high to extinguish the flames. Fighting fatigue and fear, they carried on all night, for the satisfaction of seeing the spire safe at dawn. The Bomber Command Diary summed up the raid thus: '273 Lancasters and 16 Mosquitos of Nos 1, 3 and 8 Groups to Rouen. No aircraft lost (in) a concentrated attack on the railway yards, with much destruction.'[12]

On the same night, the Diary recorded another raid by 181 aircraft on railway yards at Noisy-Le-Sec. With the yards surrounded by residential districts, the result was typical of these railway-target raids. The tracks, engine-sheds and workshops suffered great damage. Approximately 200 delayed-action bombs continued to explode throughout the week after the raid. In addition to this damage, however, the Diary noted: 'The bombing area was measured as 6km long and 3km wide – a swathe of destruction in which 750 houses were destroyed and more than 2,000 damaged, leaving 464 French civilians dead and 370 injured.'[13]

In the third raid that night, on the yard at Tergnier in Picardy, 171 aircraft bombed, but the Diary merely noted that, 'most of the bombing fell on housing areas south-west of the railway yards.'[14]

These raids by Allied air forces were justified by the planners as an important preparation for D-Day, to ensure the Germans could not speed reinforcements, especially armoured units, to the front by rail. For civilian travellers, things were becoming so difficult that the journey from Paris to Le Havre, which formerly took just under two hours, now took eighteen hours including a sleepless overnight stop in Rouen, listening for bombers overhead in the darkness.

On 3 and 4 June American fighter-bombers returned to finish the destruction of the bridges, causing more civilian casualties: fifty near-misses killed some 200 people, forty of them unidentifiable. The intensity of this bombardment is illustrated by that fact that another sixty people were never found – presumably blown to bits.[15] By then, Rouen's roll of dead and badly injured had risen to 2,500, with 9,500 homes destroyed. Nobody had any reliable count of the missing.

A man hears what he wants to hear and disregards the rest, sang Simon and Garfunkel. As with the ears, so with the eyes. Major Martin Lindsay of the Gordon Highlanders wrote a book about his experiences after D-Day. Driving through Rouen with his Highlanders at the beginning of September 1944, he noted that, 'all the bridges were blown, except one. The outskirts of the town had been badly bombed but the centre, with its famous cathedral, was untouched.' So much for eyewitness reports! Lindsay's main complaint was that the Big Red One convoys had priority on the single remaining serviceable bridge in Rouen, so the Gordons were diverted up-stream, to cross the Seine at Elbeuf.[16]

The raids on targets within built-up areas in neutral countries like France and Belgium had been a matter of controversy in the Allied camp, with Churchill against a bombing policy that was once estimated by 'Bomber' Harris as likely to cost the lives of 200,000 innocent neutral civilians.[17] The British Prime Minister's concern about bombing targets that would cause deaths of many French civilians had been expressed in an exchange with Eisenhower on 3 April:

> The Cabinet took an adverse view of the proposal to bomb so many French railway centres (in preparation for the invasion), in view of the fact that scores of thousands of French civilians, men, women and children, would lose their lives or be injured (although) the argument for concentration on these particular targets is very nicely balanced on military grounds.

Two days later, Eisenhower replied:

> I and my military advisers have become convinced that the bombing of these centres will increase our chances for success. I personally believe that estimates of probable casualties have been grossly exaggerated.

Since Eisenhower was the Supreme Commander of all the Allied armies, Churchill turned to President Roosevelt – the only person who could possibly influence him to change the bombing policy. On 7 May, he wrote to him:

> The War Cabinet have (sic) been much concerned about the number of Frenchmen killed in the raids on the railway centres in France. When this project was first put forward, a loss of 80,000 French civilian casualties, including injured, say 20,000 killed, was mentioned. The War Cabinet could not view this figure without grave dismay on account of the

apparently ruthless use of the Air Forces, particularly the Royal Air Force, on whom the brunt of this work necessarily falls. (The) War Cabinet share my misapprehensions of the bad effect which will be produced upon the French civilian population by these slaughters (which) may easily bring about a great revulsion in French feeling towards their approaching United States and British liberators. It must be remembered that this slaughter is among a friendly people who have committed no crime against us. The War Cabinet is unanimous in its doubts as to whether almost as good military results could not be produced by other methods.

Roosevelt replied on 11 May:

However regrettable the attendant loss of (French) civilian lives is, I am not prepared to impose from this distance any restriction on military action by the responsible commanders.[18]

After this exchange Churchill set an informal limit of 10,000 French civilian deaths and asked Air Chief Marshal Tedder, Eisenhower's deputy commander-in-chief, 'How does your score stand now?' Tedder replied on 23 May, fudging the issue by describing civilian deaths as Axis personnel, '(The) scoreboard reads as follows: Axis reported killed 6,062. Credit balance remaining 3,938.' On 13 July, he admitted that the 'allowance' had been exceeded, but not by very much.[19]

In fact, Churchill's 'limit' of 10,000 French civilian deaths had already been exceeded long before D-Day. He had made a political and moral point as a European politician who was concerned also with the post-war relationship between Britain and France – and had it brushed aside by Eisenhower and Roosevelt, whose plan it was, not to liberate France, but to occupy it as though the country had been an enemy belligerent, whereas it had started the war as an ally and remained neutral since the defeat, except for a few hours' resistance offered by local French forces during the Allied invasion of North Africa.

The stage was thus set for massive bombing before and after D-Day, of heavily populated French civilian centres in which were no important German targets, but the destruction of which was thought bound to impede German military movements. Ironically, in view of the British Cabinet's views, it was to be the RAF that flew many of the raids that killed and maimed massive numbers of civilians in northern France.

Rouen's next trial was the 'bloody week' of 25 May–4 June, which put out of action the fragile temporary infrastructure set up after 19 April. Water, gas and electricity were non-existent, the daily bread ration was reduced to 180 grams and the only place where one could have a hot meal was in a communal canteen. Every evening as many as 17,000 terrorised civilians walked out of town carrying their few remaining belongings or wheeling them in barrows in the belief that anywhere must be safer than their homes, even if these were still undamaged. They spent their nights in peasants' cellars and barns, or camped beneath a sheet of canvas stretched between two trees, relying on the locals' charity for food, for they had little to bring with them. And in the morning, like tens of thousands of other Norman town-dwellers who fled their homes each night in fear of the RAF bombers, they walked wearily back into Rouen, to go through the motions of normal life in school, at work or doing the housework if they still had a home.

In fact, there was no normal life now, because the American air forces bombed by daylight. Roland Lemesle was in charge of a rescue post in a school on Rouen's rue Herbière. Reporting for the day shift on the morning of 31 May, he was immediately inundated by people wanting news of relatives who had been bombed out that night. Many were still in shock from the previous day's bombardment, wandering about with suitcases containing a few rescued belongings from one building to another where blackboards gave information of survivors' whereabouts. The luckier ones received a sandwich at one place and a plate of soup at another.

At 11.00hrs a new air raid alert sounded. Lemesle ordered his wife and another woman helper to leave because the post was too near to the bridges for safety. He guessed right: the target for the incoming Flying Fortresses was the last remaining road bridge over the Seine that was still usable by military traffic. Soon fifty-eight people were crowded into the cellar beneath the school with Lemesle and his crew. At 11.06hrs he made the following entry in the log:

> The noise of aircraft motors fills the cellar, fills our hearts and our bellies. At 11.09hrs, bombs falling very near. A priest

begins the Hail Mary: *'Ave Maria, gratia plena. Dominus tecum. Benedicta tu in mulieribus ...'* For ten minutes the prayers continue as bombs fall. Then silence.

Although they knew that another wave of bombers was almost certain to arrive shortly, Lemesle and the team grabbed stretchers and went outside in search of victims. Three minutes later, they scurried back into the shelter, already shaking from near explosions. The prayer had changed. Now it was the Angelus: *'Mater dei, precate pro nobis peccatoribus, nunc et in hora mortis nostrae.'* Pray for us sinners, Mother of God, now and in the hour of our death.

At 11.24, the prayer stopped short as the shelter took a direct hit from a high-explosive bomb, killing forty-four people. The ceiling of the shelter collapsed on top of the survivors. Most were injured and some in agony, groaning and screaming in the darkness. The emergency lighting failed. The air was so thick with dust as to be almost unbreathable.

At 11.37hrs the third wave of Flying Fortresses was overhead. Unable to see a clock or find the duty log, Lemesle never knew how long this bombardment lasted. Those of his team who were still alive told themselves that very soon they would hear the noise of picks and shovels. Having so often been on the outside, digging into the rubble, they knew that rescue would not be swift. Clearing away the rubble pinning down one of his men, Lemesle found a pocket torch in his pocket. By its feeble light he took stock of the situation, but there was nothing that could be done.

Towards midday, they heard the noise of digging. It seemed very far away. Lemesle found a shattered water pipe and blew his whistle into it, calling out the location of the survivors and their names to those outside. But the rubble above them kept shifting and they knew from experience that they might have to wait hours yet, so he switched off the torch, to save the battery. The survivors were trapped in several compartments around beams that had shored up the roof. News was exchanged from one prison to another: who was alive, who was dead. Then, two injured firemen who had been given first aid in the post during the night called out that water was seeping into where they lay on stretchers. Whether it came from the hoses of their colleagues above, from ruptured mains or a holding pool nearby, it was as much a killer as fire.

First to drown were the two firemen trapped on their stretchers, unable to move. Through the pipe serving as a voice tube, Lemesle begged those on the surface to start pumping. The noise of pumps reached the trapped people. The nurse who had been caring for the injured firemen tried to crawl through to them, but was herself trapped beneath a new fall of rubble until Lemesle dug her out. The pace of digging above accelerated in response to the pleas from the cellar. At 16.30hrs one of the diggers, who had been ordained just two weeks previously, heard his parish priest call up through the voice pipe, 'Hurry, my son. The water is rising.'

But the rescuers could work no faster. Many huge lumps of masonry defied all their efforts to lift them out of the way. Below ground, the voices calling in the darkness grew fainter and fewer. The water level reached the knees of those standing upright, and then suddenly their bellies. The voice pipe was now submerged, cutting short contact with the surface. The roof started slipping again, leaving only sixty centimetres of air space. Desperate hands groped beneath the water to find bricks with which to shore it up, but the few people still alive now had to bend their heads closer and closer to the water. Rats scurried past and over them, attracted by the corpses nearby.

Up in the light of day, a priest gave absolution to all those trapped below: *'Vos absolvo ab omnibus peccatis vostris.'* I absolve you from all your sins ...

Seemingly a miracle, after ten hours the water stopped rising, but it was hard to breathe the foul air in a space just five metres square by fifty centimetres high. How long, Lemesle wondered, would two and a half cubic metres of air last? Just before midnight, the survivors felt a draught of fresh air on their faces as the rescuers at last broke through. The hole still had to be enlarged for a person to wriggle through. Seven exhausted people eventually emerged after thirteen nightmare hours in a living tomb, leaving fifty-seven corpses behind them.[20]

Chapter 13

D-Day, as seen from the other side

Since being named head of the *brigades spéciales* anti-terrorist squad in Rouen, the indefatigable hunter of *résistants* Inspector Louis Alie devoted to his work the same intelligence and energy that another detective might put into the hunt for a serial killer. After finding in an abandoned safe house a crumpled piece of paper on which was scribbled *RV 1/2 R de Caen Grand-Couronne 8/5/18*, on 8 May at 18.00hrs he snared in one blow the most important members of the CDL of Seine-Maritime *département* at their meeting in Rouen's *Place Demi-Lune* – or Half-Moon Square. Deported after torture, they died in Flossenburg, Dachau and other camps, all because of a piece of paper thrown away instead of being burned after reading.

There was in the spring and early summer of 1944 no need to be an intelligence officer or detective to deduce that an Allied invasion was imminent. The frequency and severity of softening-up air raids on the towns of northern France was typified by attacks by American B26 Marauders and P47 Thunderbolts on the coastal batteries and a radar ranging site within the Le Havre perimeter on four out of five consecutive days in the first week of June – at the cost of one Thunderbolt shot down.[1]

Every air raid – even reasonably accurate low-level daylight ones like these – produced some civilian casualties. How well the survivors were looked after depended to a large extent on where they were. In Dunkirk, Monsignor Couvreur ran a very successful section of the *Secours National* which served 1.6 million emergency meals and put in hand the repair of 1,000 dwellings in a display of unusual optimism that maybe the end was in sight – otherwise, why bother? In Pierre Courant's Le Havre, an extremely efficient resettlement service in a former savings bank employed 118 people working at twelve counter positions and behind the scenes. By the time a bombed-out person walked away from the last position, he or she had been issued with clothing tickets, an entitlement to alternative accommodation, a coal voucher, replacement ration book, an immediate resettlement allowance of 1,500F per person in the household, and with the all-important claim for later war damage compensation having been registered. Those who could take no more and requested to leave the town were immediately booked on the next train out.[2]

The scale of civilian suffering increased until, just before D-Day, the French cardinals addressed an appeal to their opposite numbers in the British Empire and the United States. It read:

> The air raids on France which are growing more intense fill our hearts with sadness and anguish. Almost every day, we and our brothers are witness to the cruel ravages among the civilian population caused by the air raids of the Allied powers. Thousands of men, women and children, totally uninvolved in the war, are killed or injured, their homes destroyed.

Despite efforts by the Germans to edit out mention of similar suffering in Britain, the text appeared in *La Semaine Religieuse de Paris* of 27 May 1944 and was published elsewhere in twenty-four languages. The BBC's reply, broadcast on behalf of Supreme Commander Eisenhower, was swift:

> Our pilots are aware that the lives and homes of our friends are at stake, and take the greatest care possible. But the scale of these attacks will inevitably add to the suffering that you – our loyal friends – have so courageously endured throughout this war. [3]

What consolation that was for the tens of thousands of bereaved relatives and injured men, women and children lying in hospitals all over France, is impossible to say. But this was total war, in which the death of civilians was just another element in the equation of a strategic bombing campaign, whose unquestioned *military* success was testified to in a report of the German transport ministry dated 15 May. It read:

> In the occupied sectors of Western Europe, particularly in Belgium and the north of France, the air raids of these last weeks have systematically interrupted all the main (railway)

lines. Supply lines to our coastal defences are cut, which is a very grave situation. Large-scale strategic troop movements by rail are practically impossible now and this situation will continue as long as these intensive raids continue ... It has (also) to be taken into account that the destruction of, and damage to, the main railway construction and repair workshops has considerably disorganised repair and overhaul of locomotives, which causes additional problems for movement by rail.[4]

On 31 May Robert Le Besnerais, director general of SNCF, was summoned to Vichy to account for the ruinous state of the French railway system, particularly in the northern *départements*, and told the same story:

The increase in bombing raids and machine-gunning (of trains) since the beginning of April is making an already bad situation worse. I shall give some examples. At this very moment, twenty-nine of the fifty-three main marshalling yards are out of action, as are seventy of the 167 depots and three of the nine most important repair workshops. Rail staff casualties total 470 dead and 1,100 injured since the start of the year. In the three previous years, we lost 464 staff members killed and 244 injured on duty by acts of war. Right now, we can run only one in five of the passenger trains that were scheduled in 1938. Freight capacity, including German transports, has fallen from 232,222 wagons per week in 1943 to 93,300 in the current week.

Asked whether he had any figures for German military traffic, he replied, 'Priority German military traffic (in the north of France) is also down to twenty-one per cent of normal.'[5]

Bomber Command would have been delighted to hear that the 'credit balance' of 13,345 Allied sorties against railway targets resulted in rail traffic between the Rhine and Normandy being virtually paralysed when the first wave of troops waded ashore on 6 June.

Movements of German military trains were by this stage in the war regularly transmitted to London, enabling carefully timed attacks by RAF and American rocket-firing aircraft, which cost the lives of many French train crews and – because the nineteenth-century railway companies had always sought to situate their termini as close as possible to city centres – of many civilians whose only fault was that they lived in working-class accommodation near the stations and marshalling yards. Not only troop transports and munitions trains were targeted: all was grist to London's mill, from shipments of cement for the Atlantic Wall to hydrogen peroxide for the V2 rockets, shortly to bring terror to Londoners.

A little-studied factor in the success of the *Overlord* invasion is how much local sabotage contributed to the German transportation snarl-up, costing far fewer civilian lives than bombing raids, although the penalty for saboteurs caught was always death, sometimes as a merciful relief from long torture. The pace of sabotage acclerated after the Code B messages were broadcast over the BBC on 4 June – the day US troops entered the open city of Rome. Those triggering the Violet Plan launched wholesale destruction of French Post Office communications centres and cables; the Green Plan cued widespread sabotage of railway tracks, rolling stock and marshalling yards. It was largely due to destruction by on-the-ground sabotage that the approaches to all the invasion beaches could not be mined before 6 June. Transportation of the necessary mines had taken, not days, but four weeks. They arrived in Le Havre at the end of May, but the minelayers were not available until 5 June, when the storm that so complicated Eisenhower's count-down also prevented the minelayers putting to sea. Therefore many beaches and approaches to the Bay of the Seine were still unmined when the troops came ashore on 6 June.[6]

Most readers will be familiar with the story of D-Day, as told from the Allied side. With dramatic licence, both documentary films and fictional recreations imply that the invasion fleet approached the coast unnoticed until just before dawn, when the sight of so many ships on the horizon alerted dozy German personnel in the coastal batteries. *Achtung! Mein Gott!* And so on.

It was not quite like that, although the severe storm on 4–5 June that delayed the departure of the invasion fleet by twenty-four hours also grounded *Luftwaffe* reconnaissance flights over southern England and confined to harbour the German patrol boats[7] along the Channel coast. Despite this, the alert was sounded in Le Havre at 01.35hrs on 6 June – it was the city's 325th alert of the year – and the war diary of the *Kriegsmarine* commander noted massive over-flights of Allied aircraft starting at 00.59hrs. A Level 2 alert was issued to the garrison at 01.25hrs after reports were received of paratroops landing in the Honfleur–Cabourg sector. At 02.02hrs all Channel coast *Kriegsmarine* units were put on full alert and the E-boat crews ordered to action stations. After 03.00hrs the noise of many powerful naval engines and gunfire was clearly audible across the Bay of the Seine to the west of Le Havre and signal flares could be seen in the sky in that quarter.

Warnings from Channel Coast HQ were received at the port commandant's office to the effect that invasion barges could be expected shortly. At 04.18hrs all military and naval forces were on full alert, with the E-boat flotilla already at sea to harass the Allied fleet of 6,000-plus vessels bringing the first wave of 300,000 men to land on the beaches: the British at Sword between Ouistreham and Lion-sur-Mer and Gold between Graye-sur-Mer and Arromanches; the Canadians at Juno between Luc-sur-Mer and Graye-sur-Mer; and the US forces at Omaha between Colleville-sur-Mer and Vierville-sur-Mer and Utah on the east coast of the Cotentin Peninsula. At 04.45hrs all German units received the coded signal meaning *Enemy troops landing*. By then, few people in

Allied troops go ashore on D-Day. For every Allied soldier killed on D-Day, two French civilians were killed by Allied bombing and shelling. Thousands more were wounded.

Le Havre, civilian or military, were still asleep as the noise of massive naval bombardments less than twenty miles away across the Bay of Seine grew steadily in volume.

Naval smoke-screens made it difficult for watchers on land to follow the developments at sea, but E-boats in contact with the motor gunboats and other fast craft protecting the eastern flank of the Allied fleet reported heavy naval bombardment of targets on land and extremely intense anti-aircraft fire greeting every appearance of *Luftwaffe* planes overhead. By 05.30hrs the E-boats were engaging a large force several miles west of the port. At 09.00hrs the flotilla returned to its bombproof pens after being driven off by Allied aircraft and having launched fifteen torpedoes without hitting a single Allied vessel.

On night duty in the town hall of Le Havre that night was Paul Latrille, employed as a runner in the mayor's office. He noted in his diary the noise of aircraft passing overhead all night long. At 02.30hrs staff sleeping in the offices were rudely awakened by eleven blasts of the warning sirens, signalling an Allied landing. At 07.00hrs the Town Clerk arrived and informed him that the Allies had indeed landed one hour previously at Arromanches, some forty miles away across the bay from where they stood. By climbing up the clock tower of the city hall, they could see the invasion fleet of several hundred warships at sea, partly obscured by smoke screens – as could residents of the upper city with binoculars and telescopes, who had a grandstand view of the incredible scene.

A detachment of German soldiers arrived at the *Kommandantur* and removed all its files to a bunker constructed in the garden. Other soldiers were wiring off additional sections of the city and patrolling the streets, with machine gun posts manned on street corners. Schools were ordered to remain closed. With the garrison on full alert, Le Havre was already in a state of siege, cut off from the world with entry into and exit from the high-security area forbidden except for authorised food convoys. Any use by civilians of motor vehicles or even bicycles was also briefly forbidden.[8]

Across the bay in Caen, the coded signal *Enemy troops landing* triggered a small bloodbath, unnoticed in the greater spilling of blood by men in uniform. *Gestapo* standing orders for an invasion were that none of its prisoners be allowed to fall into Allied hands. Plans to evacuate all the prisoners in Caen included a priority train to take them out of the battle zone *en route* for Germany via Belfort in Alsace. Before they could be driven to the main station, it was put out of action, due to Allied bombs.

Caen's *Gestapo* boss Harald Heyns ordered local army units to provide trucks, but was told they had better uses for their motor transport at this critical time.

Heyns telephoned his superior in Rouen for instructions. They were very simple. At 08.00hrs his assistant arrived at the prison with three other *Gestapo* men and a list of their prisoners who were to be shot instantly. Graves were hastily dug and the prisoners taken out of their cells 'without baggage'. They knew what that meant. In groups of six, they were escorted down the stairs to a courtyard and machine-gunned into the waiting graves. The job was done by 10.30hrs, but the killers returned four hours later with a second list. By the time all these prisoners too had been shot in late afternoon, there were no 'politicals' left alive in Caen prison.[9]

Supreme Allied Commander General Dwight D. Eisenhower had excluded De Gaulle and the staff of the Free French forces from the planning of D-Day, ostensibly because Free French security was 'leaky', but more importantly because De Gaulle was the one man capable of obstructing his plan *to occupy France as a defeated enemy state*, which it had never been, and rule it by an Allied Military Government of Occupied Territory. This would almost certainly have triggered a Communist *coup d'état* as the Germans retreated. For political reasons, there were thus

De Gaulle on French soil at last. The stress shows in his face.

very few of De Gaulle's half-million Free French soldiers permitted to fight the Germans on the beachheads. Eisenhower and Churchill also conspired to prevent De Gaulle travelling to France after D-Day. He had to requisition one of his own Free French ships two weeks later to get there.

Yet, in prisons and *Gestapo* cellars, French men and women were still dying for their country and the Allied cause. At 02.00hrs on 7 June railwayman Henri Gallois, condemned for the sabotage at Ascq on 1–2 April, wrote his last letter to his wife and 17-year-old daughter Mimi from the prison of Pont-l'Abbé, two hours before he was to be shot by firing squad. One would hope that news of the invasion had filtered into the prison, to give Gallois and his seven comrades a sense of purpose for their deaths, but he makes no mention of it in his letter and the copious black ink of the censors that defaces so many last letters is absent from this one.[10]

D-Day films place little emphasis on the undramatic *strategic* missions flown by the Allied air forces to interdict German movement of reinforcements towards the beachheads. In his capacity then as commander of Allied ground forces for the invasion, at the beginning of May General Montgomery had sent to Air Chief Marshal Leigh-Mallory, C-in-C of the Allied Expeditionary Air Force, a list of twenty-six towns in northern France that he wanted bombed flat – but only after his troops had hit the beaches, so that the location of those beaches should not be compromised earlier. The specific purpose was not to damage the population centres and kill civilians, but to create 'choke points', through which the Germans could not move troops.

Unfortunately, at the time, few towns in Europe had by-passes, having developed through the centuries at nodal points which were their original *raisons d'être*. Thus, major road junctions were in the centres of towns and, in order to prevent the Germans moving troops and equipment through those junctions, Montgomery considered it necessary to destroy sufficient buildings for the rubble thus produced to block entirely any use of the urban road system. Whether from humanitarian motives or logistics considerations, Leigh-Mallory's staff deleted six towns from the list on the grounds that the Germans could simply use alternative routes. That left twenty French towns facing Armageddon, all unawares.

Eisenhower's appointee Lt-Gen James H. Doolittle, commanding the US Eighth Air Force in Britain, had argued for a further reduction in

Lt Gen James H. Doolittle, commanding US Eighth Air Force.

the number of these targeted nodal point targets in heavily built-up areas because he knew from experience in the Italian campaign that this was of questionable military value, in that it also prevented incoming Allied troops from moving swiftly after the retreating enemy. Leigh-Mallory riposted that one does not change a plan a mere forty-eight hours before D-Day – which was then scheduled for 5 June – without causing disaster. He won the day by offering his resignation, which was refused. On the night of 6–7 June, therefore, the Allied air forces were tasked to destroy the centres of twenty towns in northern France.

Caen, capital of the Calvados region, should have been the luckiest town in Normandy that day. Montgomery's schedule was for it to be taken by the British 3rd Infantry Division on the evening of D-Day but, as his reading of Count Helmuth von Moltke's *Militärische Werke, Vol 2* ought to have told him, no plan of operations extends with certainty beyond the first contact with the enemy's main strength. Normally abridged to *No plan survives contact with the enemy*, the maxim certainly applied to D-Day. The first Allied troops in *Operation Goodwood* – the liberation of Caen – broke in five weeks behind schedule on 9 July, and the last Germans were not driven out until 19 July.

Since the initial idea was for the town to be used as a strongpoint in the British bridgehead, the original intention was simply to knock out the four bridges over the River Orne to impede a German counter-attack. One raid was planned to effect this surgical operation. At 07.00hrs on D-Day, thirty-six B24 Liberators of the US Eighth Air Force arrived over the targets to find them obscured by cloud. Some bombs were dropped more or less blind.

Two more raids to take out the bridges were scheduled for that afternoon, when fifty-eight Liberators equipped with cloud-piercing radar dropped 141 HE bombs at 13.00hrs local time on what looked on their radar screens like the bridges. Leaflets had been previously dropped warning the population that the railway and power stations were to be targeted, but the scale of the damage went far beyond what that had seemed to indicate to the Caennais.

Joseph Poirier, a councillor and head of the town's Civil Defence, kept a log, in which he recorded four bombs landing near the station in the first raid, causing one death and wounding two other people. Of the second raid, he wrote: 'Bombs in the town centre with many dead and wounded. The raid lasted only ten minutes but the damage is enormous.'[11]

The historic timber-framed medieval buildings were the ideal medium to ignite and spread the fire into the ruins of later houses built in the famous white stone from the region, but the bridges were still standing. At 16.25hrs came another short but equally violent raid by seventy-two American B26 Marauder medium bombers dropping 122 tonnes of bombs that destroyed a quarter of the town centre. An eyewitness account of this raid was written by André Heintz, a young schoolteacher and *résistant* who had heard the coded message for D-Day on his primitive crystal set, kept in an empty tin hidden among the family's food store in the cellar. He was at a loss for anything to do, since his contact, who knew where the group's parachuted arms were hidden, was unreachable due to the disruption of the railways. In the hope of finding something useful to do, André hurried to the Bon Sauveur hospital where his sister worked as a nurse, and which had already been bombed once. He helped her stain sheets with blood from the operating theatres, to improvise a red cross that they stretched out on the roof of the building. Before they had finished, a fighter-bomber roared in low

173

towards them. They feared the worst, but then the pilot veered away and waggled his wings, to their great relief.[12] André was then enlisted as an emergency stretcher bearer:

> I leaped out of the ambulance on seeing aircraft over St Sauveur Square (several hundred metres north of the bridges). Taking shelter in a doorway in rue Ecuyère, I watched the bombs spin around and finally land with a terrible whistling sound very close. The noise of the explosions was so terrible that I had the impression of being between the rails with a train running over me. I caught a glimpse of terrified people in a doorway across the street.
>
> A blast-wave slammed the big door shut and the walls seemed to move apart then stabilise as thick smoke billowed out of the building behind us. There were people screaming. The nurse and I had only to take a few paces to attend to the first wounded. In the rue de Bras, some girls emerged from a cupboard in the sewing room (of the convent, where they had fortunately taken shelter), the room itself having been destroyed. They didn't know what was going on, nor where they were. The ambulance did five trips to the hospital while I stayed there, digging out the injured with the help of a police officer, himself wounded in the arm and bleeding from a head wound.[13]

Some 500 Caennais were killed in the afternoon raids which left the bridges still standing. Meanwhile 21st *Panzer* Division had established itself between Caen and the coast, where it would stay for thirty-three days before finally dislodged.

Montgomery's written order to General Miles Dempsey, commanding British 2nd Army, read:

> Object of operation. To engage the German armour in battle and 'write it down' to such an extent that it is of no further value to the Germans as a basis of the battle. To gain a good bridgehead over the (river) Orne through Caen and thus improve our positions on the eastern flank. Generally to destroy German equipment and personnel.[14]

It all sounds so clinical, except the passage about destroying German personnel. And there is no mention of the thousands of civilians trapped between the incoming British and Canadian troops and the tenacious German defenders. It was Dempsey's job to win a war, not worry about people who theoretically ought not to get in the way.

The race to destroy the bridges continued with more raids showing the same horrific inaccuracy. By 22.00hrs, after another 157 tonnes of bombs had been dropped on the town, Poirier's log noted:

> Flames everywhere and the fires are travelling from house to house, reaching mine. From the clock tower of the Town Hall, the view is terrifying. The whole St Jean district is in flames and there are more than twenty other big fires.

To calm French people tempted to make life difficult for the occupiers, Pétain broadcast that evening:

> Battle conditions may oblige the German army to take extraordinary measures in the combat zones. We have to accept this as necessary.[15]

Beneath the debris in Caen lay more than 200 dead or dying people, with many more injured waiting to be rescued. The rescue workers toiled without rest. At 02.40hrs the nightmare scenes they were uncovering were cut short as 120 RAF Lancasters dropped another 440 tonnes of bombs on the stricken city, killing survivors and rescuers alike. André Heintz again:

> Unreal, this raid, preceded by numerous parachute flares making an artificial daylight. We know what's going to happen. In the next thirty-five minutes, the town centre is crushed flat.

To Captain Poirier:

> It seemed like thousands of Lancasters dropping thousands of tonnes of bombs all over the town area. There are fifty dead in the square alone. The hospital will be treating

1,750 seriously injured. Already more than half the town (intact this morning) has been destroyed.[16]

By this stage, he noted, people still able to run, did so, rather than walk, because the soles of their shoes were burning from the melting asphalt of the road surfaces.

There was precious little laughter or humour of any kind in Normandy in the days following the landings, and what there was, was unconscious – like one small event on Utah beach on D+1. David Bruce, the London representative of the American OSS, told how General 'Wild Bill' Donovan, his ultimate boss, insisted on being allowed ashore, allegedly to meet some agents. The agents were conspicuously absent at the rendezvous. After a German plane strafed the DUKW in which the two OSS officers were travelling, they continued on foot. With Donovan wearing his Congressional Medal of Honour, no one dared stop them as this was American territory, until they came under fire from a German heavy machine gun.

Donovan said to Bruce, 'David, we mustn't be captured. We know too much. Have you got your (suicide) pill?'

Bruce had not.

'Never mind,' said Donovan. 'I have two of them.'

Still lying flat on the ground, he disgorged the contents of all his pockets. There were a number of old hotel keys, a passport, currency of several denominations, photographs of grandchildren, travel orders, newspaper clippings, and heaven know what else, but no pills.

'Never mind,' whispered Donovan. 'We can do without them, but I must shoot first.'

'Yes, sir,' I responded. 'But can we do much against machine guns with our pistols?'

'Oh, you don't understand,' he said. 'I mean, if we are about to be captured, I'll shoot you first. After all, I am your commanding officer.'[17]

By the evening of D+2, more than 4,000 Norman civilians had been killed in British and American air raids – a figure almost twice as high as all the Allied soldiers killed on D-Day, for which the figure of 2,500 is generally accepted. And still the air raids continued, Montgomery's rationale being that, if Caen could not be liberated, it must be reduced to the point where reinforcements could not be moved through its streets.

So, more bombs fell in the night of 7–8 June, and the dawn came to light a scene of smoke and desolation as another raid pummelled the town from 06.30hrs to 07.00hrs, with another at 11.00hrs. And they fell, not just on the town, but on the suburbs and outlying villages held by the Germans, where 500lb and 1,000lb bombs caused severe cratering.

Again and again, Allied aircraft dropped bombs, turning the just recognisable ruins into a field of dust and rubble that bore no relation to streets and houses. At least the population could be alerted just before an air raid – providing the electricity was working – but there was no way of warning them when the 16-inch guns of the battleship HMS *Rodney*, the 15-inch guns of the monitor HMS *Roberts,* and the smaller guns of several cruisers standing well offshore opened fire, and their huge shells arrived like bombs in the absence of any aircraft overhead.

In theory, all this destruction was supposed to be making difficult the passage of German troops through the town, but all it meant in practice was more deaths. The prewar population had been just over 62,000. It was now down to a hard core of 35,000 people who either feared looting of their homes more than death or who had nowhere else to go because there was no local, regional or national body able to relocate them. With so many homes destroyed or uninhabitable, thousands of homeless survivors lived and slept on the streets or in the crypts of churches, eking out starvation rations well below their theoretical entitlement. Bread, if they were lucky enough to find any, was rationed to 100 grams per adult per day. Meat was conversely in reasonable supply because hundreds of animals killed in the bombing had been butchered for human consumption, but so many people were homeless and without means for cooking it or anything else that the staff of the main emergency restaurant were serving 18,000 meals to traumatised and hungry people each day.

The nights were the worst time, with everyone waiting for the sound of aero engines. On the night of 12 June, 118 RAF Lancasters returned at 02.30hrs to drop 401 tonnes of bombs on the ruins of the town. On 15 June Joseph Poirier noted that it was impossible to fight the fires that constantly flared up from beneath the rubble, for lack of men and equipment, so they had to be left to burn themselves out. After more bombing on the night of 16 June, he wrote despairingly in the log, *Will there be anything left of our town?*

Four weeks later, the air raids and artillery bombardments were still going on. On 18 July, one of the youngest officers in the Guards Armoured Division, Robert Boscowen, woke up about 06.00hrs and waited for the day to start:

> Suddenly the silence was broken by the rising crescendo of guns breaking into a roar all along the line. A minute or two later the heavy drone of bombers could be heard. And there they came, hundreds of them sweeping in from the coast in an endless untidy stream, protected by a few Spitfires, flashing and wheeling like hawks high above them. Soon they were over their targets and one heard the muffled crumps of their bombs. The air boomed and the ground shook as these showered down, while a dense cloak of grey dust rose slowly over the battlefield. Soon, nothing but a continuous roar could be heard.[18]

Chapter 14

Tidal waves and terror

On the night of 7–8 June, the E-boats in Le Havre repeated their sorties to harass Allied shipping and lay mines in the Channel. One flotilla was driven off by Allied patrol boats, but the other returned to base having sunk two landing craft of 900 tons and two of 400 tons. On 10 June the patrol boats claimed several Allied ships of 2,000 tonnes and one of 5,000 tonnes before being driven off by destroyers. All over Le Havre, the garrison was still on full alert, aware that the success of the E-boats based there would bring Allied reprisal.

It came in the evening light of 14 June, when twenty-two Lancasters, escorted by Spitfires, targeted the concrete pens of the submarine and E-boat base, which suffered considerable damage. A direct hit from one of the giant Tallboy 'earthquake' bombs designed by Barnes Wallis of Dambuster fame pierced the 3-metre-thick reinforced concrete roof. Dropped from 17,000 feet, these enormous engines of destruction hit the ground at something like the speed of sound. They were designed to pierce several metres of reinforced concrete, with the high-explosive charge detonating several seconds after impact, when the bomb was already inside the target, so that the blast effect was intensified by the walls.

Even near-misses from bombs like this caused considerable damage. On this raid, one near-miss created a local tidal wave that surged into a pen with such force that several German vessels were literally driven up into the roof, killing all those on board. Subsequently some pens in the Atlantic coast pockets were fitted with metal doors to prevent this. In what the Bomber Command campaign diary noted as 'a successful raid with no unexpected difficulties', fifty-seven *Kriegsmarine* vessels were sunk or rendered unusable, with 200 dead and 100 wounded among the naval personnel.

The accuracy of this raid was considered to merit the award of a VC to Group Captain Leonard Cheshire for his role as leading pathfinder. Yet the raid also cost seventy-five French civilian lives; a further eighty-four civilians were so injured as to require hospitalisation; and 700 buildings were destroyed. With next-day photo-reconnaissance showing fifty-seven *Kriegsmarine* vessels sunk in the harbour and considerable destruction to the base, Harris and his crews could afford to be pleased.

Nobody in Le Havre was laughing later that evening. With the German flak batteries fortuitously ordered to stand down to permit the over-flight of aircraft from *Luftflotte* 3 heading for the Allied bridgehead, RAF Lancasters paid two more visits. After Pathfinder Force Mosquitos fired marker rockets not only on the port but also into residential areas of the lower town, before strafing some streets with machine gun fire, the accompanying Lancasters dropped 800 tonnes of bombs in Le Havre's worst raid of the war thus far, causing heavy civilian casualties.

With the warning sirens disconnected since the whole pocket was placed on permanent alert on 6 June, the curfew may have saved some civilian lives, as not only the port, also residential areas around the cathedral, were also heavily damaged. Driven by a strong wind, so serious were the fires fought with seawater pumped from the harbour that in places the Germans ordered the fire brigade away and dynamited the premises most affected in an attempt to literally blow out the flames, but it was in vain. Fanned by a gale-force westerly wind, fires continued to erupt from the ruins and spread to previously unaffected streets over the following two weeks.

The heavily fortified pocket of resistance around Cherbourg was now cut off from reinforcements and re-supply by the advancing American forces. The town and port had been strongly fortified in the nineteenth century – against invasion by the English, of course. In the four years of the occupation, the Germans had considerably improved on these older fortifications. Learning from the surrender of Singapore, where the British had omitted to think of defence against an attack from the landward side until it was too late, they prepared a defence in depth around the perimeter, with an interlocking network of reinforced-concrete bunkers and strong-points, in which they sat, awaiting the inevitable assault.

Two weeks after D-Day, US troops under General J.L. Collins reached the outer defences and paused to wait for the necessary artillery and other logistics to catch up. On 22 June they broke through the outer defences on high ground overlooking the port, but it was still necessary to progress by neutralising bunker after bunker with bazookas and hollow charges. The bunkers were manned by an assortment of men in various uniforms, including civilian employees of the *Todt* Organisation conscripted at the last minute by fortress commander General Karl-Wilhelm von Schlieben, and whom he attempted to motivate by liberally bestowing Iron Crosses that were parachuted into the pocket. This heterogenous mini-army held the Americans for four days before collapsing under the sustained pressure. That evening, von Schlieben cabled Rommel, 'Further sacrifices will achieve nothing.' The inevitable reply was: 'You will continue to fight until the last cartridge, as ordered by the *Führer*.' With a clarity of vision that does him credit, von Schlieben took Rommel's reply for what it was – whitewash – and surrendered to the 9th US Infantry Division.

Hitler was furious. It is true that the demolition of the port was so severe as to render it of no immediate use to the Allies, but he had personally intervened the previous day to signal von Schlieben: 'I expect you to conduct yourself in this battle as Gneisenau did in the defence of Kolberg' (during the Napoleonic wars, and hold out, come what may).

Von Schlieben's reward for his rational behaviour was thus a court martial sentence of death *in absentia*, with his immediate superior General Friedrich Dollmann writing a letter of protest and then committing suicide as the only way out of the situation that he could see.[1]

Coming where they did, the D-Day landings wrong-footed not only Hitler, but also the French emergency services, which had assumed an invasion further east, to which they would respond by moving the civilian population by train, bus and coach westwards, away from the assumed direction of an Allied thrust towards the *Reich*. In all the confusion of disrupted railway services, destroyed telephone exchanges and scarcity of motor fuel, these plans could not be amended. Bicycles became the fastest way to send emergency messages and the many injured were transported sometimes in farm carts drawn by horses. Yet, within days, sixty reception centres were improvised, with children making collections of food and local women volunteering to cook it for hungry mouths. In the four months following D-Day, 2 million meals were served in these centres. With the stocks of the *Secours National* destroyed by bombs, more than 150,000 tons of food, 1,250,000 items of clothing and 86,200 pairs of shoes were somehow obtained and distributed in all the post-invasion chaos – as well as furniture, pots and pans, crockery and cutlery.[2]

With additional E-boats arriving in Le Havre from Boulogne and elsewhere, joined by others based in Dieppe, the harassment of Allied shipping and mine-laying sorties continued, with German *Neger* one-man piloted torpedoes being particularly effective against the defences of the *Mulberry* harbours. Their greatest single success was in the early hours of 6 July, when the Captain Class frigate HMS *Trollope* had its bow section completely severed, with considerable loss of life, and had to be scrapped. This prompted the Admiralty to ask Bomber Command to destroy their base. On Monday 31 July, after five Pathfinder Force Mosquitoes fired marker rockets, fifty-two Lancasters bombed the port and city centre in Le Havre's 108th air raid of the war. At 18.55hrs on 2 August a single RAF Mosquito fired marker rockets to indicate targets for a wave of fifty-five Lancasters of Groups 1 and 8, which bombed the port and residential areas for twenty minutes. In addition to sinking two E-boats and damaging two others, the raid caused civilian deaths and substantial damage to property. Local historian J. Guillemard recorded the scene in the cellar where he took shelter that night:

The women were praying aloud. Doubtless, men were also praying, but silently. Someone said, 'Don't be afraid. It doesn't help.' But you can't stop people clinging to faith when they are facing death. After an exceptionally violent explosion, one of the ladies said desperately, 'We must all pray aloud together, men as well. It's the only thing that can save us.'

Eyes shining in desperate hope, she prayed at the top of her voice and ten other voices joined in above the infernal shriek of bombs, the explosions and crack of the anti-aircraft batteries.

The street door of the shelter had already been blown away by a blast-wave. Hearing the shriek of the falling bombs getting closer and closer, I cried out, 'Everyone, get into the middle of the shelter!' Instinctively, everyone huddled there together, just in time. With a noise beyond description, an avalanche of rubble completely blocked the exit. We thought the whole house must have fallen on top of us. The praying had just begun again when another bomb completely demolished our house and the one next door.[3]

Once the Resistance in the northern zone was fully activated on D-Day, no less than 2,000 acts of sabotage were committed in the north of France. This led to a wave of arrests, resulting in appalling conditions in the overcrowded prisons, with military courts passing sentences like a production line in a factory of death. More than half their victims in this period were men under thirty, including many from non-Communist groups. The 218 memorial plaques on the bullet-pitted brick walls of the citadel of Arras give a fair idea of the spread of class and political conviction of the victims. Just over half were miners: the youngest aged sixteen; the oldest sixty-nine. Although most were French, the remainder came from eight other nationalities.

After the first V1 flying bombs landed on London on 13 June, the RAF's priority was changed. Neutralising the launch sites became more important than anything else, but the interruption in area bombing of Norman towns brought another kind of terror from the skies. Faults in the steering mechanism – believed due to sabotage by slave workers making the circuitry – saw numerous V1s launched in northern France divert from their course towards London and crash shortly after launch sometimes in the country, but also in villages and towns.

Operation *Charnwood* was the final assault on the German positions north of Caen, in which for forty-eight hours beginning on 7 July a total of 1,598 Allied aircraft were to drop 2,570 tonnes of bombs on the suffering Caennais. War correspondent Michael Moynihan was at Montgomery's press briefing:

> Monty put us in the picture, with the aid of maps and diagrams, in the clipped didactic tones of a lecturing headmaster and the young staff officers in attendance on him could be seen as favoured senior prefects, all-rounders, jolly good chaps. There was no whiff of death or destruction in the air.[4]

The following morning, he was up before dawn, waiting for what he termed 'the Greatest Show on Earth with a cast of thousands' from the vantage point of a hillside with a safely distant view of Caen:

> In airfields throughout England, nearly 6,000 Allied aircraft – heavy bombers, medium bombers, fighter-bombers – were

preparing to deliver the most shattering blow ever inflicted in the history of warfare.

It was 5.45 – zero hour. A Mosquito, marker for the greatest force of destruction in history, was over the Mondeville factory. From the bulky humped mass of the factory two pink clouds were sprouting, spreading in smoke. Behind us, to the north and south, an artillery barrage broke into a cacophony of noise. Thunder was rolling across the sky.

We (correspondents) held our breath at the sight of the approaching air fleet – heavy bombers pouring in from behind the horizon until the sky seemed to shudder. Across the river, as the first bombers went in, gouts of black smoke poured from the factory. For each of two particular targets 450 Lancasters and Halifaxes were detailed. The rising sun vanished behind a vast canopy of black smoke.

Now the ground under our feet was shaking, and from the western skyline night was creeping up across the sky. The smoke rose, impenetrable, blue-black against the ripening corn before us, until it was no longer possible to see bomb-burst or marker. Soon, even the incoming bombers were veiled behind the drifting clouds (of smoke). It was night now, a night of smoke and thunder. The landscape was blotted out and the fog of destruction was creeping to the road where we stood.[5]

Beneath the bombardment, the civilians could only cower in their cellars. With two of her neighbours blinded by flying shards of glass, a mother nearly suffocated her baby by pressing a pillow to his face as the only protection she had for his eyes. The ground, trembling from the sustained bombardment, continued moving for fifty minutes. André Heintz again:

The sky was a solid mass of Lancasters and Halifaxes, flying very low. The German anti-aircraft fire was at first intense, then slackened off. The planes came on and on, wave after wave in impeccable formation. There was something so grandiose and yet terrifying about it that I took out my camera, but the inhuman level of noise from all the explosions made me think we should all be killed, so that seemed rather a futile thing to do. The bombing lasted half an hour but, after a few minutes, more planes flew in lower still. This time, the green and red markers limited the damage but our town is now reduced to an unhealthy no man's land. [6]

Unhealthy, of course, because of the human and animal remains rotting in the debris. One of the doctors caring for the wounded wrote of this day:

> The bombing was pointless. There were no military objectives (in the town). All the bombs achieved was to block the streets even worse and impede the movement of the Allied troops through the town.[7]

Fifty years before the rolling newscast, this was the age of the cinema newsreel. On 25 June 1944 cameramen of *France Actualités* captured this total destruction of a French town that had begun on 6 June. Against a background of solemn funeral music, the commentator spoke of twenty days of horror destroying the capital of Calvados. Immediately before D-Day, Caen had boasted 70,000 inhabitants; 40,000 fled, abandoning their homes and all they had. They were right to do so, of the 30,000 who stayed hundreds were corpses before the bombardments ended, with many bodies still to be unearthed beneath the wreckage of their homes. Two-thirds of the city was destroyed. The images filmed were of ruins as far as the eye could see, with street after street blocked by unidentifiable piles of masonry that had been houses, offices, shops in a scene of destruction exceeded in no German city.

'These are French homes destroyed, French civilians killed, a French town obliterated,' the commentator intoned. The commentary was pro-Vichy, as was the coverage of a column of Allied prisoners marching through Paris being attacked by a crowd of people – whether angry for their own suffering or staged for the camera, no one now knows – to show the rest of France what liberation meant. However, the truth was not far different. Similar images of death and devastation could have been filmed in several other towns and cities of Normandy. What had they in common to merit such savage attack that British historian Anthony Beevor came close to calling this carpet bombing a war crime? The answer is simple. These historic towns were road junctions, nothing more. To the planners of Bomber Command and the American air forces, there was no question that those town centres had to be so thoroughly destroyed that the Germans could not force a way through for their reinforcements heading to the Allied bridgeheads. This meant total destruction.

Operations *Charnwood* on 7–9 July and *Goodwood* on 18–21 July killed about 2,000 civilians in Caen and so damaged the city centre and communications as to hamper the British advance through the city. Some days after the 'liberation' of Caen, Major Lindsay of the Gordons took an afternoon off to visit the city with another Gordons officer, who had been placed in charge of Civil Affairs there. Lindsay wrote of his visit:

> There was awful desolation after our bombing. Usher said that there were 1,000 killed and 2,000 wounded (French civilians) and 600 bodies still buried under the debris; there was certainly an unhealthy stench there.[8]

He also visited nearby Lisieux:

> ... and found that the town had been so badly bombed that the centre was a field of ruins. Later in the day I heard that we bombed it on D-Day to prevent the Hun bringing reserves through it, after dropping leaflets to warn the inhabitants, but most of the leaflets drifted elsewhere and few took any notice of those that did arrive. 'Lisieux is a famous religious centre, the British will never bomb such a place,' the French said.[9]

After the soul-destroying job of directing the Civil Defence of Caen for the last thirty-three days, Joseph Poirier recorded the arrival of the first Canadian troops in the town:

> These French Canadians march in single file. The tanks arrive. Our Canadian friends all speak excellent French and deluge us with chocolate and sweets. Women kiss them and men shake their hands. But it's all very restrained and dignified. We have all suffered far too much to go overboard for those whom the war obliged to do us so much harm.[10]

Forgotten in the macrocosm of war are all the individual tragedies. In addition to bombing the V1 launch sites, the RAF was charged with shooting down the flying bombs that made it across the Channel. Jean Mirador from Le Havre had been taken off flying duties due to stress, only briefly alleviated by his engagement to an officer in the WAAF. Joining 91 Squadron after D-Day he became something of an expert on shooting down the V1s, then causing damage and heavy casualties in London. On 22 June he scored two victories in one day, before learning that another RAF pilot had found a better solution: de-activating the gyro compass of a V1 by nudging it off-balance with his wing-tip, after which the rocket crashed harmlessly on open countryside.

On 3 August, Maridor was doing just that when he saw that the destabilised V1 was now diving straight at Benenden school in Kent, requisitioned for use as a military hospital. To save the hospital, Maridor went in close and shot it to bits at point-blank range, killing himself in the explosion.

The wedding invitations had already been sent out. His fiancée's parents had to send a follow-up note:

> We regret to inform you that the marriage of our daughter will not take place. We have just been informed that Wing Commander Jean Maridor of the Free French Air Force was killed this morning.[11]

Shaven-headed Frenchwomen 'guilty' of having a relationship with a German exhibited on a truck for public humiliation.

Bereavement was the lot of so many women that summer. In France there was also the public shaming of women whose German lovers had retreated with their units. A 22-year-old soldier from Iowa, Donald Willis, recorded what he saw driving through Normandy with the US 3rd Armored Division on 3 August:

> The Nazi sympathisers are paying for their past friendly relationships with the enemy. We see many women being shaved of their hair and this is a very mild treatment. Male collaborators caught by the *maquis* or Free French usually get a one-way trip down the road. The *maquis* like to guard the captured enemy but we must keep our eyes on them or there will be no Germans left alive.[12]

PART 4

LIBERATION AND DEATH

Chapter 15

The silent city

On 20 August 1944, Montgomery tasked 2nd Canadian Division with the capture of Dieppe, Boulogne, Calais and Dunkirk, code-named Operation *Fusillade*. Since Dieppe was where so many Canadians lost their lives in the raid of August 1942, some of the survivors of that raid were looking for satisfaction, if not revenge. Monty's succinct comment was, 'I am sure that 2nd Canadian Division will attend to Dieppe satisfactorily.' But first the Canadians had to get there.

Behind the façade of Allied unity, political battles were being fought. Supported by Churchill, General De Gaulle was adamant that the liberation of Paris must be seen to be done by French forces. His argument was that, should the Americans in the southern thrust drive in as the Germans retreated, they would be seen as just another wave of occupiers. He had already frustrated President Roosevelt's plans to install by force the American 'sixty-day wonders' – civil affairs officers given a two-month crash course in Maryland that supposedly equipped them to govern France under an Allied Military Government of Occupied Territories (AMGOT). He now got his way again, since the logic of his argument was impeccable. Agreeing that the US armoured spearheads would halt in the suburbs of Paris and allow General Leclerc's 2nd Free French Armoured Division to pass through and drive ahead of them into the city, Eisenhower imposed one condition in keeping with the US armed forces' colour bar: that none of the troops wearing French uniform in the liberation of the capital be drawn from France's coloured colonial forces who had played an important part in the fighting.[1]

Five days after this carefully staged all-white liberation of Paris on 25 August, the Canadians reached the Seine at Rouen, the ancient capital of Normandy, but Dieppe was still 50km distant and in a state of anarchy. When Hitler designated the ports of Dunkirk, Calais, Boulogne, Le Havre, Cherbourg, Saint-Malo, Brest, Lorient, Saint-Nazaire, La Rochelle and the Royan-Pointe de Grave complex at the mouth of the Gironde as *Festungen* – or fortresses that must never be abandoned in the event of an Allied invasion – Dieppe was omitted from the list. Although the port was fortified and its hinterland placed under strict security, OKW never issued a to-the-last-man order because the town and port were not officially on the list of *Festungen*.

After being bombed by the *Luftwaffe* during the retreat of 1940 and undergoing raids by the RAF and USAAF during the occupation and the softening-up raids preliminary to D-Day, the town and port were unrecognisable. In this wasteland, braving Allied bombs and the extensive German demolitions in the port area, a number of Resistance groups unearthed their caches of arms and began harassing the garrison troops. On the night of 31 August, *résistants* risked their lives to cut German demolition cables before the charges could be detonated. Thanks to their courage, parts of the port would be back in service immediately after the German withdrawal, handling 6,000 tons of supplies a day. Nevertheless, at 03.15hrs that night everyone in Dieppe and for miles around was awoken by a series of enormous explosions in the port and town. Substantial damage was caused to civilian property due to huge blocks of reinforced concrete from dynamited harbour installations flying through the air, killing and injuring many civilians, the injured being treated in first aid posts and hospitals. At dawn, the sun could hardly penetrate the smoke from burning fuel dumps and ammunition dumps, both in the town and the nearby forest of Arques.

As the smoke gradually cleared on the 1,590th day of the German occupation, the sleepless Dieppois surveyed their ruined town, in which 1,800 houses were destroyed or severely damaged. The castle was partly destroyed; the town hall was razed to the ground; the main bridge had been cut into two separate halves, the *gare maritime* was completely demolished, as was the fish market, the telephone exchange and the power station. In the port area, bridges, locks and quays were ruined, and the waterways were blocked by twenty-five ships, sunk either by bombing raids or scuttled by the *Kriegsmarine* demolition squads. Fifteen huge cranes were tangled wrecks, the warehouses gutted and the floating dock destroyed. Fuel storage tanks were ablaze

Soon after dawn, the German 245th Infantry Division, the *Kriegsmarine* units and *Luftwaffe* anti-aircraft crews leaped aboard any motor transport that was passing, or stole civilians' bicycles to get out of town fast, the last men in field grey having to walk, without any apparent orders or officers present, robbing housewives at gunpoint for the food they would need in the retreat. The various uncoordinated groups of *résistants* who had taken up arms managed to capture a thousand German personnel, afterwards handed over to the incoming Canadians. That so many surrendered without resistance to irregulars wearing FFI armbands – many of whom had for four years been more interested in assassinating Germans than observing the rules of war – shows the preference of the average *Wehrmacht* soldier, especially the non-Germans, to become POWs rather than continue a war they already considered lost. In the chaos, atrocities were inevitable, with some *résistants* killing soldiers whose only concern was to get out while the going was good and Germans taking an 'insurance policy' with them in the shape of hostages. In Arques, seven farm labourers had their wagons commandeered at gunpoint and were then shot for reasons unknown. At Bellengreville, retreating soldiers rounded up five men, lined them up and shot them. Reprisals? Unprovoked savagery? It is impossible to say.

However, as far as the advancing Canadian forces knew, Dieppe was to be held to the last man, like the other Channel ports. The ground assault was therefore to be supported by two battleships standing offshore with lesser vessels to mount a devastating naval bombardment, plus RAF bombers, all of which were to be cued by the arrival of the Canadians outside the Dieppe perimeter. On 1 September at 10.30hrs two reconnaissance motorcyclists from 2nd Canadian Division rode warily towards the outskirts of the town and were amazed to find no German presence, apart from the prisoners being held by the FFI. In the streets, the 3,000 stubborn Dieppois who had refused to be evacuated greeted their liberators with open arms.

The naval and aerial bombardments cancelled, it was for once the men in battledress who had tears in their eyes, as survivors of the 1942 raid recalled the slaughter on the beach two years and two weeks before. Kneeling by the graves of comrades who had died there, they wept.

De Gaulle's provisional government banned all newspapers that had been published during the occupation, treating their editorial staffs as collaborationist until proved innocent. Thus, the last edition of *La Vigie de Dieppe* went on sale on 31 August. On 1 September it re-emerged as a free paper calling itself *La Vigie Nouvelle*, full of emotional accounts of the liberation by the Canadians. But this too died after three issues, and was replaced by the untainted *Les Informations Dieppoises*.

All over the liberated areas, street signs such as *Boulevard du Maréchal Pétain* were being torn down. A new *sous-préfet* arrived, direct from Paris, where he had participated in the liberation, and Dieppe's popular mayor Monsieur Levasseur, automatically relieved of his functions for having served under the Vichy regime, was replaced by the president of the local *Comité Provisoire de Libération Nationale*.

Not until August 1949 could Dieppe publish its own reckoning, counting 207 civilians killed and 584 injured, plus 117 soldiers and FFI men killed and thirty-eight shot by the Germans or deported, never to return. The various bombing raids had completely destroyed 718 dwellings, equivalent to thirty-five per cent of homes. As the Channel ports went, it was not a heavy price.

Even the coming of freedom was tarnished for the general population by the senseless deportation, a few hours before the liberation of Lille on 1 September 1944, of hundreds of detainees in the prison of Loos-lès-Lille to concentration camps behind the retreating German armies. Bronze plaques on the memorial in front of the prison commemorate the 871 men concerned, of whom only 275 survived. Deportations from the two *départements* of Nord and Pas de Calais during the occupation totalled 7,700, including 1,772 Jews transported into the *Reich* for extermination within the Final Solution.

Hitler's vaunted Atlantic Wall was effectively now reduced to the chain of heavily fortified *Festungen* manned by a total of 140,000 men provisioned in food and munitions to survive for months after being totally cut off from re-supply. After 8,000 first-line troops in Le Havre were transferred to active service against the Allied bridgeheads, leaving largely second-rate troops to garrison the pocket, on 14 August the new *Platzkommandant* Lieutenant-Colonel Eberhard Wildermuth arrived from Italy to assume the unenviable role of commander of the pocket, which would inevitably be cut off by the Allied advance.

Allied intelligence had the garrison down as 'full of fight, and their commander a fanatic, whose wife and children had been killed in Berlin'.[2] Wildermuth was in private life a bank director and no fervent Nazi. He was, however, a conscientious reserve officer, who could not afford to put a foot wrong after suspicion of being peripherally involved

Lt Col Eberhard Wildermuth.

in the July plot. Under interrogation after his surrender, he defined his mission as 'to deny the Allies the use of the harbour for as long as possible, and to tie down the largest possible number of enemy troops meanwhile'.[3]

He found most of his subordinate officers to be reservists even older than himself, and was largely unimpressed with the quality of the 11,300 troops under his command, which included 3,000 *Kriegsmarine* personnel servicing the U-boat and E-boat pens – who were busily re-wiring the demolition circuitry damaged in the RAF raids. The ground forces charged with defending the perimeter included many Russians, Poles, Ukrainians and other nationalities forcibly conscripted in Eastern Europe, and therefore of doubtful morale and loyalty. Wildermuth also considered the physical defences less than adequate in many places, although the flooded valley of the Lézarde and the wide and deep anti-tank ditch stretching from it most of the way to the coast presented formidable problems even for tracked assault vehicles. The problem was the shortage of 88mm and 75mm anti-tank guns: how many dual-role 88s could he afford to take from the anti-aircraft positions, to use as tank-busters on the perimeter? The extensively mined and obstacle-strewn foreshore, overlooked by the coastal batteries, made a seaborne assault unlikely, but when he asked how many of the long-range guns in concrete emplacements could be revolved to engage targets on land, he was informed that there was only one.

He was particularly dismayed to find a large civilian population still living within the perimeter, although thousands had left, evacuated in an orderly manner with supplies for the journey and help in finding accommodation in areas thought to be safer. Why had so many chosen to stay, Wildermuth asked, when it was obvious that the Germans were not going to relinquish Le Havre without holding out for as long as possible and that civilian casualties would be inevitable during its prolonged defence?

The chief reason was their memories of the widespread looting of, and damage to, private property when they had fled their homes as instructed by the military governor of Le Havre during the German invasion in summer 1940. Another was that the speed of the Allied advance since the breakout from the Normandy bridgeheads made even many high-ranking military men think that the war would be over by Christmas, when the pockets would surrender in any case without the Allies needing to attack them. Even if the Allies did attack the pocket, most people in Le Havre assumed that their liberators would use minimal force against targets of low military priority like the city centre and residential districts. Many were influenced to stay by a local Resistance network operated by a Serbian refugee named Tsirich Svetisav. Svetisav had fought in the Belgian army in the First World War and afterwards come to live in the Ste-Adresse district. His network distributed and posted on walls leaflets signed *Le Vagabond Bien-Aimé* urging the Havrais not to leave and find themselves trapped in the middle of German and Allied artillery duels. The result was a report dated 16 August 1944 from the head of the *Renseignements Généraux* to the *Direction Générale* of the Sûreté Nationale:

> As previous reports of my service have indicated, evacuation has not been popular with the Havrais. Despite repeated air raids on the town itself, they prefer to stay in their homes – which is why the population of the town alone still numbers 70,000 men, women and children.[4]

To Wildermuth, all these civilians were 'useless mouths' who would have to be fed and provided with medical care, drinking water, etc, during what could be a long siege. In addition, it was obvious from experiences elsewhere in France since D-Day that a population of such a size must include several hundred *résistants*, some with hidden stores of parachuted or stolen firearms anxiously awaiting the opportunity to metaphorically stab the German defenders in the back once the main attack came in.[5]

All over France young men and a few women were putting on an armband with the letters FFI and grabbing a parachuted Sten gun or a pistol to confront battle-hardened *Wehrmacht* and *Waffen-SS* troops as the German retreat became a rout. As far as the troops were concerned, these hit-and-run irregulars were terrorists, entitled to no mercy. Sgt Pieter Kahl was a platoon leader in the 202nd Mountain Battalion. These entries in his diary show the gradual escalation of bitterness on both sides:

12 August – The population is calm and has behaved peacefully. All of us can understand they'd rather see us leave than arrive. But you only have to imagine if the situation was reversed. It remains to be seen whether the new occupying forces – the English and Americans – will treat them so humanely.

26 August – Shortly before evening, terrorists are reported. There are losses on both sides and 100 of our Italian allies with a captain desert to the terrorists.

7 September – The French here are a terrible people. You seldom see a person when passing through villages. Closed doors and windows, a sign that they do not have a clear conscience. We're in a gorge being shot at by terrorists who have their hiding place above us. Two are caught and shot dead on the spot. One of them is silent and resigns himself to his fate. The older one calls out before the bullet hits him, *'Vive la France!'* Actually, they should have been hanged but the leader of the transport column doesn't want to do that.[6]

Partly in the hope of avoiding that sort of confrontation within the pocket of Le Havre, on 18 August Wildermuth had posters put up all over town warning that the coming battle would bring down on the civilian population 'terrible losses by bombardment, lack of food and illness because availability of water, electricity and food will be severely restricted or non-existent'. He backed this up next day by summoning Mayor Courant and ordering him to evacuate the entire population before the pocket was cut off by the Allied advance.[7]

Courant was universally popular for steering his city through the political minefields of Vichy France and for dealing efficiently with the German occupation authorities. His administration was also widely considered, even by its political enemies, to have made the best possible choices for handling the casualties in the many air raids the city had suffered by construction of underground shelters, including surgical facilities, setting up emergency services and in the distribution of food and other comforts to victims of the bombing. For once, Courant was in complete agreement with the German occupiers. After his meeting, notices in French bearing Wildermuth's name were posted by the Germans:

> Humanitarian concern forces me to order the evacuation of Le Havre and its suburbs. No German military authority will prevent anyone leaving. The German authorities can make available limited transportation facilities for the evacuation of the sick, pregnant women and mothers with small children.[8]

Although British territory, the Channel Islands are called *les îles normandes* in French. More than two months after D-Day, the calm relations between the islanders and the Germans are reflected in the diary of the Baron von Aufsess, a key occupation administrator, and by no means a Nazi:

> 12 August – On the beach complete amity still reigns between the German soldiers and the local girls. With a few exceptions, the girl will surrender to her partner readily enough, provided this can be effected in proper secrecy. While the Frenchwoman involves herself in the game of love, which she likes to be conducted along intellectual lines, for the Englishwoman here it is a surprisingly straightforward physical matter. This direct and uncomplicated fashion of making love is not to be underrated.

> 14 August – We discussed the delicate question of reprisals against the civilian population for sheltering escaped prisoners (by this he meant the Russian slave labourers imported to build the massive fortifications). I am the only

one in favour of restraint. We should not, on account of a couple of unimportant escapees, drop the velvet glove which we have used with such success in the past.[9]

Velvet gloves were not the fashion of the month in Vichy, where Marshal Pétain was arrested by the SS on Sunday 20 August and driven into exile across the Rhine, as a hostage for his people's good behaviour during the German retreat. Before going, he recorded his last radio chat:

> By the time you are hearing this, I shall no longer be free. I have had one sole aim, to protect you from the worst. If I could not be your sword, I wanted to continue to be your shield.

Central government in France had now ceased to exist for most purposes. With no national infrastructure to take care of tens of thousands of evacuees from Le Havre, 35,332 people nevertheless did apply for exit permits, but few left. On Monday 21 August a single train-load, mostly of women from the categories enumerated by Wildermuth, assembled in the bombed-out main railway station, where not a pane of glass was intact. The evacuees were calm and resigned. There was no shouting, no pushing. Helped by Red Cross and *Secours National* officials and volunteers, they clambered aboard and the last train to leave the pocket slowly gathered speed and disappeared along the main line towards Rouen. After its departure, the mayors of the suburban communes joined Courant in asking every citizen able to find accommodation outside the perimeter, to go there immediately.

What of the town they would leave behind? By 22 August, when an RAF reconnaissance photograph showed large areas of the city centre with more blotches of bomb damage than intact buildings, all the cafés had put up the shutters and the vast majority of shops were also closed, although a small number of bakers, grocers and butchers was formally ordered to remain open, to feed those not leaving. Eighty other non-food shops were also ordered to stay open. An interesting comment on changing social habits is that these included tobacconists and stationers, considered vital at the time.

With the sealing of the Falaise Gap on 21 August, German forces west of the Seine who had succeeded in escaping the Allied pincers conducted a disciplined retreat, formed into *Kampfgruppen* after their original units no longer existed. Eisenhower could now launch his drive on Germany, with American forces in the centre and right wing and Montgomery on the left, or northern, wing of the advance.

On 25 August – the day Paris was liberated – elderly and infirm Havrais were placed on board a convoy of trucks to take them out of the pocket. But the Allied approach to the Seine was delayed after Field Marshal Walter Model succeeded Field Marshal Günther von Kluge as Hitler's C-in-C Western Front, von Kluge committing suicide halfway back to Germany on August 18 after implication in the plot to assassinate Hitler. Model managed to get 67,000 infantry and 98,300 men from his armoured divisions with 25,000 tanks and other motor vehicles across the river by night and day between 24–29 August. They would literally 'live to fight another day', facing the Allies again in the Ardennes and Holland, but their comrades left dead or wounded on the left bank among the wrecks of 12,000 vehicles of all kinds were the price paid to delay the arrival of the Allies.

On Monday 28 August, young Jack Hugill was advancing east of Caen with 30th Assault Unit, commanded by future author Ian Fleming. He caught two instances of compassion that day among the advancing troops:

> In Lisieux I was surprised by Marine Powell. We saw three old women sitting on their bundles by this pile of rubble that had been their home. They'd just got back. Powell, who is normally talkative and keeps up a stream of Cockney wisecracks, suddenly stopped and said, 'That sort of thing always wrings me, yer know,' pointing to the old women.
>
> On the road today, when we paused for a 10-minute halt, the MP corporal in charge of all the DRs (despatch riders) also surprised me by a sudden show of humanity. A Frenchman was driving a couple of horses in front of a large shay (a 2-wheeled cart), on which were perched all his household goods, and his family, in the opposite direction to us. Two large Army lorries came hooting along and tried to get past him. The MP went straight out, stopped the lorries and waved the Frenchman ahead of them. As he came back, he said in a slightly shamefaced way, 'Don't see why they shouldn't be allowed to drive on their own fucking roads, do you?'[10]

Model planned to halt the retreat by constructing a new defence line on the northern bank of the Seine, with its right flank anchored on the fortress of Le Havre, but the line was never established, the German retreat turning to a rout that permitted Montgomery's forces to advance 400km in six days, reaching Brussels on Monday 4 September. Rather than slow the Allied advance, Eisenhower had already decided to leave mixed blocking forces of FFI and Allied military units containing the pockets of resistance around most French ports, inside whose heavily defended perimeters hundreds of thousands of French civilians remained trapped under German military law. His logic was that the pockets could be reduced later, if the commanders could not be persuaded to surrender – an act for which OKW had ordained the death penalty. But Montgomery had designs on beating his American allies in the race to Berlin, and for this he needed at least one of those ports fast, to bring in the necessary supplies.

Hitler had ordered a zone of devastation to be created 15km deep around all the pockets of resistance. As Wildermuth told his Canadian interrogating officer Major Milton Shulman – later to become a celebrated London theatre critic – he simply did not have sufficient sappers to demolish all the built-up areas within that radius. Instead, using 400 Italians and a company of conscripted French labourers, he used the little time left to fill in gaps in the minefields and to strengthen anti-tank obstacles. As to the extensive demolition of the port facilities, he claimed not to have been involved, since that was the responsibility of the *Kriegsmarine* engineers.[11]

The task of liberating the Pays de Caux – roughly, Le Havre, Dieppe and the area between – was allotted to General Henry Crerar's 1st Canadian Army, which included 1st British Army Corps. On 30 August, the Canadians crossed the Seine at Rouen by the bridge that had withstood all the attacks of Allied bombers. The paucity of bridges and the priority given to the Red Ball Express trucks carrying everything needed at the rapidly advancing front meant that troops for a sideshow like Le Havre had low priority. Many other units crossed the Seine down-river, nearer to Le Havre, using any raft or boat, military or civilian, that could be found. It was not easy because the river was several hundred meters across – too wide for Bailey bridges and unsuitable for a pontoon bridge because it was subject to violent flood currents from up-river at low tide and from the sea as the tide came in, with only short calms as the incoming tide briefly balanced the outflow. Even then, craft sank in the eddies, men drowned and vehicles were lost. Once across, orders were to prepare for sustained house-to-house combat, with the issue of additional supplies of small arms, ammunition and grenades.

Wildermuth having ordered a complete evacuation of civilians by 21.00hrs on Tuesday 5 September, Mayor Courant's go-between Paul Latrille noted that he, the mayor, some councillors and the secretarial staff would be the last to leave, having worked 24/7 in the Town Hall to ensure that everything proceeded in an orderly fashion. On Friday 1 September *Le Petit Havre* published the evacuation order, informing those who intended leaving that they must first claim their entitlement to provisions for the journey from certain shops that had been ordered to stay open for the purpose.

However, Wildermuth could not *force* all the population to leave without physically rounding them up, which would have required taking far too many men away from their positions on the perimeter and the preparations to destroy the docks. In the city itself, approximately 40,000 people refused to go, with another 25,000 in suburbs lying within the perimeter. Inside the city limits, German troops were augmenting the number of bunkers with smaller strong-points dug-in at strategic places in expectation of last-ditch street fighting. In the port, thousands of demolition charges were placed on the wharves, cranes and the all-important lock gates in what was to be an orgy of destruction rendering the whole area useless to the Allies.

Millions of French people had now been liberated – at what cost in lives and injuries, no one is certain. As they would the following year in Britain, when the book *Living Together Again* was a best-seller – hundreds of thousands of wives all over France were now asking what their husbands would be like, returning from more than four years in the POW camps. A popular song, always sung by a female artiste, asked, *Que reste-t-il de nos amours?* – What is left of the love we shared? But in Le Havre there was no liberation yet and it was as well that no one could have guessed the price that would have to be paid there to see the back of the last German. On Saturday 2 September, the single-sheet *Petit Havre* carried a summary of how things stood:

> Le Havre is a silent city. Life has slowed down in the city
> centre, cut off with rarely any news from the outlying villages

and towns. It is a week now since our ears were last battered by gunfire, except for some anti-aircraft fire at passing aircraft. Ahead of us lie some difficult days. For three days now, all talk has been of the evacuation, whether total or partial.[12]

As Crerar's Canadians walked and rode unscathed that day into Dieppe, abandoned by its German garrison, he tasked Lieutenant-General John Crocker, commanding 1st British Corps, with the reduction of the pocket of Le Havre, supported by 51st Highland Division and 49th West Yorkshire Division under Major-General 'Bubbles' Barker. The reaction of Allied commanders detailed off to attack the pockets around the Normandy ports was frustration at missing the greater glory of the drive on Germany. In the words of Major Martin Lindsay of the Gordon Highlanders, written in his diary on 3 September at St Valéry:

> We had a big dinner party at the hotel, entertaining the mayor and local worthies. It was rather spoilt when the Brigadier whispered that we were going west to Le Havre, where 10,000 Germans were still resisting. It was not much fun to be going backwards when the big news was all of the drive forward into Belgium and Holland, and it looked as though we should be out of the hunt for some time. I remained depressingly sober for the rest of the evening. In the morning I had to preside over a field general Court Martial. We tried two deserters, whom we sentenced to five years and eighteen months, and reduced a CQMS to sergeant for *giving away* Army rations.[13]

It was not much fun inside the pocket, either. Also on 3 September, Wildermuth attempted to stiffen the resolve of his hotchpotch collection of troops by sending a Roneo'd notice to all units:

> Private Lubetski has been condemned to death by court martial on 3 September 1944 for having spread defeatism, in particular on 1 September. I have confirmed the sentence and ordered it to be carried out this day. This notice is to be brought to the attention of every unit and afterwards destroyed by burning.[14]

The defenders also received a Nazi pep talk, of which Dr Goebbels would have been proud. Although signed by Wildermuth, it was probably written by some fanatical underling, for its Nazi fight-to-the-death message caused the colonel no problems after he was taken prisoner.

> The military situation (of the pocket) permits neither conferences nor discussions. National-Socialist officers and commanders must visit every strongpoint and infuse each soldier with Nazi ideals, so that he fights the coming battle like a Nazi, with no looking back, but fighting with heart and soul for our homes and our State. Our daily paper *Die Festung* will also be used for this purpose.[15]

Loyalty to Hitler was not the only reason why men did not desert. Able Seaman Günter Lautmann spent long hours lying in the grass on the cliffs watching the distant invasion fleet with a French friend, whom he knew to be in the Resistance. He visited the friend's farm in uniform and was warmly welcomed, but resisted all blandishments and offers to help him desert because of the consequent shaming of his family, back in Germany.

The crossroads at Gainneville, a village lying just outside the perimeter, was famous throughout Normandy as the place where a locally-recruited militia had soundly trounced a flying column of Prussian cavalry on 11 January 1871. The same road junction was to be where the first shots of Le Havre's liberation were to be exchanged. M. Pimont, the mayor of the commune, was going about his normal business which, on 2 September at 14.00hrs, was celebrating a marriage of two young residents. Just after their arrival with family and friends in attendance, Pimont happened to look out of the window of the conference room and saw a squad of German soldiers laying mines around the building, which was also the village school.

'My friends,' he said calmly, 'I think it would be better to celebrate this marriage on the other side of the main road, in my farm.' With his secretary carrying the all-important register of marriages, he then led the way across the road through the busy Germans, one of whom had said to him that morning, pointing at the next village, 'The British are just over there. Tomorrow morning, I shall be dead.' He was right.

Further along the main road, another squad was chopping down a row of trees, to block the road to light vehicles. The marriage duly celebrated, the secretary walked back to the mayor's office with the register, to find several soldiers lying down in the playground in full combat kit, covering the crossroads with their weapons, and several others bashing firing-holes through the classroom wall facing the junction. Calmly, the secretary called his wife and children, and led them out of what he rightly considered would soon be a battlefield. It was the lull before the storm.

That same afternoon, Wildermuth ordered several salvoes to be fired at around 16.00hrs into residential areas just outside the perimeter where FFI men succeeded in capturing some German soldiers who had become cut off. Inevitably, the gunfire killed and injured a number of innocent people. Another diary-keeping civilian, M. Patouillard, noted repeated explosions in the direction of the docks lasting all afternoon as the *Kriegsmarine* engineers continued the demolition, while nearer at hand long queues still waited patiently outside the stores issuing provisions for the evacuation.

It is easy to overlook the enormous amount of horse-drawn transport used by the *Wehrmacht* in the Second World War. Hundreds of thousands of draught horses and farm animals grazing in the fields had been killed by both sides' artillery and Allied strafing. As Allied troops moved closer to the perimeter of the pocket, they passed through areas where the air was rendered foul by the masses of human and animal corpses and body parts lying rotting in the warm sunny weather. They found many German positions abandoned in haste, with paperwork, food and ammunition left in place. Many *Wehrmacht* men surrendered – both to Allied patrols and armed FFI groups – surprising their captors with freely given information, especially when they were eastern Europeans wearing German uniform as the lesser of two evils after their countries had been overrun, and had no loyalty to the German cause.

To all those who were hoping that the garrison might capitulate once faced with overwhelming odds, on 4 September the commanding officer of 2nd Battalion of the 1041st Grenadier Regiment circulated another Nazi pep-talk to all troops in the pocket:

> The battle for the fortress of Le Havre, which it is our duty to defend, is about to commence. Not an easy task, but an honourable one! We grenadiers of the army of the National-Socialist nation believe unshakably in the victory of German arms and, in this outpost of the western front, our hearts will beat more proudly than ever for our Führer Adolf Hitler!

He also cautioned against the temptation to desert using the safe conducts dropped by the RAF over the pocket. What the Poles, Russians, Ukrainians and other non-Germans made of this, one can guess from the high percentage that used the safe-conducts. Wildermuth's last message to his troops before the onslaught was more sober, echoing Nelson's *England expects* signal at Trafalgar:

> In accordance with our mission to defend Le Havre, I have declined the (Allied) offer to surrender. I expect each man in the fortress to do his duty.[16]

Chapter 16

The deadly oranges and lemons

Starting in the late afternoon of Saturday 2 September at Gainneville a series of probing attacks were already taking place and more artillery duels were in progress. The meticulous M. Patouillard noted these in his diary, adding that explosions also continued all that day as the *Kriegsmarine* artificers continued demolishing port installations including the ship repair facilities of the Électro-Mécanique Company. The explosions, he wrote, shook houses and rattled windows all over Le Havre, with considerable damage to civilian premises from blast and flying debris. To this was added the noise of battle as some German-occupied areas lying outside the perimeter were liberated, tightening the screw on the garrison.

Colonel Wildermuth knew that the main Allied attack could not be long in coming. It being now more than two weeks since he had ordered the evacuation, he summoned Mayor Courant to meet him at 19.00hrs in the German HQ – normally a no-go zone for civilians. There, Courant was given explicit instructions to evacuate the population the following day from the coastal zone of the pocket by two designated safe-conduct passages, one at Octeville in the north and the other at Harfleur in the south-east. At Harfleur, too, special arrangements were to be made for the whores who had been working there for the German garrison. Posters announcing these arrangements were posted in the areas concerned next morning, but once again many of the people affected decided for themselves that, with liberation at hand, they had little to fear by staying at home. After some refugees preparing to leave via Octeville were injured by Allied artillery, the evacuation order was cancelled, sealing the fate of those inside the perimeter.

That Sunday afternoon the heat was so torrid that mines began spontaneously detonating in a field over which British infantry was shortly tasked to advance. At a planning and coordination conference in the tactical HQ of 1st British Corps at Foucart, General Crocker briefed representatives of the Royal Navy, RAF and the British and Canadian ground forces under his command on the requirements of Operation *Astonia* – the reduction of the pocket. Logistics problems prevented the launch of the ground attack before the 147th Brigade and the Gordon Highlanders of 51st Division arrived at earliest on 8 September – by which time Crocker wanted the defences reduced by artillery and air raids to minimise his men's casualties in the final assault.

The official minutes of the conference reveal Crocker's hope that showing the Germans the scale of the irresistible onslaught being prepared would pressure Wildermuth into surrendering, and thus make unnecessary a full-scale ground attack with heavy Allied casualties. The first step in this plan was to give the German garrison an ultimatum to surrender or suffer massive air raids and naval bombardment within forty-eight hours. After the first air raid, codenamed *Astonia One* and scheduled for Tuesday 5 September, a second ultimatum would be extended. If rejected, a second massive intimidation raid codenamed *Astonia Two* would be called in on 6 September. If the Germans still did not surrender, the main attack codenamed *Astonia Three* would go in on Friday 8 September, supported by the Royal Navy and the RAF. In the event that Crocker's ultimatum was accepted, a message would be sent to Bomber Command, calling off the whole plan: *Astonia. Enemy capitulated. Cancel bombing (of Le Havre)*.

The meeting moved on to a discussion of the bombing, and the RAF liaison officer Group Captain A.H.S. Lucas was given precise coordinates of eleven targets, said to be German command points and troop concentrations in the city itself. These he was to forward to Bomber Command HQ at Stanmore, where the aiming points would be calculated. Exactly how, why, and by whom the specific targets had been chosen, remains unclear.

On the evening of Sunday 3 September, Mayor Courant, who was spending his nights in a small bedroom in the town hall so as to be on hand for whatever emergency, was admiring the gardens in the Place de l'Hôtel de Ville, thus far spared by all the air raids his city had undergone. About the same time, around 21.00hrs, on the perimeter to the south of Harfleur, Brigadier J.F. Walker summoned German representatives by loud-hailer to a meeting under flag of truce in Gonfreville l'Orcher.

There, he delivered the first ultimatum which included the warning about the scale of the coming attack and the dangers both to the German defenders and the civilian population.[1]

At 09.20hrs on the Monday, with the local armistice for negotiations still in force, a British tank flying a white flag from the radio mast was observed by locals advancing towards the German positions, followed by a jeep bearing General Barker smoking his trademark pipe, and three other officers. Both vehicles stopped at a red-brick house on the main road. From the other side of the lines came a German staff car bringing a lieutenant with Wildermuth's rejection of the ultimatum. Instead, he asked for a 24-hour truce to permit safe evacuation of French civilians resident in the pocket.[2] Failing that, he needed time to ensure their removal to areas where there were no military targets. Both requests were refused as stalling manoeuvres that would upset the *Astonia* timetable, and the point was made by Allied artillery shelling several areas of the city that afternoon, against a background noise of demolition explosions from the port area that lasted until 21.15hrs – after which, the night was relatively calm, with no Havrais realising that it was the last night on earth for many of them as the count-down clock for Operation *Astonia* ticked away.

Next morning *Le Petit Havre* newspaper announced that the evacuation had been halted. When a deputation of priests and local politicians begged Wildermuth to surrender, to save the population, his reply was understandably, 'You should all have left by the end of August, as I ordered, but your people didn't want to leave. Now, it's the British who have refused to permit the evacuation. So, it's nothing to do with me. I am here to fight.'

The civilians in the pocket were more interested at that moment in bread – now available only on Tuesdays, Thursdays and Saturdays. A limited distribution of cooking oil was available, as were tins of condensed milk for those with the right ration cards, plus 150 grams of ersatz coffee. All over the city, people queuing outside the thirty-seven butchers and thirty *charcutiers* with whom they were registered could clearly hear the artillery fire from the perimeter, and took this as a favourable sign that the Allies' final assault was beginning, with their liberation only hours away. What point was there, they asked, in the Germans continuing to hold out in Le Havre when British spearheads had already reached Antwerp in Belgium and the Americans were approaching Reims?

The answer was that the very speed of the Allied advance and the competing demands for motor fuel had made it an urgent priority for Montgomery to capture some of the Channel ports along the line of advance. Supply lines already stretched 400km to the rapidly advancing front from the *Mulberry* harbours and the French terminal of the PLUTO pipeline at Port-en-Bessin, north of Bayeux[3] – which carried 4 million litres per day from a pumping station on the Isle of Wight. Capturing Le Havre also meant control of the Seine estuary, making available the already liberated riverine ports of Rouen and Paris. With the overstretched supply lines thus drastically shortened, it seemed to many in the Allied chain of command that it would be possible to end the war by Christmas.

This was the pressure now on Crocker: to get the job done as rapidly as possible, using whatever force was necessary. But some of the troops under his command, like the Hallamshire Battalion, commanded by Lieutenant-Colonel Trevor Hart Dyke, had suffered up to seventy per cent casualties since landing in Normandy and most of the survivors were suffering severe combat exhaustion. It was therefore understandable that Crocker was prepared to use any means to keep Allied casualties in Operation *Astonia* to a minimum.

Throughout the morning of Tuesday 5 September the Havrais could not ignore the heavy shelling outside the city, accompanied by the continuing demolition explosions in the port area. A moment of unconscious humour was provided by Wildermuth's Order of the Day:

> It is suspected that agents inside the *Festung* are in contact with the enemy by carrier pigeon. Any pigeon seen flying out of the *Festung* is to be shot down.[4]

The Allies' experience in Normandy since D-Day had shown the importance of building in last-minute confirmation or cancellation of bombing raids that were planned several days in advance, in order not to kill one's own troops by 'friendly fire' or waste bombs on a position that had already been neutralised. In this case, the RAF raid code-named *Astonia One* was to be either confirmed or cancelled by midday on 5 September by a simple transmission, in which *oranges* meant *Go!* and *lemons* meant cancellation, with another 'target for tonight' being selected from the list.

At midday, when *oranges* was transmitted, the die was cast. General Barker, commanding 49th Division, belatedly protested to Crocker that 'history would judge severely' a massive air raid on a target largely occupied by neutral French civilians, but it was in any case too late to cancel the raid then. According the RAF Bomber Command campaign diary, on that day:

> 348 aircraft – 313 Lancasters, thirty Mosquitos and five Short Stirlings (of) Nos 1, 3 and 8 Groups – carried out the first of a series of heavy raids on the German positions around Le Havre which were still holding out after being bypassed by the Allied advance. This was an accurate raid in good visibility. No aircraft lost.[5]

Shortly after 17.45hrs the Mosquitos from No 8 Group roared over the city from north to south, firing green marker rockets into the designated target areas. This was no night raid, nor did cloud obscure the target. At the beginning of September it was broad daylight and visibility was excellent – in technical terms: '9/10 THS cumulus, cloud base at 9,000 ft on take-off, with the cloud clearing on approach to target to 3/10 cloud cover and cloud base at 6,000–7,000 ft.'

The Mozzies were followed after an interval of five minutes by the first wave of bombers, all bearing the roundels of the RAF. People on the ground counted six waves of forty Lancasters each – although many traumatised Havrais counted eight or more waves, each lasting a terrifying six minutes. A total of 1,820 tonnes of high explosive and 30,000 incendiary bombs were dropped on squares 4826 and 4827 of the navigators' maps, described impersonally in Crocker's plan for *Astonia* as: 'Night 5/6 September. Bombing of the harbour area.'

Those two squares denoted residential areas in the lower town and the city centre around the Town Hall, in the cellars of which, reinforced by wooden beams supporting the ceiling, Pierre Courant and his team had taken shelter, knowing from experience that the interval between the dropping of the TIs and the first bombs was too short for them to reach a bunker. At 18.05hrs they though their end had come. In fact, time did literally stop when the hands of the Town Hall clock stuck as a memorial to the raid.

For two whole hours, the firing of the German flak – rendered less intense than in previous raids by the prior removal of many 88s to the perimeter for use as anti-tank guns – the shriek of falling bombs, the noise of the explosions, the shock waves and crash of falling masonry stopped thought on the ground – or, rather, below it, where the civilian population huddled together in the cellars, communal shelters and slit trenches dug in their gardens. The last noise many of them heard was the dopplered scream of the bomb that hit their home and the crash of the entire building falling in and burying those still alive in the cellars, together with the corpses of their neighbours and families. A few people more courageous or more desperate than the others managed to scramble through holes leading into neighbouring cellars and climbed up to the open air in the brief intervals between waves of bombers. Under a sky turned dark by clouds of smoke and dust from the explosions billowing hundreds of feet into the air, they ran desperately through streets littered with broken glass, dodging between huge masses of unrecognisable smoking fallen masonry, hardly able to breathe for smoke as incendiary bombs set fire to buildings ripped open by the preceding high–explosive bombs.

At 18.15hrs Jacques Chantrelle, leader of a team of rescue workers, was in a cellar opposite the Town Hall when incendiaries fell into the entrance. Two of his young men attacked them with extinguishers, but these were soon exhausted. A direct hit collapsed the exit staircase. The next building

Le Havre? Cherbourg? Dunkirk? Calais? Actually St-Lô, but it could be any northern French city after the Allied invasion air raids.

was hit and collapsed, with a single person emerging through the escape hole into Chantrelle's cellar. Swirling dust making the air unbreathable, they held wet handkerchiefs over their noses. The only lighting was from acetylene lamps, whose flames were blown out by the blast waves, leaving them in darkness. Across the square, the town hall was split from roof to ground level. At 18.18hrs, precisely on schedule, the Lancasters of No 8 Group headed for home, the Group diary noting: 'The whole sector covered in smoke and dust. Several fires burning.'

The next wave hardly needed to navigate because the rising column of smoke and dust, visible before they crossed the English coast, was their beacon. Conveniently, the wind blew it away to the north-east, so that the markers were clearly visible when they arrived overhead squares 4826 and 4827. At 18.20hrs a stick of fourteen bombs fell within a few metres of the Sanvic emergency hospital, killing the surgeon, tearing off the doors of the operating theatre and leaving his attendant staff flat on the ground. A rescue worker stationed above ground, with just a steel helmet for protection, ordered a distraught woman to take cover, only to be told that she had to find her missing children first. A group of people sheltering in a garage with stout beams shoring up the roof opened the door to allow desperate neighbours to enter – and found a phosphorous incendiary bomb blazing just outside. A man shovelled it hastily further away, but not before choking fumes had filled the garage-shelter. A series of terrible explosions blew the door open in a storm of shattered glass. The roof beams shuddered under a violent shock. A woman was ill. A stranger offered her a swig of rum. Another weeping woman ran in, begging for help to dig out her husband, trapped in a collapsed slit trench in the garden, and had to be restrained from running out again.

Overhead, all was relatively calm, the target area completely invisible beneath the cloud of smoke and dust. At 18.25hrs the master bomber calmly ordered the incoming wave simply to aim for the centre of the smoke. Five minutes later one of those bombs blew out the wall separating Chantrelle's cellar from the neighbouring one, the blast hurling everyone into the corridor and burying him, two other men and fifteen nurses under a mass of debris. By the time he pulled himself out, wounded people were screaming, and others were lying still, killed by the blast that had only deafened him temporarily.

In another cellar rescue post, shared by several civilians and a lone German soldier, a direct hit on the house above brought the entire structure down on top of them, blocking the exit. Trapped in the suffocating darkness, screaming and thrashing about in panic, most calmed down when someone switched on a small torch – its weak beam revealing swirling masses of choking dust. Only the German had a gas mask, which he put on. Someone found a bucket of water, into which the others dipped their handkerchiefs and held them over their nostrils with one hand while desperately pulling away at the debris blocking the stairs. Just as a glimmer of daylight was seen, several more bombs exploded close nearby, blocking the opening. Under the weight of all the fallen masonry, constantly disturbed by new shock waves, the beams shoring up the roof started to split and give way. A new terror was added to all the others as smoke from the burning timbers above them infiltrated into the cellar. Young people collapsed from shortage of oxygen: one, two, three. And then, a miracle as another bomb blasted enough of the fallen masonry skywards to leave a narrow gap, through which they dragged the three unconscious youths.

But not to safety. The world was in darkness except where there was fire. Phosphorous was burning holes in the tar of the street and melting the tram rails, twisted like spaghetti, and the metal street lamps. Trees, stripped of their foliage by blast, burned like fiery crosses. So too did the hair of a woman, running with her baby clasped to her breast. Another woman, covered in blood and minus an arm, sat in the rubble, staring blankly ahead in shock. Unrecognisable heaps of flaming and smoking masonry and timber that had been homes less than an hour before were piled high all around. On every side the explosions continued. When the wind blew a brief hole in the smoke, a shaft of light made people look up to see a sky full of bombers with gaping bomb bay doors delivering more death from the sky. People staggering, confused, through the smoke and dust found themselves confronting nervous, trigger-happy, gas-masked German soldiers manning machine-guns on street corners, as though fearing an uprising under cover of the bombs.[6]

Driven by a strong westerly wind that rapidly gusted to 50mph and above, the flames of the initial fires spread rapidly, engulfing rescue workers trying to save screaming people trapped in the ruins of their homes, their clothes on fire. People who had been dug out alive subsequently died with their rescuers in first aid posts overtaken by the flames. With water mains destroyed, the fire brigade used every man and all its paltry five mobile pumps, running on diesel fuel begged from passing German trucks, to pump seawater from the harbour onto the flames until low tide prevented even this. At 20.00hrs fire chief Dumont noted in the station log:

> The sea itself appears to be on fire. Everything is covered by a cloud of fire and smoke. Everything is on fire as far as the Town Hall, itself burning like a torch. The sky is red. The air is all smoke. Wounded people are filling up the cellar of the fire station, where one surgeon and a wounded nurse operate on them, one after another.[7]

Shortly after writing that, he found a small group of people sitting in the open near the war memorial. In deep shock, none of them could speak or show any reaction when he addressed them, but they followed docilely like sheep when he rounded them up, to lead them to the fire station.

Borough engineer Pierre-Donatien Cot also kept a diary. At 23.00hrs he recorded another colossal explosion – not a bomb, but a German petrol dump going up in flames only fifty metres away from him. At 02.00hrs some of his team had already fallen asleep where they stood from sheer exhaustion. Mayor Courant arrived with a fire crew and the men threw themselves into attempting to create a fire break in the rue Maréchal Galliéni. As though in some small miracle, the wind shifted, slowing the approach of the flames. It took two hours for the fire crew to connect hoses along streets where they would not instantly catch fire, so that they could begin pumping water from the harbour again. Cot left them to it and collapsed on a mattress. By then, the medical teams, many of them injured or suffering burns, had been operating for eight continuous hours on severely injured people, some of whom were so shocked they could not be anaesthetised before an operation. Under the stress, a surgeon suffered a massive heart attack and was carried out with the other corpses by two young volunteers.

At 03.00hrs, Cot was on his feet again, logging the progression of the flames with the wind changing direction again: 'Smoke and dust hurt the eyes. Throats are so dry that we can hardly speak. The fires are slowing down in the northern sector.'[8]

The rescue workers were slowing down, too – some sleepwalking until they collapsed and covered themselves with the same dirty, blood-stained blankets in which corpses had been wrapped. Others went home as the dawn broke, anxious about their own families and all too often arriving at the rubble that had been their homes to find everyone dead.

Chapter 17

Tunnelling through bodies

The morning air of Wednesday 6 September was fouled all over Le Havre and for miles downwind by the acrid stench of smoke and the unmistakable smell of charred and burning human flesh. Debris transported by the superheated column of air was still landing many miles away. As soon as the fire teams turned their backs, flames extinguished on the surface broke through again from underneath fallen buildings. In the Henri IV shelter, a German surgeon was operating on civilian victims, helped by a French Carmelite nursing nun. In the cellars beneath the burnt-out shell of the Grand Théatre, rescue workers found the corpses of more than 150 *résistants* who had gathered there to take up arms in the anticipated liberation of their city by the Allied troops, and there been burned alive or suffocated by the smoke, unable to escape.

Underneath the ruins of the Guillaume Tell café, they dug out the corpses of ten *equipiers nationauux* – teenage boys who had volunteered to work as stretcher bearers. Even that term was a euphemism: stretchers were in such short supply that many wounded had to be carried on wrenched-off doors over the heaps of rubble to an emergency hospital. Similarly, corpses lacking heads and/or limbs were carried to the provisional morgues on whatever support was available. Blinded and singed dogs and cats crawled or ran in panic through the ruins.

The heat was in many places still so intense that roof timbers and furniture ignited before any flame reached them. Young volunteer rescue workers watched comrades crushed by falling walls while trying to save trapped people. With heavy lifting equipment lacking, two women were trapped by a corpse in rigor mortis locked around them, of which flesh and bones had to be cut away with a pocket knife to free them. Above ground, distraught survivors wandered numbly through the ruins:

mothers looking for their children, children looking for parents. In a landscape where even the street lines could not be traced with certainty, it was hard for people to find where their homes had been.

People were still burning, but also drowning. On the Place de Gobelins, most of those taking refuge in the centre of a cellar were crushed to death when the weight of the five collapsed storeys above broke through, leaving a small triangular space in each corner of the cellar, where the few survivors huddled. As water from a broken water main seeped in, they slowly drowned, unable to move hand or foot. It was many days after the raid before clearance work uncovered the bodies, some having burned before the water reached their nostrils, so that their lower halves were intact and bloated while the upper body was reduced to a few charred bones. Meanwhile, they awaited removal standing upright in water that was covered in a layer of human grease.

Having moved his surviving staff into the boys' secondary school, Courant tried to maintain a semblance of local government, recording names of survivors and casualties, although hundreds were simply listed as missing because unidentifiable bodies had to be hastily buried. Monsieur Cayeux, superintendent of the municipal parks and gardens, had every man in his department digging graves under the lawn of the Pasteur hospital and in the main square under the shattered pavement and road surface. Everywhere was the smell of death and decomposition, which they could not remove at the end of their shifts because it was forbidden just to tip a corpse into a hole and cover it. Every pocket had to be emptied and the body itself inspected for rings and jewellery, which were placed in a labelled bag. Where a body was so badly burned or shattered that no other identification was possible, pieces were cut from each article of clothing in the hope that a relative would recognise them. Any looting of bodies or homes was heavily punished.

In addition to his cares as garrison commander, Wildermuth had to receive a delegation of Protestant and Catholic clergy, trying to persuade him that he should capitulate with honour in order to save the thousands of civilians in the city, having done all that could be expected of a soldier. Wildermuth received them politely, but showed them his bulging files covering arrangements for evacuation of the population. 'I have done all I could,' he said. 'It is not my fault that, in defiance of my orders and advice, the people have stayed. It's too late now.'

As a compromise, the clergy asked for permission for one of their number to cross the lines under safe conduct, to ask the Allied commanders for a truce to enable evacuation. 'I'll let you know,' he replied. Later that morning, his reply reached them. It was, *'Nein!'*

To his staff, Wildermuth said openly that Germany would soon have lost the war. Already he was without any direct communication with friendly forces outside the pocket, the last remaining channel to OKW being a *Kriegsmarine* transmitter in the port. However, his duty was to continue immobilising the maximum number of enemy forces in the siege. As to how long he could hold out against a sustained ground attack, his estimate was, no longer than three days – time that must be used to continue destruction of the port, so that it would be of no use to the Allies. By now, deserters surrendering to the British forces said that morale was so low inside the pocket that the only thing stopping all their comrades on the perimeter surrendering was fear of having to cross their own minefields![1]

Understandably, in this chaos, various estimates of the dead and injured conflicted. The modern conservative account is that *only* 781 civilians died in this one raid, with 289 missing – meaning that their bodies were too damaged to be identified, or simply never found. To this total of 1,070 casualties in the two-hour bombardment must be added the unknown hundreds of civilians injured and all those traumatised by what they had lived through. To some extent, coming to terms with such trauma is helped by understanding the reasons for the traumatic event. In this case, that closure was never available because no one could ever explain why the city centre was targeted.

As if the horror of Tuesday evening was not enough, at 11.00hrs on Wednesday morning a fateful decision was taken in General Crocker's HQ. The *Astonia Two* mission was confirmed to Bomber Command, targeting a different sector of the city with reference points 510300, 542297, 547278 and 510282.

Several hundred people had been living for days and even weeks in one of the many tunnels excavated over the centuries below the city. Construction of the Jenner road tunnel to connect the upper and lower towns had stopped at the beginning of the war. In 1942 Courant's administration decided that it would make an ideal air raid shelter for up to 7,000 people. The secondary reason for the decision was that the labour force working on it would be exempted from conscription for compulsory labour service in Germany. By the beginning of 1944, one end of the tunnel was in regular use as a shelter. For weeks, in some cases months, families brought mattresses, furniture and simple cooking facilities, and slept there each night, apparently untroubled by the fact that the two ends of the tunnel had not yet been joined up, so that there was only one way in or out.

At 18.00hrs on the fatal Wednesday a mixed force of four RAF Mosquitos followed by four Lancaster bombers roared over the stricken city, dropping their target indicators. For eight minutes the stunned Havrais watched the red and green firework display, fearing the worst yet having no idea how bad that could be. Terrified by the previous night's raid, many hundreds more people than usual arrived after the markers were dropped. Among them was 13-year-old Daniel Canu, whose grandmother panicked on seeing the target indicators and persuaded the whole family not to go down to the cellar they had previously used, but to join the stream of people heading for the tunnel. The 'permanent residents' having occupied all the best places, there was little room left for all the newcomers. Undecided what to do, they milled about inside and outside the entrance.

At 18.01hrs the first wave of forty-six from the 344 RAF bombers tasked with this mission flew in low, west-to-east across the Bay of the Seine, to discharge their loads of high-explosive bombs in accordance with the co-ordinates they had been given. Unlike the previous evening, there was little German flak, the batteries having been largely neutralised by Allied artillery. Seeing the first bombs falling apparently straight at them, the crowd at the entrance of the Jenner tunnel forced its way in, with several hundred people overflowing into a section of the tunnel that was closed to the public as being dangerous. None of them knew just how dangerous. Daniel and his family were trapped in the middle, unable to go any further, or to make their way back against the pressure of those behind.

Above ground, some people still watched the approach of the second wave, seemingly filling the sky with their dark silhouettes. It was a terrifying sight. With 10/10 cloud cover above 6,000 feet, the Lancasters came in low, pilots and bomb-aimers having perfect visibility of the ground below. But the Canu family was feeling quite safe, although clearly hearing the bombs explode and feeling the shock waves travelling through the ground.

The night watchman was making his way to the tunnel, taking shelter each time he heard a bomb dropping and from what he thought was a hail of machine gun bullets, but was probably shrapnel fragments falling to earth. Just before reaching the tunnel, he heard the scream of a bomb falling directly overhead and hurled himself inside a concrete street urinal. From that odiferous shelter, he saw a 1,000kg bomb explode directly beside the tunnel entrance, making a crater ten metres wide, completely blocking the entrance and bringing down the roof for twenty-five metres inside.

Inside the tunnel, Daniel Canu and his family were knocked down by the blast. The diesel-powered electricity generator, sited near the entrance so that the poisonous exhaust fumes could escape, was overturned and smashed. In the darkness, there were only a few pinpoints of light where individuals had an acetylene lamp, or some cooking oil in a saucer with a piece of string for a wick.

Before the raid was over, the force of 311 Lancasters, thirty Mosquitoes and three Short Stirlings in three waves dropped 1,728 high explosive and incendiary bombs. The chaos was in places even worse than the previous evening – so that fire chief Dumont had to stand his men down because so many collapsed buildings and craters prevented them reaching the fires. With coal stocks at the power station exhausted, the city's electricity supply failed for good, after which the only lighting was by small generators in the hospitals and oil and acetylene lamps elsewhere. At 19.31hrs precisely a fourth wave of bombers arrived overhead, but the cloud base had dropped even lower and torrential rain now obscured the target, so that the master bomber was obliged to tell the last wave of Lancasters to return to base with their bomb loads – an order disliked by the crews in case of problems on landing while still bombed-up. The Bomber Command Campaign Diary report of the raid read: 'Bombed German fortifications and transportation targets at Le Havre without loss.'[2]

Where the entrance to the Jenner tunnel had been, men started to dig, at first with bare hands and empty tin cans, into the rubble and earth that was rapidly turning to a sticky mud under the downpour. A boy was dug out alive after being completely buried. Then the horrors began when a man and a woman were found literally stapled to the tunnel wall by a steel rail from the construction workers' narrow-gauge wagon-run. The rescuers continued uncovering bodies until the air in their working space was too foul to breathe. Inside the tunnel, conditions were far worse.

Daniel Canu recalled afterwards how his entire family huddled together in pitch darkness, waiting for the end.

That night the downpour continued, making the rescuers' work even more difficult, and Allied artillery continued firing into the city. Underground, thousands of tons of wet earth, liquefied by the explosions, turned into a subterranean mudslide inside the tunnel, engulfing no one ever knew how many of the living. In the gloom and the rain above ground, volunteers started digging down to the roof of the tunnel, six metres below ground level, watched by a silent crowd of relatives. At 08.30hrs a fire team arrived under Lieutenant Lacheray, all gaunt with exhaustion and without any tools to cut through the thick tunnel roof shuttering. A handsaw was found, with which a hole was cut and the planks lifted clear. Among the survivors below, the Canu family could hear the desperate digging and sawing somewhere above them in the darkness.

Lieutenant Lacheray was dropped through the hole on a rope with his foot in a bowline and swiftly hauled up again with the news that it would be necessary to carve a way through the mass of impacted bodies immediately below the roof in order to make enough space inside the tunnel to start digging properly. He refused to order any of his men to do this, but two of them volunteered and went down, to be replaced by two other volunteers when they could take no more.

By 10.00hrs the air inside the tunnel was almost devoid of oxygen. A baby near Daniel Canu died. All around him was the sound of death rattles and people fighting for breath. Some men started fighting, with the idea of being first to escape. Another man strangled his dog to stop it breathing precious oxygen.

One of the firemen removing bodies under the roof called up to rescuers above that he could hear groans. Thirty minutes later, they broke through into empty space and a draught of deliciously cool air rushed into the tunnel. People began shouting that they were all going to be saved. Then came anti-climax as debris fell into the narrow opening, blocking it. Lieutenant Lacheray was the first to find a living person: a woman who was hoisted up and carried on a stretcher through the downpour to a first aid post. Below, there was now so little oxygen that no flame could burn. In the pitch darkness, Daniel heard his father say that his grandmother and uncle were dead, but he had lost touch with the uncle's wife. Shortly afterwards, his father died too and Daniel huddled closer to his mother, unaware that she was already dead.

It was mid-morning before a sufficiently powerful winch was found to permit easier removal of the bodies from the tunnel through the hole in the roof. A team of tired and traumatised grave-diggers from the Parks and Gardens department arrived to help with the grisly excavation of bodies. As space was gradually cleared beneath the tunnel roof, more hands could be used to disengage bodies from the rubble and haul them to the surface. Volunteers working by the light of electric torches found themselves facing whole families, including the baby in its pram, compressed into one mass by the blast-waves.

At the far end of the gallery, Daniel thought his head was going to explode. Hardly able to move, he crawled under a wagon, saw the light of a torch and heard a man say, 'No point in going further. No survivors here.' With just the energy to cry out, Daniel recovered consciousness in the Joan of Arc chapel, being used as an emergency hospital, and was told that his aunt had also been saved. She was the only relative he had left.

The work continued, helped by a fan pumping air into the vault. There were only six survivors. An accurate body count was difficult, many of the bodies near what had been the entrance being vaporised or dismembered by blast and those who died suffocating under the mud-slide being locked together in rigor mortis. Eventually the number of dead in the tunnel alone rose to an estimated 319 killed by a single bomb, many unidentifiable and buried immediately and anonymously in the mass graves. Back in his office late that morning, Dumont wrote to the mayor:

> I've just got back from the Jenner tunnel. Bodies are being removed at the rate of one every five minutes. I demand that the fire teams be relieved by civil defence personnel, so that they can continue the work of fighting the fires. We need a larger morgue and stretcher bearers for the huge number of victims. It will be necessary to tunnel in (through the blocked entrance) to provide a second exit.[3]

The continuous downpour hampered the grim work of penetrating further into the tunnel next day against a background of artillery fire outside the city limits, with some shells landing on residential areas. That evening Jeannette Leroy and her mother crawled out of the cellar where they had spent forty-eight hours without food or water, too terrified to come out even during the short periods of calm. During this time in the cellar, one woman had given birth and another woman had gone mad. Jeannette and her mother could not recognise any landmarks in the devastation above ground, where piles of rubble still smouldered. Instead of seeing streets, shops, churches and apartment blocks, they had a clear view all the way to the sea. Guessing their way in this foreign landscape, they reached their home at the public baths in the rue Louis-Blanc, hoping to find Jeannette's father there. The baths had been used as a clearing station. Corpses lay on stretchers in the entrance hall, in the changing rooms and in the offices but Monsieur Leroy was not among them. He was lying beneath the mud of the Jenner tunnel, and would remain there until rescue teams wearing breathing apparatus against the stench dug out his decomposed body two weeks later.[4]

At 19.15hrs on 8 September the Mosquitos returned to fire marker rockets into outlying villages north of the city near the German gun emplacements and minefields of the perimeter. Of the 333 Lancasters and Stirlings that took off, only 109 were able to find the targets in conditions of low cloud and heavy drizzle, but they managed to drop 539 tonnes of bombs in ninety minutes with relatively minor civilian casualties, compared with the previous raids on more densely populated areas, but caused considerable damage to homes and farms.

In addition to the ground artillery of the investing Allied forces pounding the German strong points, the minefields and villages near the perimeter and the murderous air raids, civilians now had another arm to fear. The battleship HMS *Warspite*, and the heavily armed inshore support vessel HMS *Erebus,* took station outside the minefields in the Bay of the Seine, their 15in guns outranging any of the German artillery in the coastal batteries under the cliffs. Their combined bombardment of more than 300 massive shells severely damaged the German positions in and around the Sainte-Adresse fort, with near-misses landing in the surrounding residential districts and causing more casualties. In any case, the usefulness of the naval bombardment was questionable, since only a shell landing *inside* the carefully constructed embrasure of a gun would put it permanently out of action, as already proven by the RAF raids on 10, 13 and 26 April, in which 380 tonnes of bombs were dropped, doing little damage to the guns that were the real targets and considerable destruction in nearby residential districts.

On land, six medium and two heavy Allied artillery regiments suppressed the German flak during air raids. In the city centre, the

109 exhausted men of the municipal fire service still patrolled the ruins in the attempt to prevent fires burning underground from spreading – a task made nearly impossible by their ability to only pump water from the harbour with the five remaining pumping engines at, or near, high tide.

On the morning of Saturday 9 September the deluge continued. Bewildered survivors wandered into the makeshift emergency centres, unaware that the weather was sparing them a further planned air raid, of which only a few aircraft turned up, targeting the coastal batteries. Of the shops still standing, few had any stock left to sell. Some bakers managed to make bread, seized upon by the hungry. German soldiers stuck up posters regretting the damage and casualties, but disclaiming any responsibility. At the boys' secondary school, a constant stream of shocked and grieving people came begging Courant's exhausted team for help, but there was little the harassed officials could do for them, except note names of missing and dead relatives and neighbours and instruct grieving relatives and neighbours where to take bodies for burial in the many provisional cemeteries. All along the perimeter, artillery duels continued, with 'overs and unders' hitting residential districts, killing and maiming more people. Typically, in the little village of Fontaine-la-Mallet, only two houses remained standing, and they were both heavily damaged.

A final ultimatum was delivered to Colonel Wildermuth – and rejected like the others. At midday the rain eased after four days and nights of misery and the sun was seen at last. Outside the siege lines, the British and Canadian commanders hoped the rain would hold off long enough for the waterlogged ground to dry out and permit use of armoured vehicles. The weather thus delayed for forty-eight hours the final attack. Meantime, artillery duels continued, with the inevitable civilian casualties.

On Sunday 10 September few Havrais slept after 04.20hrs when the final assault began with sustained artillery fire on the German lines. The day dawned sunny and beautiful, but the naval and ground bombardment of the German defences continued, with waves of bombers in Operations *Alvis, Bentley, Buick* and *Cadillac* pummelling the German positions for nearly three hours. At 10.00hrs *Erebus* and *Warspite* again engaged the coastal batteries. Despite many of the flail tanks and AVREs[5] falling victim to mines while clearing the perimeter minefields, all primary objectives were reached, with gaps in the minefields taped for infantry follow-up and the anti-tank ditch bridged in several places. Many concrete bunkers were cleared by the Crocodile flame-thrower tanks of 79th Armoured Division, later credited by Wildermuth as the most terrifying weapons used in the attack.

By now, apart from volunteers helping the emergency services, few civilians ventured into the open air, but stayed in whatever shelter they could find, praying that the end of their suffering was near. To their discomfort in many places was added rainwater from the heavy downpours flooding them out of cellars and underground shelters.

Another night was made hideous by sustained artillery fire and explosions to the north-east. At 07.30hrs on Monday 11 September the air raid delayed by the weather finally commenced, with RAF Hawker Typhoons dropping 857 tonnes of high-explosive on tactical targets in the German coastal defences and defence perimeter. Seeing the marker rockets coming in, civilians near the targets panicked too late to save themselves. So thick and high was the cloud of debris, dust and smoke that the master bomber ordered the last wave of aircraft to return to base without dropping their loads. It was after this raid that Crocker wired 'Bomber' Harris: 'All ranks unanimous in their praise of absolute accuracy of bombing and timing on every occasion.'[6]

No one could deny that the raids had been impeccably timed, but as to accuracy, the final record of Le Havre's civil defence log was that 12,000 tonnes of bombs had been dropped on the pocket, killing some 5,000 people, mostly civilians, and leaving eighty-two per cent of homes destroyed. But what does it mean in human terms when records speak of seven-tenths of Caen and 300 acres of Rouen being completely destroyed by Allied air raids and artillery? The devastation is beyond comprehension. Even the figures for killed and seriously injured are hard to take in, and made harder by conflicting estimates, complicated by the casualties among conscripted workers, refugees, people with false papers and thousands of human remains that were quite impossible to identify with the technology then available.[7]

Chapter 18

We greet you in mourning

Infantry in the second wave attack on the pocket were protected inside Ram Kangaroo armoured personnel carriers[1] of 1st Canadian Armoured Carrier Regiment. As they advanced, many blockhouses surrendered, the men flocking out with raised hands after seeing what the Crocodile flame-throwing tanks had done to their comrades. The Gordons alone took 500 POWs that day. When they reached the city itself, coloured recognition flares were fired to warn off RAF aircraft, but not before more homes had been destroyed and yet more civilians killed. Major Lindsay of the Gordons considered that the RAF had done a good job: some craters were 100 feet deep. His diary records that he found, hiding in one blockhouse:

> ... two Frenchwomen (who) looked so pleased with themselves that I told them they would be handed over as collaborators and have their heads shaved. Whereupon one of them promptly went inside and produced six bottles of champagne. I said, 'Thank you, but it won't make any difference.'[2]

About midday the sound of artillery lessened, encouraging people to leave their shelters in search of food. There was little to be found. Instead, news travelled by word of mouth that *les anglais* (sic) were already in the city centre, guided by *résistants* to, or around, German strong-points. Sadly, in the midst of all this grief – as in the London Blitz – some people judged this the right moment to enter damaged homes and steal furniture and personal belongings.

With parts of the town liberated and others still under German control, that evening volunteers distributed the last reserves of food that Mayor

Courant had kept hidden, passing through German positions without any interference from the troops still holding out there. Mopping-up operations continued the next day, marking the end of the nightmare week, with British and Canadian infantry picking their way through a wasteland of rubble and smouldering ruins, wondering where was the euphoria to which they had become accustomed in other liberated towns. Many of the tricolor flags draped over the ruins were edged with black crêpe and the population was, for the most part, too numbed and too traumatised to welcome the liberators. This was a city where everyone was in mourning, for their loved ones, for their neighbours and for their native city, large areas of which had been erased from the map. The incomprehension of the victors was unwittingly expressed by Major Lindsay's entry in his diary:

> All the restaurants and cafés were closed and I cannot help feeling that the French are rather wet; we should never have allowed bombing of one part of a town to have closed down all life in the rest of it. (The bombing) had made us highly unpopular. We had none of the rapturous welcome that we had received elsewhere, and when (the chaplain) made a few tentative enquiries about getting up an officers' dance, he was told that the whole town was in mourning and (the population) would have nothing to do with it.[3]

Uncannily untouched, the memorial to the dead of the First World War stood in the city centre, surrounded by smoking ruins being hosed down by the fire brigade and improvised graves dug into any level space. This was the setting for a brief ceremony, for which a path had to be cleared through the ubiquitous rubble and at which some British officers joined the mayor and members of the Committee of Liberation laying wreaths and singing the *Marseillaise*. In the middle of the brief ceremony at Le Havre, a single aircraft flew overhead, presumably for photo-reconnaissance. The sound of its motors caused the small crowd around the memorial to fall silent and gaze anxiously up at the sky.

The atmosphere towards the end of the day is best captured in the Hallamshires Battalion War Diary:

> As A Company crossed the canal bridge into the docks, enormous explosions took place, parts of the lock gates and

rubble were hurled high into the air and crashed down among the men. After several hours of hard and hazardous work (mopping up German pill boxes) C, B and later D companies successfully cleared the whole area with the exception of the South Mole – a strip of land about a mile long and 100 yards wide, studded with large concrete pill boxes. Most of them were not defended and over 80 German officers and men surrendered. By 22.00hrs, when it was quite dark, the whole mole had been cleared and with that the capture of Le Havre was complete. A total of 1,005 POWs, one submarine and three Dornier aircraft were captured (by the Hallamshires). It was fortunate that the enemy offered little resistance.

However, right up to the last minute men were being wounded and dying: Lt Col Hart Dyke took a piece of shrapnel in the head; another officer was shot through the head by a sniper. There are conflicting accounts of the sniper's fate, but since both sides in Normandy routinely shot captured snipers out of hand, it can be assumed that he was executed shortly after capture. On 9 September Wildermuth had modified Hitler's 'to the last man' order: 'Fighting tanks with bare hands is useless. Resist any infantry attack, even if you have only personal weapons, but faced with armour, it's up to you to decide what to do.'

He himself retreated into a bunker in the town centre, where he surrendered at the approach of the first British tank. Lying wounded on a bunk, clad in his pyjamas, but wearing his medals, he formally handed his pistol to a young lieutenant and was driven to General Barker's command caravan on the Place de la Liberté.

Barker smartened up for the occasion: full uniform, down to his kidskin gloves. Through an interpreter, he ordered Wildermuth to require the strong points still holding out to lay down their arms. Wildermuth refused, on the grounds that he was a prisoner of war and thus had no authority. When asked what was the point of that, he replied, 'To tie down the maximum number of your troops for the longest possible time.' Only after the fruitless conversation was he passed over to a surgical team, which proceeded to remove shrapnel from his left thigh and abdomen.[4]

The Sainte Marie tunnel, where so many Havrais had spent their nights during the early raids, had been requisitioned by the Germans in 1942 as an ammunition dump, with concrete blast walls. As the last Germans left, people of all ages clambered into the tunnel and carried away as much loot as they could. Food, bedding, tobacco, but also German stick grenades, guns and ammunition – just in case.

The requirements of Montgomery's plans for operations *Market* and *Garden* – the air-drop on Arnhem and the fatally delayed armoured breakthrough to link up with the paratroops – were already causing the redeployment of troops from Le Havre before the last German personnel in the port and the Ste-Adresse fort surrendered on 13 September. Civilians searched through the ruins of their homes for anything still usable. Homeless people moved into any empty house that was still habitable. Volunteers helped rescue workers to search the ruins for bodies, aided by the stench of decomposition. Others joined the exhausted fire teams still pumping seawater onto the ruins when the water-level in the harbour was high enough. With all newspapers which were printed during the occupation now banned, a new local paper appeared, but for one issue only on 13 September. In *Havre Matin* was an article beginning *Vous êtes venus enfin.*

> So, you have come at last. We awaited you with joy, but we greet you in mourning. We had hoped to see our flags flying joyously in the wind of liberation. Instead, they hang heavily beneath the burden of mourning crêpe and the thought of joyous days of freedom to come cannot appease the sadness in our hearts. However, you who have liberated us are welcome in this, our ruined town, bled nearly to death. Lost beneath our grief, we can no longer find the words we should have said to you, but if our greeting was not joyous, it was nonetheless fervent. We waited so long for the day when you appeared through the morning showers – both members of the FFI, among whom we recognised old friends, and you British soldiers returning after four long years to the sound of machine-guns firing nearby and of tanks firing point-blank at the German blockhouses. Le Havre is free again. Le Havre will live again.[5]

The port was reduced to a wilderness of masonry and twisted metal, 18km of quays having been blown up by the *Kriegsmarine* sappers, with 320 wrecks sunk in the waterways. The ship repair facilities were non-existent, as were the refuelling quays. The four maritime railway stations were destroyed, together with long stretches of the tracks leading to them. Half of the dockside warehouses were irreparably damaged and of the 285 cranes functioning in 1939 only one floating crane was still operational. The locks on the Tancarville canal had been destroyed, letting the Seine water flood in.

In the previous two weeks 2,042 aircraft had dropped 11,000 tonnes of bombs on Le Havre. In all, the fifty-one months of occupation had seen four-fifths of the town destroyed in more than 120 air raids, leaving 31,000 people homeless; 12,500 buildings were reduced to rubble and another 4,500 severely damaged, 2,500 having to be demolished, making a total of 3 million cubic metres of rubble to remove. Almost all the public buildings had been destroyed: the town hall, the exchange, the main post office, the main Catholic and Protestant churches, the Grand Théatre, the museums and the central market. The two general hospitals had suffered great damage. Of forty-four schools, only ten remained, damaged but usable.

In human terms, 5,126 Havrais had been killed by Allied bombing since the first air raid on 19 May 1940,[6] compared with a total of twenty-eight shot by the Germans and 2,850 deported to camps in Germany for various reasons during the same period. Two weeks after the 'liberation' of the town, a search team found one small group of survivors in a cellar on the Boulevard de Strasbourg, where they had stayed, too terrified to emerge, drinking water from the radiators and eking out their store of food until none was left.[7]

On the other side of the balance sheet, *Astonia* involved nearly 45,000 Allied soldiers, of whom some 400 were killed. General Crocker's British and Canadian forces took 11,292 POWs and, despite the appalling destruction by demolition, bombing and the naval bombardment, the port was back in limited use within days. *Astonia* could therefore be considered an overall military success.

But what part had the air raids played in this? In October 1944 an RAF Bombing Analysis unit made one of the first on-the-ground evaluations and estimated that:

Only between a quarter and a third of all coastal batteries had been silenced in the air raids, (but that) the attack (of 5 September and later) on the town itself contributed little to the success of our ground forces, *having killed just nine German personnel in addition to all the French civilian victims of the raids.*

In addition to Crocker's congratulatory message to Harris, maps appended to official accounts of the *Astonia* raids bear out that the areas bombed were indeed the targets communicated after the planning conference of 3 September.[8] This was despite much information about German dispositions being smuggled out of the pocket to the besieging Allied forces before the raid. Deserters, especially non-Germans, also freely gave information when interrogated; and RAF photographic reconnaissance before 6 June showed that the only German targets of real importance within the town centre were the two forts.

In London the *Daily Telegraph* – usually supportive of Bomber Command – qualified the air raids as 'partially successful', while *The Times* dismissed the bombing as a 'meaningless sideshow', giving all the credit for the liberation of the pocket to the ground forces.[9] As to the vague claim that the devastation of the city centre demoralised the German garrison, making the final assault less costly, not only is it clear that attacks of this scale on on the perimeter defences would have had far more effect but, in his interrogation by Milton Schulman, Wildermuth considered accurate ground artillery fire and the use of flame-throwing tanks to kill his men inside their bunkers as far more effective in this respect than the bombing or the naval bombardment.

Pierre Courant was, like all mayors and other functionaries who had served under the Vichy government, automatically debarred from political office when De Gaulle's provisional government returned to Paris in September 1944. To show that the blanket disqualification did not reflect what his constituents thought about him, he was carried shoulder-high at his last official function: to place a wreath on the Monument aux Morts. His successor as mayor in the interim left-wing liberation committee that governed Le Havre until elections could be held admitted that Courant's humanitarian record during the occupation was untainted by his appointment under Vichy. His continuing popularity saw his 'list' of candidates elected at the municipal elections in April 1945. In 1947 Courant again became mayor of Le Havre in his own right.

Tsirich Svetisav survived the bombing and liberation, but died three months after liberation, apparently crushed by guilt that he had caused the deaths of so many people, by convincing them through the *Vagabond Bien-Aimé* network to remain in the pocket to the bitter end.

Eberhard Wildermuth was not considered by the post-war French authorities as a war criminal or as having acted in any way that could be construed as anti-French. He was, on the contrary, selected to act as an adviser to the authorities of the French-occupied zone of Germany, and went on to pursue a respectable political career in the Bundesrepublik after the Allied occupation of Germany ended.

In July 1945 the municipal council approved the plan of city architect Félix Bruneau for the reconstruction of the devastated urban area. The magnitude of the job was quantified in the 1946 census, which reported fifty-eight per cent of the population of Le Havre as homeless.[10] Of France's 38,000 municipalities, 1,838 were officially declared as having suffered damage to, or destruction of, a third of all their buildings, but Le Havre headed the list and was hailed as *'la ville martyre'* – France's most damaged city. However, the wishes of the population were ignored in Paris, where the Ministry for Reconstruction was so effectively lobbied by Auguste Perret, an aggressively vigorous proponent of reinforced concrete architecture, that he was given the job. Perret arrived in Le Havre with a team of eighteen disciples who, with the Ministry's backing, rode rough-shod over the wishes of the population. The result is today's 'skyscraper city'. Although no visitor can tell, it is built on a 1-metre-thick layer of rubble – all that remains of prewar Le Havre.

Festung Boulogne, the next port along the path of Montgomery's thrust north-east wards towards the Rhine, was commanded by Lieutenant-General Ferdinand Heim with a garrison of some 10,000 *Wehrmacht*, *Kriegsmarine* and *Luftwaffe* personnel. Among Heim's first acts, when taking command at the beginning of August, was a final, forced, evacuation – in which 8,000 civilians were sent out of the pocket for their own safety, leaving only 1,000 who would stay to the bitter end in the eastern sector of the town, the uninhabited western districts being a no-go zone for civilians. Planning to use the port to bring in supplies for his drive to Antwerp, Montgomery told Crerar, 'I want Boulogne badly.' Although the port itself was out of commission until 12 October, one of its beaches was used to site the continental terminal of another pipeline, dubbed Dumbo, bringing the vital motor fuel under the Channel from Britain, far closer to the advancing front than PLUTO.

Operation *Wellhit*, the ground attack on the German positions by a combined Canadian and British force, supported by heavy air raids that inevitably added to the destruction of the town and port being busily demolished by the *Kriegsmarine* engineers, did not begin until 17 September, by which time sufficient troops had arrived from Le Havre. On 18 September, as the first Canadian soldiers entered the outskirts of Boulogne, their welcome was cool and they were surprised that no particular gratitude was shown by the 1,000 people who had refused to leave in the evacuations. As local historian Guy Bataille commented, 'How could it be otherwise? Liberated we were, but we Boulonnais had no heart to make a song and dance about it. We had suffered too much for that.'[11]

After four days of fighting, Heim retreated to, of all places, Le Portel, where he surrendered on 22 September. Interrogated by Milton Schulman after arrival in Britain, Heim explained why he had not obeyed the to-the-last-man order of Hitler:

> It is difficult for Westerners to sacrifice our lives when the situation is hopeless and that is why my troops preferred to surrender, rather than die in their bunkers. The further east you go, the less people fear death: the Japanese not at all and the Russians not a great deal, either. In England and America, life is precious and in time of war you do everything, not to waste lives for no reason. We Germans are halfway between the two extremes.[12]

The returning population of Boulogne found a wasteland: of the 9,800 homes inhabited in 1939, 5,000 had been totally destroyed and 3,967 others were so damaged that only 533 remained fully habitable, leaving 25,000 people homeless and 24,000 others eking out an existence of sorts in what remained of their homes. The port was wrecked, with less than one in ten of the wharves usable, one crane out of sixty-one still working and every building demolished, every metre of railway track torn up. The scene of desolation was complete.

Next on the list of Channel ports to be liberated was Calais. On 6 September, Lt Col Schroeder, commanding *Festung* Calais, ordered a massive evacuation of civilians. As at Le Havre, hardly anybody complied. After 13 September, with no water, electricity or gas, the civilians stayed in their cellars and shelters night and day except for brief forays to specially organised public canteens, the only places where they could eat a hot meal. Besieged by the Canadians, the pocket then underwent artillery bombardments and massive raids by RAF Bomber Command on 20, 24, 25, 26, 27 and 28 September. To avoid the casualties of the final assault, which had been so horrific at Le Havre, the Red Cross arranged a mass evacuation of the civilian population on 29 September, which was followed by a massive artillery bombardment.

When the garrison surrendered on the following day, three-quarters of the town had been destroyed, but the suffering of the Calaisiens was not over. Five months later, on 27 February 1945, a force of American Mitchell bombers took off from nearby Vitry-en-Artois to bomb Dunkirk, where the German garrison was still holding out. Due to heavy cloud cover, most returned to base, but thirteen pilots glimpsed houses through gaps in the cloud at 17.30hrs. Believing themselves to be over Dunkirk, the pilots failed to ask themselves why, in that case, no anti-aircraft barrage was coming up at them. They dropped their loads on long-since liberated Calais. The body count was ninety-seven dead and 150 injured needing hospitalisation. For this gross error, Air Marshal Arthur Tedder in his capacity as C-in-C of Allied air forces in Europe personally apologised to General De Gaulle, now acting as the French Prime Minister.

Although not complete until January 1946, the gist of the Le Havre Bombing Analysis report was unofficially circulated earlier and decided Harris to oppose similar intensive bombing of the port of Flushing. On paper, he argued to Tedder that:

> Many civilian casualties will occur, especially as air raid shelters will be flooded. A similar instance occurred at Havre (sic), where many French civilians were killed and much damage done which did not materially help our forces to take the port.[13]

This did not stop the disastrous RAF raid on 5 January 1945 destroying the town of Royan at the head of the Gironde estuary in south-west France, when the town, crowded with refugees as well as its normal inhabitants, was targeted – and not the German positions on the perimeter of the pocket of resistance. The mission teletype clearly gave the object of the operation as *TO DESTROY TOWN STRONGLY FORTIFIED BY*

ENEMY AND OCCUPIED BY GERMAN TROOPS ONLY, when it was known that the German positions were *outside* the town.

A total of 1,576 tonnes of high-explosive and thirteen tons of incendiaries destroyed the town centre. Little damage was done to the 249 blockhouses on the perimeter of the Royan pocket. With napalm and conventional incendiaries used, the bodies of 284 female and 158 male French civilians – *and just thirty-seven German personnel*– were trapped, alive or dead, in the burning debris.[14] A final total of dead and wounded French civilians was rendered impossible by destruction of all the town's records in the raid, and the declared figures of the dead were modified as body parts were recovered during reconstruction up to five years later.

Allied embarrassment after the raid resulted in alibis ranging from poor visibility over the target confusing the marker aircraft to an accusation that the French casualties must have been *collabos* and deserved what they got. As to the first alibi, the town was clearly visible to the bomb-aimers during the raid, due to the target indicators and parachute flares. Even more embarrassingly, navigators' maps found in the seven Lancasters shot down by the German flak showed aiming points exclusively in the town area, where there were no German targets of importance.[15]

Chapter 19

The last town in France

Dunkirk was the next Channel port along the line of Montgomery's thrust. Its inhabitants were spared the agony of another *Astonia* – not in consideration of the casualties and damage to the town before, during and after the evacuation of the BEF in summer 1940, nor because De Gaulle's provisional government in Paris had protested strongly to the Allies at the scale of civilian casualties in the reduction of the Le Havre pocket.

Montgomery was in a race with the Americans in the central and southern thrusts, each of the several commanding generals hoping to be 'first in Berlin'. Since D-Day, the Allies had landed more than 2 million men in Normandy, suffering losses of 40,000 against *Wehrmacht* losses of 700,000. Monty decided on 15 September not to waste time and lives reducing Dunkirk, designated by Hitler as a no-surrender *Festung*, but to place all his bets on capturing Antwerp, which would give him his 'own' port of entry for supplies and reinforcements. He decided therefore that it was sufficient to leave a strong containing force around the Dunkirk pocket of resistance manned by a heterogeneous garrison of some 13,000 *Wehrmacht*, *Waffen-SS* and *Kriegsmarine* officers and men.[1]

Two days later, a joint British-Canadian force was probing the perimeter of the pocket and tidying up a few bulges and weak points on the line, with casualties on both sides. Further progress was made difficult by the extensive German minefields – in places flat *Teller* mines were laid three and four deep, one on top of the other – and the widespread flooding, renewed at each high tide to depths of up to five metres by the garrison opening the sea locks. The flooded areas limited the possible lines of attack and forced the besiegers to patrol much of the perimeter in assault boats and amphibious vehicles. Had there been any Allied intention to fight a way into Dunkirk town, further obstacles were provided by the numerous

235

canals, whose bridges were wired for demolition and defended by bunkers. In the heart of the town, there was a POW prison that eventually contained some sixty British, Canadian and French military personnel – and two US aircrew, one of whom might qualify as 'the luckiest guy in the war' after being shot down inside the severed rear turret of a B17 that landed in a minefield, from which he had been extracted by the garrison.

German fast patrol craft known as *S-Boote* guaranteed communications with the pocket after it was cut off to landward, bringing in supplies for the garrison by running the gauntlet of Royal Navy vessels while at sea and shelling by Allied artillery on the coast to the east of Dunkirk during their approach to the port, as well as air raids once moored in their concrete, supposedly bombproof, pens in the harbour.

In February 1944, when OKW was preparing for an Allied invasion somewhere between Calais and Dunkirk, 50,000 'useless mouths' had been forcibly evacuated from greater Dunkirk by the French authorities acting on German orders. A further evacuation was imposed on all males over the age of sixteen in the suburb of Rosendaël on 6 September, following an attack on a *Kriegsmarine* officer there two days previously by an ill-organised group of *résistants* in the *Voix du Nord* network – seven of whom were executed, including a father and son. One way and another, by the time the pocket was surrounded the civilian population had already been reduced to 25,000 people.

The garrison commander was Lieutenant-General Wolfgang Von Kluge, brother of the disgraced field marshal who had been implicated in the July plot, but *Kriegsmarine* units inside the pocket were commanded by 49-year-old Rear Admiral Friedrich Frisius, lately arrived from Boulogne. He was known to be no fanatical Nazi, despite his tall, slim, fair-haired, blue-eyed Aryan appearance. Before entering the navy as an 18-year-old cadet, his studies in German, Bible studies and mathematics would have better fitted him to follow in his father's footsteps as a Lutheran pastor. He went everywhere with a walking stick in his right hand, to avoid having to return the Hitler salutes of his subordinates, which he acknowledged with curt nods or not at all. Frisius was a career naval officer who had spent most of the war efficiently exercising various responsible functions along the Channel coast fortifications. In December 1942 his zeal was rewarded by the appointment to *Seekommandant* of the Pas de Calais region – commanding officer of all naval forces between Zeebrugge and the Somme. He was a man awaiting the call of destiny.

Fortunately for the record, Frisius kept a personal diary, in which he wrote up each day's events in the life of the German garrison of Dunkirk during the 8-month-long siege. Fortunately also, after the surrender on 9 May 1945, he was immediately flown without baggage to Special Camp 11 in Wales, where senior German officers were held for interrogation, and could therefore not take the diary with him. It was recovered after his departure and passed to the senior French naval officer in liberated Dunkirk. Twelve years later, he in turn delivered the manuscript diary to the naval archives service at Vincennes. Whether or not Admiral Frisius regretted leaving behind this rather personal document is unclear, but there is a postscript. Seven years after his departure from France a young German appeared at the villa outside Boulogne in which the

Commanding the garrison of Dunkirk, the devout Lutheran Admiral Friedrich Frisius refused to give the Nazi salute but hanged soldiers for defeatist talk.

admiral had been quartered during his stint as regional *Seekommandant*. Identifying himself as the son of Admiral Frisius, he said he had come to recover his father's suitcase, left there on the admiral's last-minute posting to Dunkirk on 3 September 1944. Was this some kind of attempt to recover also the diary? No one can say.

Extracts below from Frisius' diary[2] are revealing about the mindset of a fanatically obedient German commander. They are replete with pious thanks to God, worry about his family and descriptions of flowers, which he adored. As a naval officer, he noted the weather conditions on most days.

> <u>3 September 1944:</u> It's at least fifteen years since I kept a diary, and I'm starting again because it seems that these will be my last days and I feel a need to communicate to my wife and children my daily activities, although it is unlikely that this will ever reach them.

The journey this afternoon (after the posting to naval commander of the Dunkirk pocket) went as planned. The roads were full of retreating troops, a sight to break a soldier's heart. I never liked Dunkirk. It's true that the landscape resembles my own East Friesland, but the town has no character. It is ugly and made bleaker by the war damage. Nowhere is there a garden, however small, where flowers are lovingly grown. The intended size of the pocket of resistance was too small to hold out for long, which is why I did my best from Boulogne to push the Dunkirk perimeter outward. The work was just starting as I arrived. It may seem strange to my family that the *Kommandant* of the fortress is a colonel, whom I outrank, but ground warfare is the *Wehrmacht's* responsibility.

Frisius was an unforgiving perfectionist who frequently criticised the *Oberkommando der Kriegsmarine* (OKK). He also had a naval officer's disdain for all ground forces, considering most *Wehrmacht* officers incompetent and their men badly motivated and led. Nor was he polite about the failure of OKW to adapt to the changed realities in Normandy after the successful Allied landings.

15 September 1944: OKK asked me today over the radio whether I was prepared to take command here. I replied yes, on condition that I am sole commander, including the ground forces. I was aware that problems could arise immediately after I take control – as they did already this evening, when we had to give ground on the western perimeter. I cannot see why reinforcements were not rushed there from the central reserves. That's what you get for having two commanders!

16 September 1944: No decision yet on the question of handover of command. The morale of the ground forces is not good. From the top down, they are lethargic. As to whether this can be changed, time will tell.

It's been a magnificent autumn day, a clear blue sky and warm as summer, making me think of spending time with my family, going for a walk and picking fruit. What worries they must have. May the Lord God let them live and be in good health.

<u>17 September 1944:</u> This afternoon fighter-bombers dropped bombs on the HQ area, blowing my door off its hinges and onto the bunk where I was taking my siesta. I suffered no damage, but our so-called mess was a shambles. Bad news from Boulogne. It seems that the British have penetrated into the town.

<u>18 September 1944:</u> Shortly before 11.00hrs a Frenchman appeared to ask for our surrender, which was, of course, refused. I learned later that this was the result of the divisional commander sending the mayor of Rosendaël to the British to arrange the evacuation of civilians on his own initiative. With the mayor able to tell the British how things are here, is there a better way of giving intelligence to the enemy?

This evening a flotilla of S-boats arrived with munitions and hospital supplies. The crews made an excellent impression on me: calm and keen. They departed during darkness, taking with them General Von Kluge and his adjutant. I thank God for letting the boats come and leave safely. A somewhat unique occurrence, to spirit away in the middle of combat a general whose soldiers are surrounded by the enemy. Command passed (automatically) to the senior regimental officer, a likeable fellow, but no tough commander. Are they going to make me commander-in-chief of the pocket?

<u>19 September 1944:</u> Sky overcast, not so good for the fighter-bombers. The new so-called *Kommandant* came to present his compliments. On the ground in front of the HQ, which already looks to me like a prison camp, a single dahlia is growing. Although it is in the shade, it has a singular beauty, and a mixture of colours: dark violet, bright red and white. I found an important bridge, prepared for demolition, but with the charges gone. We should hang those responsible for this situation and not their subordinates. With great joy I heard over the radio that our blockade runners made it safely home.

<u>20 September 1944:</u> In late afternoon the *Kommandant* and his adjutant came to visit. I asked them to inform me before any important decisions, so that I could make my views known to them. After an embarrassing silence, they agreed.

A truce arranged through the Red Cross enabled another 6,000 Dunquerquois to leave the pocket. Frisius was not above interfering in the defence of Boulogne, which was no longer his responsibility.

<u>21 September 1944:</u> My cold, due to always sitting in draughts, seems to be getting better. During the afternoon, the enemy penetrated into Wimereux (a suburb of Boulogne) and forced Dieckmann to retreat. I radioed him to fight his way through to the nearest battery. During the evening I learned from Schilling that Dieckmann was trying to get through to him – thus heading in the wrong direction. Since we lost radio communication, there was nothing I could do. I am now very worried for his honour as a soldier. Even if he has not deserted, he has abandoned his position and his men. I trust he has good reasons for this, which I shall require him to furnish.

<u>22 September 1944:</u> Dieckmann broke through to Schilling with 250 men, which confirms my worries for his honour. He had three dead and thirty wounded, and considers the 500-strong attacking force took 120 dead and numerous wounded. Why, in that case, did he retreat?

In early afternoon I was named *Festungskommandant* of Dunkirk. Now I have a mission – unfortunately at an unfavourable moment because Boulogne has practically fallen, which will permit the enemy to move more forces here. One thing alone gives me confidence: I have so often wondered why the Lord God has allowed me to emerge unscathed from so many dangerous situations. And why have I never really had a combat command during the war? I can see now that this means He has spared me for this task, with which He is testing me.

The weather is beautiful: sunny and warm with a slight drizzle.

On that day, Boulogne surrendered to the Canadians. In Dunkirk, a bomb killed the senior *Wehrmacht* army officer and wounded his staff, so that the new *Festungskommandant* had no direct chain of command to the ground forces until replacements were appointed. Frisius commented:

> This made me wonder whether the Lord God wanted to make my task here nearly impossible. Did He intend to make me a laughing stock by letting the enemy carry out a successful attack at the very moment of my taking command and transferring the HQ with all the organisational changes made necessary by the loss of these important officers? Then everybody could point the finger at the (new commander) of the fortress. These thoughts really got me down until, God be praised, my confidence in the Lord God and my mission gained the upper hand. Perhaps He wanted only to clear the way and enable me to organise everything as it should be.

> 23 September 1944: A few salvoes of enemy artillery fire in the night. In the morning I felt calm, and immediately reorganised the HQ staff. Enormous resistance to my taking command, which was concealed, of course. But I shall be ruthless and establish a clear chain of command with as few intermediate HQs as possible. It will take a few days yet, but then I shall have a smoothly running machine, although at the moment I still have to commute between the naval and army HQs, each time running the gauntlet of attack from the air and crossing three bridges that are regularly shelled.

> 24 September 1944: The air is cool, sky overcast, strong wind. My first action in my new post was to attend the funeral of (the two officers killed by the bomb). I had ordered minimum attendance and forbidden commanding officers to come, since the cemetery is exposed to enemy fire and I did not want to risk losing them for sentimental reasons. But I myself attended so that the troops could see that I placed myself in danger to honour their late commander.

> 25 September 1944: Weather stormy and overcast but improving. I forgot to mention my visit to the hospital, where

241

there are 300 wounded, some seriously, for whom I made a special allocation of food from our limited stocks.

27 September 1944: Bright intervals and a strong wind, thus many attacks by fighter-bombers, which made it necessary to get back swiftly under cover each time I went out. News from Calais and Cap Gris Nez – the fighting is over and men like Schilling, Dieckmann (and others) are dead or taken prisoner, although I still hope that some may have escaped. I have given up hope of reinforcements/supplies getting through to us. The mosquitoes are a plague here. The best thing is that I am gradually freeing more men for duty on the perimeter. It is difficult, but I must persist.

On 30 September Frisius was congratulating himself in the diary for freeing 370 men from the central areas for service at the perimeter and splitting up units with a poor fighting spirit. He continued:

Had I taken command earlier, all this could have been done a fortnight ago. As it is, we can undertake only small-scale raids to bring back prisoners (for interrogation). The troops' low morale is the cause of the failure of the operations I ordered. But I think a wind of change is blowing. Good leadership always brings its fruits. This evening I received a signal confirming my promotion to Vice-Admiral. I hope that my wife and children hear of it. It's all the more pleasurable because I had long since renounced all hope of this promotion. It would be wonderful if we could (somehow) get out of the pocket.

The following day, all the senior officers of the garrison came to congratulate him on his promotion, but Frisius' disdain for the *Wehrmacht* was plain in the diary entry:

In the course of the evening Colonel Wittstadt got so drunk that he could neither speak nor think and passively resisted all attempts to make him leave. Finally I threw him out at 04.00hrs. I stayed sober as befitted my new responsibility. All this confirmed my feelings that the *Wehrmacht* officers get drunk more easily than we do in the *Kriegsmarine*. They are simply less civilised.

Inside the pocket, he entered on a furious reassessment of the defences, moving units, re-siting artillery, stationing on the perimeter supposedly elite *Kampfgruppen* composed of men from units that had ceased to exist in the fighting since D-Day and stepping up the toughness of the battle school that was training groups of commandos to raid the Allied lines at night, bringing back prisoners for interrogation and identifying new targets for the German artillery. The garrison soon found that he would accept nothing less than perfection and, since the quality of the different units under his command varied widely, there was considerable friction between Frisius and his officers.

2 October 1944: After a visit to the front that necessitated a half-hour walk at risk from Allied fighters but no artillery fire, in the evening we received a letter from the enemy HQ via the Red Cross agreeing to the evacuation of the remaining civilians and asking permission to send a representative to arrange the details. This means that the bombing will intensify. I was always against these evacuations for that reason, but since General von Kluge made the offer I could hardly refuse because that would have been used as propaganda against us. It is always an error to initiate dealings with the enemy. General von Kluge and his staff had not learned this lesson and I must carry the can.

3 October 1944: It's a pity that I can't have my vice-admiral's insignia brought here, although they have very kindly parachuted the German Cross in gold. The evacuation truce began at 18.00hrs. In the beneficial calm I took a long walk.

4 October 1944: Just before dinner, I took a bath in the hospital. The water was a dark brown and, to tell the truth, it was all rather rudimentary, but still refreshing. In the evening the enemy negotiator returned, making problems about the wounded. He wanted to take only English (sic) wounded. I refused and said we were handing over severely wounded

Civilians leaving Dunkirk after hearing what happened at Le Havre.

regardless of their nationality. I also refused an exchange of prisoners because we should have received only deserters in return. My refusal means that the enemy will be killing his own men here when bombing us. It is plain that most Englishmen (sic) are not gentlemen.

The truce of 5 October saw most of the remaining civilians leave the pocket, having heard what had happened to those who did not leave Le Havre in time. Between 6 and 9 October Major-General Alois Liska's Czechoslovak Independent Armoured Brigade Group (CIABG) took over the perimeter. The Czechs were deliberately allotted the stay-behind task because the Allied High Command foresaw a problem with the anti-Soviet attitude of Liska's men, should they be allowed to confront the advancing Red Army whilst it was 'liberating' their homeland. CIABG's strength of 4,260 men was complemented by miscellaneous British, Canadian and French units. Local knowledge was provided by several hundred FFI men, many from the Communist networks, to whom De Gaulle had given the choice of continuing the fight by enlisting in uniform for the duration of hostilities or going to prison. By comparison with regular Allied troops, they were unfit and undernourished, not being placed on the official ration strength until 1 January 1945. They were also poorly trained and ill-disciplined for regular warfare: at the end of January 1945 a whole company of 200 men went AWOL for several days, to visit their families and/or simply live it up in Lille.

Liska's little army had its own armour, plus tracked and half-tracked personnel carriers, some of them amphibious. Its anti-aircraft batteries had few *Luftwaffe* targets, but could use air-burst shells to break up German infantry attacks. To any logical civilian mind, there was no point in the garrison holding out any longer, with the front already 200 kilometres to the east at Antwerp. But Frisius was not a Von Schlieben, the *Kommandant* of *Festung* Cherbourg who considered his men's lives more important than a senseless order from OKW.

The truce had to be extended until 6 October after the main bridge being used by the evacuees collapsed under the unaccustomed load. Among the 17,522 Dunqerquois evacuated were all young men of military age, whom the *Feldgendarmerie* rightly suspected of including numerous *résistants* and potential trouble-makers. The few civilians left in Dunkirk were either too old to be moved, or were employed in the fish factory, where locally caught herrings were smoked, the beet-sugar refinery or otherwise in the vast machinery of food production for the thousands of Germans in the garrison, whose morale plummeted after this final evacuation. To counter the natural assumption that they were in for a long and arduous siege under a commander to whom the vow of obedience to Hitler was a sacred oath, Frisius went on a tour of units, particularly at the front, telling the men that they would only have to hold out until the end of October before being relieved. Whilst he may have convinced himself of this, there was no military likelihood of it, as the officers at least must have realised.

> 5 October 1944: This evening I had to sign yet another death sentence. An NCO had been making defeatist propaganda, exceeding the worst English leaflets and radio broadcasts.[3] The NCO confessed and was sentenced to be confined to quarters. I twice refused to confirm the sentence

and summoned a court martial. Since I am trying to raise morale among the garrison – and it is really poor – anyone in the fortress defying my efforts is a traitor who deserves death. In any case, I have no men to spare to guard him or ensure he ceases his demoralising work. Sad for his family, but necessary.

On 6 October Frisius was complaining about the problem of getting his laundry done. On the following day, his main complaint was that the garrison was reluctant to fight. He summoned the commanding officers, who told him outright that their men were demoralised and saw no point in dying for a cause that was already lost. Frisius was determined to overcome this. His consolation was reading a family Bible that his grandmother had packed in his luggage, especially the 103rd Psalm. It is hard to see why, unless the lines that appealed to him were: *As for a man, his days are as grass, for he flourisheth as the flower of the field; the wind passeth over and it is gone.*

Believing only the official, rigorously censored, German news broadcasts, he seems to have been completely out of touch with the truth of Germany's dire situation, particularly the shortage of fuel due to Allied bombing that kept most of the *Luftwaffe* grounded and most submarines in base. When an Allied convoy sailed past *en route* for Ostend, he railed against the failure of OKK to send out a wolf pack and destroy it – as he did against the *Luftwaffe* for failing to send fifty fighters to attack the swarms of Allied bombers that strafed the German positions and pounded Dunkirk into dust day after day.

Given the permeable nature of much of the perimeter, it was not difficult for desperate or simply discontented *Wehrmacht* men to 'get left behind' on the Allied side of the lines when on a night patrol. Some deserted singly; others in groups. Another way of achieving the same aim, with less risk if it should go wrong, was simply not to resist an Allied attack. In this way, on 28 October almost a whole battalion allowed itself to be taken prisoner. Frisius blamed the poor quality of the officers and consoled himself with the thought that he was better off without such subordinates.

To supplement the stock of rations, no less than 170 acres of potatoes and 500 acres of grain were grown, with another 400 acres producing fodder for the 400 cattle, kept for slaughter, and the 800 horses, used both for transport and meat. Fishing from boats salvaged in the harbour was also practised when the weather permitted, as was the use of *carrelets* – nets in square frames that were let down into the watercourses and craned rapidly up when fish swam over them. Officers also shot game birds on the marshes. In theory, everything was to be handed into central stores. Frisius' disapproval of private enterprise in this respect did not stop him eating rather better than most of his men on occasion.

The occasional courageous *Luftwaffe* pilot overflew the pocket, dropping canisters of food and medical supplies, as well as bags of mail, many of which fell into the flooded areas, with disastrous results. Even the roads within the fortress were flooded to a depth of one metre. Frisius learned on 25 November that his elder daughter had become engaged to the son of Admiral Erich Förste and was continuing her studies at university. Mail from home is a prime source of the fighting man's morale but, as their commander recorded in the diary, unfortunately, many of his men received no mail.

On 30 November, his main concern was that there was not enough fodder for all the 1,000 horses used on the farms. It would be necessary to slaughter a great number in order to feed the others. The dilemma was what to do with the meat, in the absence of any cold store or even sufficient salt to preserve it. As usual, he laid the blame on previous commanders, who ought to have arranged things better. Two days later, he commented on a new weapon, which appears to have been a forerunner of the cluster bomb:

> 2 November 1944: Cool, overcast, good visibility, cold westerly wind. Aircraft have been bothering us more lately, both fighters and bombers – the latter with a new and dangerous (!) tactic. The bombers come over singly at such high altitude that you can't hear or see them – and, if you do, they are taken for reconnaissance flights. Suddenly they release their bombs in the form of a container suspended beneath a parachute. After reaching a certain altitude, the container opens and releases thirty or forty little bombs of about 2kg each that land all over the place. What makes this so dangerous is that the bombs hit the ground long after the passage of the aircraft. If one is not vigilant, it seems that all is safe when the real danger is just beginning.[4]

It ill behoved a German officer to complain of this, since the original such weapon was the German *Sprengbombe Dickwandig*, also of 2kg, first used in a raid on Ipswich in 1940. Known as 'butterfly bombs' from their strange shape after deployment of the fins, as many as 108 were packed into the container, some having delayed-action or anti-tamper fuses.

3 November was the first day of Advent, prompting Frisius to reflect on what the years of National Socialism had done to Christianity in Germany, even before the start of the war:

> The majority of priests were unconvincing, the churches empty. Completely lacking was the magic of a full congregation all praying together. Will the war change all that? Will the magic come back? And when? We must wait and see.

On 5 December he discovered that illicit distillation of schnapps by his troops was widespread, and ordered the senior officers to stamp out this practice. At the same time, his orderly was scouring deserted houses to find toothpicks, toothpaste, crockery and other creature comforts left behind by the evacuees. On 8 December there was a barrack concert, which Frisius found 'nice but too long'. Of two soldiers who acquitted themselves convincingly, playing the female parts, he commented with no apparent irony, 'I am not exactly certain that they are very good soldiers.'

His tours of inspection were complicated by the fact that some units were composed largely of Alsatians – whose homes had been liberated by the American advance, and who were therefore legally French citizens again – and of Poles and Russians who could not speak German. The state of mind of these men, trapped in German uniform and fighting for a cause which was not theirs, is easy to imagine.

On 26 December, rumours were circulating among the German troops in Dunkirk that Hitler's Ardennes offensive, aimed at recovering the port of Antwerp from the Allies,[5] would sweep westwards far enough to relieve Dunkirk. Frisius was more concerned with the fact that the officers' mess had nothing of the ambiance of a wardroom. Each officer left as soon as he had eaten, prompting Frisius to deplore that alcohol and tobacco were necessary for men to relax together after a meal. He likewise inveighed against soldiers who poached or otherwise obtained extra food illicitly – something he was determined to stamp out. Frisius' killjoy philosophy extended also to the hospital, where he considered the doctors lacking in discipline. As for the few women still working there, he wrote:

> I learned by chance that they spend the night with the men. Cars are even sent to collect them and take them home about 05.00hrs. I intervened very forcibly, imposing a celibate regime and told the senior doctor that, if I heard of any other such errors, I should install a military commander in the hospital, to ensure my orders were obeyed.

The year ended with him yearning for prewar *Sylvesternacht* celebrations: a candle-lit church packed for the midnight mass, and the journey home along snow-covered streets to the sound of church bells. Reality was his stiff and mirthless officers' mess, where everyone listened at midnight to Goebbels telling them how well the war was going, followed by Hitler's equally irrelevant speech. Everyone present was 'very serious', not surprisingly, since the Ardennes offensive had visibly failed – and with it Germany's last desperate gamble that might just have relieved the pocket. There was no further point to be served by continuing to hold out, but Frisius had sworn an oath.

On New Year's Day, visiting some wounded officers, Frisius went ballistic on learning that two girls with VD and a Russian had escaped from the hospital. The girls were soon caught, but the Russian vanished and Frisius implemented his threat to impose a military commander over the medical staff. The nearest he came to relaxing in the whole eight months of the siege came on 17 January, when his birthday was celebrated with the entire headquarters staff:

> Given our living conditions, it was an almost unjustifiable meal. I nearly forbade it. First, there was an entrée of smoked herring, then starling soup, then roast cod. At last, the turkey and – because it was insufficient for sixteen people – two hares also. There was also a pudding. Although not all from the rations, it seemed to me excessive. But they told me that one only celebrates his fiftieth birthday in an encircled fortress once in a lifetime!

In February Frisius decided to group all the remaining civilians in three internment camps within the pocket, not because they represented any threat, but for their own safety, the coordinates having been communicated to the Allied artillery. There were thus 571 people living in theoretically safe but restricted conditions, plus 173 old people in a retirement home run by the Little Sisters of the Poor at Rosendaël.

Even Frisius was depressed after two aggressive patrols achieved nothing except the loss of every man in them. With continuous Allied loudspeaker propaganda all along the perimeter, desertion continued to sap the garrison's strength. Unsuccessful attempts were summarily judged by court martials handing down sentences of death, as on 20 February 1945, when personnel passing through the town centre were treated to the sight of a former comrade hanging from a gibbet on the second floor of the gutted town hall.

What effect on morale the awards of Iron Crosses and other decorations had is impossible to judge, but Frisius continued to go through the motions of conferring promotions and awards. After one such ceremony on 3 March he was nearly killed when several shells exploded on his way back to HQ, causing him to reflect yet again that the Lord was preserving him for tasks as yet unknown. On 28 March two two–man midget submarines arrived, laden with batteries, Teller mines and blocks of lard. That evening, he invited the two officers and two NCOs to dine with him, but the evening was spoiled when his guests explained how little submarines could do to help the *Festung*.

And so life dragged on for the men in the pocket: boredom and hunger, interspersed with death from a random shell or a bomb, or in one of the raids that Frisius insisted on continuing, despite the mounting casualties and the fact that any ground gained had soon to be relinquished:

> 1 May 1945: We learned this afternoon that the Führer is dead and that Grand Admiral Dönitz has succeeded him. One cannot dismiss the meaning of Adolf Hitler's life. Fate has been cruel to him. His aims were pure, but perhaps he had grown presumptive, or even took himself for God, at least in the early days. Who knows whether he blasphemed or tolerated blasphemy? Yet, does Stalin not offend God every day? Are not the Anglo-Americans sacrilegious? Will the German people emerge purified from their ordeal?

On 5 May Allied aircraft dropped over the pocket hundreds of copies of that day's *Nachrichten für die Truppen* (*News for the Troops*), a German-language paper that reported surrenders everywhere: Hamburg had been declared an open city to save it from further destruction; in Mecklenburg on the Baltic coast German forces had laid down their arms; the commanders of the southern armies had signed a surrender document; in the north, British armoured columns had already reached Denmark.

At midnight on 5 May, German-speaking officers in Laska's HQ heard over a captured German radio set that OKW was sending a negotiating team to Reims, to agree the details of the general surrender of all German forces. Having already written in the diary that further resistance was pointless, had Frisius been sane, he would almost certainly have at least offered a cease-fire until the outcome of the negotiations was known. Instead, he ordered the positions of the besiegers to be pummelled night and day with every calibre of shell in the garrison's ammunition dumps. For two days and two nights it was unsafe to move about above ground in the Allied lines and men died for no military reason whatever.

> <u>7 May 1945:</u> My chief of staff and several other officers came to persuade me to initiate surrender negotiations because the continuing heavy shelling is costing lives every day and because the men cannot be relied on, now they know that the Grand Admiral has said there is no point in continuing the fight against the western powers at the cost of further German blood being shed.
>
> I made (the officers) understand that we have only our honour to lose and must be prepared to sacrifice victims for that. If we wait a few days and receive orders to capitulate, our honour will be intact. We shall be able to hold our heads high because we shall not have been beaten. My effort succeeded, but left me exhausted. I have spent every effort to influence the soldiers, but all they want to do is give up. I have given orders to those I can trust to shoot any cowards, as may be necessary.

The surrender of the German forces in north-western Europe had been signed at Montgomery's headquarters on Lüneburg Heath on 4 May. After the official surrender of all German forces was signed at Eisenhower's headquarters in Reims, in the presence of Soviet, British,

American and French representatives, the war in Europe was officially ended at midnight on 8 May.

Even Frisius could not argue with fate the next day, when orders were finally received from OKK in Flensburg to surrender the pocket. After meeting two Allied officers in the hospital to discuss the details, at 09.00hrs on 9 May he was driven in an Allied vehicle to Liska's HQ and there signed the document surrendering the pocket. As a senior officer, he asked for the traditional courtesy of being allowed to keep his side arm and personal possessions, and to be accompanied into captivity by his orderly. Permission was refused on the grounds that he was to be immediately flown to Britain for interrogation, with no space on the aircraft for more than one small item of hand luggage. Whatever that item was, it did not contain the diary.

While Frisius' troops were rounded up and despatched to POW camps, with the exception of sapper teams kept back to help lift, and dispose of, all the thousands of mines and other munitions inside the pocket, the inhabitants of Dunkirk were returning on foot, hitching lifts on trucks and old farm carts, to find a wasteland where their homes had been. Even after the streets were cleared of the millions of tons of rubble blocking them, it seemed impossible that the town could ever live again. Of the

Frisius reduced the major town of Dunkirk to a wasteland. After the rubble was cleared, only the widest street lines survived.

3,362 residential buildings, 1,524 were completely destroyed and a further 805 so damaged as to be uninhabitable. As at Le Havre, but using different materials, the architects imposed by the Ministry of Reconstruction and Town Planning for the reconstruction that lasted three decades paid little attention to the wishes of the Dunquerquois. Outside the urban area, returning farmers found many of their livestock dead and, even worse, their fields rendered sterile for years by the successive inundations in salt water.

The pointless eight-month siege of Dunkirk had cost German losses of some 1,000 dead and 890 taken prisoner in various raids, with 11,238 eventually surrendering one day *after the end of the war*. On the other side of the lines, casualties were 167 dead, 461 wounded and 40 missing in action.

Has one man's perverted sense of honour ever cost more casualties for no military gain at all? Sadly, the answer is yes, but not in recent European military history.

Epilogue

The first seed of this book was sown when the *assistant français* at my grammar school told a class of the complete destruction of Caen, his home town, by the Allied air forces in the summer of 1944 with the loss of thousands of innocent lives. Some know-it-all said, 'No, that must have been the *Luftwaffe*.' But it wasn't. This was the first I had heard of it, for it was not a subject for public discussion in postwar Britain.

The point of the anecdote is that, long before Professor Lindemann was able to 'raise doubts' in Churchill's mind about bombing accuracy in late 1941, RAF Bomber Command aircrew knew – even if they did not talk about it – that most bombs were dropped well wide of the target. The reasons ranged from an understandable desire to spend as little time as possible coned by searchlights over the target in an aircraft lurching and bumping through air disturbed by near misses – and where the next shell-burst might not be a miss – to badly positioned TIs, bombs jettisoned because of a reluctance to return to base with them still on board and a host of other reasons which may sound inadequate when set out in black and white, yet be totally compelling at the time.

Few Bomber Command aircrew can have been surprised by D.M. Butt's examination of 4,065 photographs taken on raids, proving statistically that three-quarters of the aircraft on a 'good' raid dropped their loads wide by five miles or more. As Churchill wrote, *'The air photographs showed how little damage was being done (to the target)'*.[1] Even that appalling record of inaccuracy was for nights with moon and good visibility. On nights with no moon, only one in twenty got even that close. When their targets were in or near built-up areas of occupied France, the implications in terms of civilian deaths were obvious.

Certainly, 'Bomber' Harris knew the score when he replaced Sir Richard Peirse as chief of Bomber Command after the Butt Report. It is impossible today to put oneself into the mind of Harris, who by day and by night sent thousands of his own men to face death in the skies with the result that, although containing approximately seven per cent of British military manpower during the war, Bomber Command suffered a quarter of all British military deaths.[2] How could Harris allow thoughts of collateral civilian casualties to distract him from the job in hand when no other air force at the time could prove a better record of placing bombs on the target and not miles away from it?

True, there was in place the policy that the priority and the choice of targets were 'established with great care for the well-being of the population in these countries' and that 'pilots failing to observe these rules lay themselves open to severe penalties'. But, what use is a policy if it cannot be enforced? In the case of Le Portel, because the Fort de Couppes to the north of the town and Cap d'Alprech to the south of the town were extremely close to built-up areas, reference was made in the planning stage at the Air Ministry and COSSAC to the policy laid down by the Assistant Chief of Air Staff (Policy) in the previous October, but reference to a noble policy made no difference to the ignoble execution of the raid.

Churchill's predictions in April and May 1944 that 'scores of thousands of French civilians' would be killed or injured in the area bombing of Norman towns before and after D-Day were simply brushed aside, with Eisenhower accusing him of 'grossly exaggerating' the figures. In fact, they were an under-estimate. Nor did the protests of Lt Gen James H. Doolittle, commanding US Eighth Air Force, achieve anything. Having led the first raid on the Japanese home islands, he was no shrinking violet, but his experience in the Italian campaign indicated that area bombing of enemy-held towns before the ground attack went in both killed large numbers of civilians and was of questionable military value because, if it prevented the enemy moving troops to the front, it obviously also prevented Allied wheeled and tracked vehicles moving swiftly after the retreating enemy. Leigh-Mallory's threat to resign trumped Doolittle's voice of experience and twenty Norman towns were bombed flat after D-Day. Even that was six fewer towns than Montgomery had asked for.

Bishop Bell did not have the support of his fellow-prelates of the Church of England because war is a moral no-man's land, whether it be launched 'against tyranny' (Second World War), 'to make the world safe for democracy' (Cold War) or 'against terror' (Iraq and Afghanistan). As a churchman, Bell was in a privileged position to make his protests against civilian casualties, but the senior service commanders were under military discipline and extreme pressure from their political masters to get results fast with the minimum losses in Allied personnel, already unacceptably high soon after D-Day in some units by today's standards, due to the tenacity of the German resistance.

The same thinking ran all the way down the chain of command. During the reduction of the German pocket of resistance at Le Havre in September 1944, local Allied commanders like British Lieutenant General Crocker and Canadian General Crerar were faced with a morally insoluble equation: *how many of my men do I want to see killed or maimed, for the sake of an unknown number of civilians who may be killed, maimed or made homeless in the preparatory bombing of our objective?*

Crocker was personally concerned to minimise casualties among his own combat-exhausted men, some units of which had lost more than half their strength in the two months since landing in Normandy. His final ground assault was delayed by logistics. Had he known that it would also have to be postponed by two further days because of the weather, he might have agreed to give Wildermuth forty-eight hours for a general evacuation, but at the time of the parleys he could not know that the weather was about to change for the worse. Once it did, he was under even greater pressure to 'get the job done'. In any case, he could reasonably ask why the civilians were still inside the pocket, when they had had plenty of time to leave it – which leads to a perhaps unvoiced assumption that they 'had it coming to them'.

General 'Bubbles' Barker cannot have been the only Allied officer in the sector who knew that the town centre being targeted was inhabited by civilians with few German military personnel at risk there, but even he must have been horrified when the on-the-ground RAF Bombing Analysis evaluation of the *Astonia* raids concluded that the air raids of 5 September and later probably contributed nothing to the success of the ground attack because they killed just nine German personnel and did little damage to German defences – at a cost of 5,000 French civilian deaths.

At that point even De Gaulle's cold rationale that thousands of French civilians must die from 'friendly fire' in the liberation of their country wavered. As did Harris' previously unflinching determination to use area bombing as a tactical weapon when it was proposed to bomb Flushing flat.

By then, however, it was too late to save the 130,000-plus Normans killed or severely injured by British and American air raids, without counting the vastly larger numbers traumatised, made homeless, bereaved, orphaned, rendered insane or otherwise damaged in the raids.

Acknowledgements

Occupation by a foreign power is not an episode of history in which a nation takes pride. The many museums in northern France recording the Allied liberation of 1944–5 are big tourist attractions, but the few museums dedicated to the occupation are closing down, one by one, for lack of support after receiving little encouragement from local, regional and national authorities.

In the European community, history is constantly being re-written to avoid upsetting yesterday's enemies who are today's commercial and political partners. Thus, when French memorials to local people who died in front of German firing squads are refurbished after more than seven decades of weathering, the wording is sometimes changed. Instead of the crystal-clear *fusillés par les Allemands* – shot by the Germans – French mayors may decide to exonerate today's partners across the Rhine and change the wording to, for example, *tués par l'occupant* – killed by the occupiers. In a generation or two, will anyone remember what that means?

There was also, for many years after the Second World War, a long silence on both sides of the Channel about the embarrassing fact that France's British and American allies killed far more civilians in the north of the country than the Germans ever did.

As the survivors of France's war become rarer, it is more important than ever to record their experiences. For their help in various ways, I salute Philippe Delaurin, who invested his own money and many years of his life to run an unsubsidised museum of the occupation, and freely gave me the benefit of his extensive knowledge. Professor Andrew Knapp, Director of European Studies at the University of Reading, generously allowed me access to his comprehensive on-the-ground research as a post-graduate student in Le Havre. Fellow BBC pensioners Don Craven

258

and Brian Johnson unravelled for me the origins of the Morse V-sign used for so many broadcasts to occupied Europe. Major Len Chaganis dug up material on Operation *Cockade* and Chris 'Biggles' Turner identified aircraft in fuzzy photographs and unearthed sources aviational. I am grateful that historians Robert Aron, Annie Lacroix-Riz and Robert Paxton have kept open the windows on France in the Second World War. My greatest gratitude and admiration is reserved for Guy Bataille in Boulogne, R-G. Nobécourt in Rouen, J. Guillemard in Le Havre and other local historians who overcame their terror to record the events they lived through.

At Pen and Sword Books Ltd, for this edition I should like to thank commissioning editor Claire Hopkins, production manager Janet Brookes and copy-editor Graham Smith.

With all this help, it goes without saying that any errors are mine alone.

Douglas Boyd,
Gironde, south-west France,
Summer 2019

Further Reading in English

R. Atkin *Dieppe 1942* London, Macmillan 1980

D. Boyd *De Gaulle – the man who defied six US Presidents* Stroud, The History Press 2013

D. Boyd *Voices from the Dark Years* Thrupp, Sutton 2007

G. Corrigan *Blood, Sweat and Arrogance* London, Phoenix 2007

M. Cumming *The Starkey Sacrifice* Thrupp, Sutton 1996

T. Draper *The Six Weeks' War* London, Methuen 1946

M.R.D. Foot *Resistance* London, Eyre Methuen 1976

A. Furse *Wilfrid Freeman* Staplehurst, Spellmount 2000

J. Haswell *The Intelligence and Deception of the D-Day Landings* London, Batsford 1979

M. Lindsay *So Few Got Through* London, Arrow 1970

H. Probert *Bomber Harris* London, Greenhill 2006

A. de Saint-Exupéry *Flight to Arras* London, Pan 1975

Notes and Sources

All translations are by the author, unless otherwise attributed.

All illustrations are from the author's collection.

Every effort has been made to trace copyright owners. In the event of any infringement, please communicate with the author, care of the publishers.

Introduction

1. W.S. Churchill *The Second World War*, *Vol V* London, Penguin Classics 2005, pp. 456–7
2. W. Shakespeare *King Henry V* Act III, Scene I (abridged)

Chapter 1

1. E.R. May *Strange Victory* New York, Hill and Wang 2002, p. 477
2. ibid, p. 309
3. ibid, p. 388
4. G. Corrigan *Blood, Sweat and Arrogance* London, Phoenix 2007, p. 252
5. Report by E. A. Montague in *Manchester Guardian* of 29 May 1940 (abridged)
6. W.S. Churchill *The Second World War*, *Vol II* London, Penguin Classics 2005, p. 103
7. B. Myers *Captured* London, Harrap 1941, pp. 22, 23, 58
8. E. Williams (ed) *The Escapers* London, Collins/Eyre & Spottiswoode 1953, pp. 270–88

9. Deported to Bergen-Belsen in 1944, he survived and returned to France, but not to political life.
10. *1940 La Défaite* Paris, Tallandier 1978, pp. 284–5
11. ibid, p. 288
12. ibid, p. 300 (abridged)
13. See Corrigan, pp. 172–270 for a comprehensive account of troop movements May–June 1940

Chapter 2

1. C.D. Freeman and D. Cooper *The Road to Bordeaux* London, Readers' Union & Cresset Press 1942, p. 189
2. A. de St-Exupéry *Flight to Arras* London, Pan 1975, pp. 71–75 (abridged)
3. H. Amouroux *La Vie des Français sous l'Occupation*, *Vol 1* Paris, Fayard 1961, pp. 15–16
4. Article by J. Tronel in *Arkheia Revue No 20* Castelsarrasin 2008
5. ibid *Revue No 22* 2010
6. Amouroux, *Vol 1*, p. 25
7. See Article 5 of the agreement between Bousquet and Oberg dated 16 April 1943.
8. Article by L. Chambrun et al in *L'Express* 10 October 2005
9. H. Le Boterf *La Vie Parisienne sous l'Occupation*, *Vol 3* Geneva, Famot 1979, p. 241
10. Except in a few sections of the Maginot Line, which held out pointlessly for a few days.
11. For a comprehensive description of the defeat as experienced by civilians, see D. Boyd *Voices from the Dark Years* Thrupp, Sutton 2007, pp. 1–89
12. *La Défaite*, p. 280
13. P. Burrin *Living with Defeat* London, Arnold 1996, p. 253
14. *La Défaite*, p. 492
15. ibid, p. 293 (abridged)
16. Quoted in H. Diamond *Fleeing Hitler* Oxford, OUP 2007, p. 123
17. P. Webster *Pétain's Crime* London, Pan 2001, p. 88
18. Burrin, p. 420

Chapter 3

1. R. Chaussois *Le Dernier Round* quoted in E. Florentin *Quand les Alliés bombardaient la France* Paris, Perrin 2008, p. 610
2. D. Pryce-Jones *Paris in the Third Reich* London, Collins 1981, p. 63
3. Amouroux, *Vol 1*, p. 263
4. ibid, p. 221
5. T. Kernan *France on Berlin Time* New York & Philadelphia, Lippincott 1941, p. 36
6. Amouroux, *Vol 1*, pp. 201, 208
7. Pryce-Jones, p.94
8. H. Diamond *Women in the Second World War in France* London, Longman 1999, p.23
9. Article by L. Chabrun in *L'Express* 10 October 2005
10. ibid
11. Le Boterf, *Vol 3*, p. 7
12. Testimonies of Admirals Schniewind, Schulz, Boehm, Kranke and Schuster in G.H. & R. Bennett *Hitler's Admirals* Annapolis, Naval Institute Press 2004, pp. 32–5, 43–5, 49, 78–9, 138

Chapter 4

1. W.S. Churchill *The Second World War, Vol IV* London, Penguin Classics 2005, p. 250 (author's italics)
2. Corrigan, pp. 385–6
3. Florentin *Quand les Alliés*, p. 15
4. Pryce-Jones, p. 92
5. Florentin *Quand les Alliés*, pp. 22–3
6. ibid, p. 25
7. ibid, pp.29–31
8. ibid, p.19
9. ibid, p. 21 (abridged). The nun's prayer was seemingly granted. In the following year, when bombs fell on the operating theatre and a ward, neither exploded. In 1942 incendiaries hit the hospital, but no one was killed
10. ibid, p. 21 (abridged)

11. ibid, pp. 27–8
12. Burrin, p. 75
13. The colour that car headlamps and bicycle lamps had to be painted in the blackout

Chapter 5

1. Le Boterf, *Vol 1* p. 37
2. Amouroux, *Vol 1* p. 205
3. ibid, pp. 210–11
4. *Collaboration and resistance*, ed. L. Frankel, New York, Abrams 1998, p. 98
5. Personal communication with the author
6. See www.cheminsdememoire.gouv.fr
7. *1941–1942 Collaborateurs et Résistants* Paris, Editions Tallandier 1979, pp. 916–20
8. Webster, p.141
9. Burrin, p. 264
10. Amouroux, *Vol 2*, pp. 82–4
11. W. Thornton *The Liberation of Paris* London, Hart-Davis 1963, p.118
12. L.H. Nicholas *The Rape of Europa* London, Macmillan 1995, p. 292 (abridged)
13. Pryce-Jones, p. 124
14. ibid, p.120
15. *La Vie à en Mourir – Lettres des Fusillés 1941–1944*, ed. G. Krivopissko, Paris, Tallandier 2003, pp. 59–60
16. ibid, pp. 46–8, abridged
17. ibid, pp. 57–8

Chapter 6

1. Article by Jean Daigre in *Le Petit Havre*, 12 September 1941 (abridged)
2. *La Vie à en Mourir*, pp. 71–4
3. ibid, p. 78

4. ibid, pp. 79–81
5. ibid, pp. 93–7 (abridged)
6. ibid, p. 85 (abridged)
7. Amouroux, *Vol 1*, p. 185
8. *Semaine religieuse du diocèse d'Arras*, 11 September 1941
9. At the Liberation, Drieu La Rochelle committed suicide. Brasilach was executed.
10. *La Vie à en mourir*, pp. 99–103
11. *1942–1943 Années Noires* Paris, Tallandier 1987, pp. 1153–5
12. Amouroux, *Vol 1*, p. 199
13. Le Boterf, *Vol 1*, pp. 34, 36
14. ibid, p. 67
15. ibid, p. 40
16. Article by L. Chambrun et al. *L'Express* 6 October 2005
17. Mathilde's story is told in L. Paine *Mathilde Carré, Double Agent* London, Robert Hale, 1976
18. article by G. Smajda in *L'Humanité*, 8 October 1966
19. He was fatally injured in an attack by PCF prisoners while in detention awaiting trial for collaboration.
20. Burrin, pp. 245–9
21. Florentin, *Quand les Alliés*, pp. 338–44

Chapter 7

1. Article by L. Chabrun *et al* in *L'Express* 6 October 2005
2. e.g. Exodus 20,5 ; Numbers 14,18 ; Deuteronomy 5,9
3. Article by J.-P. Guilloteau in *L'Express* 31 May 2004
4. Burrin, p. 207
5. *La Vie à en Mourir*, pp. 158–60, (abridged)
6. Between 4 October 1940 and 16 September 1941 twenty-six laws, twenty-four decrees and six *arrêtés* were published in the *Journal Officiel* diminishing the status and limiting the activities of Jews. In 1947 Vallat was condemned to ten years' imprisonment, but released two years later.
7. Many people considered they were still too well treated. One typical letter addressed to Darquier on 26 January 1943 recommended intending travellers being obliged to produce an identity card when

buying their tickets so that Jews could be prevented from travelling on trains. *Archives Nationales*, Paris under reference AJ 38/67 CGQJ

8. *La Vie à en Mourir*, pp. 167–74 (abridged)
9. M. Jullian in *Résistants contre SS 1943–1944* Paris, Tallandier 1987, pp. 1507–8
10. Florentin *Quand les Alliés*, p. 76
11. ibid, p. 213
12. Report by Pierre Villette in *Je Suis Partout* 16 April 1943
13. S. Klarsfeld in *Le Monde* 14 March 1979
14. The letter is preserved in the *Archives Nationales*, Paris under reference AJ 38/67 CGQJ
15. Amouroux, *Vol 2* p. 29

Chapter 8

1. R. Atkin *Dieppe 1942* London, Macmillan 1980, p. 32
2. R. Doherty *Normandy 1944 – The Road to Victory* Staplehurst, Spellmount 2004, p. 22
3. ibid, p. 15
4. Previously code-named Operation *Rutter*
5. *1942–1943 Années Noires*, pp. 1193–1200
6. J. Gardiner *D-Day – Those who were there* London, Collins & Brown 1994, p. 33 (abridged)
7. ibid, p. 31 (abridged)
8. ibid, pp. 33, 34 (abridged)
9. Atkin, pp. 250–52
10. W.S. Churchill *The Second World War*, *Vol IV* pp. 459, 467
11. PRO WO 106/4223 Encl 10A GHQ Home Forces letter HF/00/136/G (Plans) and reply in DDMO (H) War Office, both dated 31 March 1943 – quoted in M. Cumming *The Starkey Sacrifice* Thrupp, Sutton 1996, p. 9
12. *1942–1943 Années Noires*, p. 1200
13. See at length J-M. Berlière et F. Liaigre *Liquider les traîtres, la face cachée du PCF, 1941–1943* Paris, Laffont 2007
14. Designated No 340 'Ile de France' squadron
15. For biography, see www.jean-maridor.org
16. M. Jullian in *Résistants contre SS 1943–1944*, pp. 1507–8

Chapter 9

1. *La Vie à en Mourir*, pp. 223–4
2. Published in *Le Journal Officiel* of 13 September 1942
3. J. Barzman & E. Saunier *Migrants dans une Ville Portuaire XVIe– XXIe siècles* Rouen, Publications des Universités de Rouen et du Havre 2005, pp. 113–6
4. Amouroux, *Vol 2*, p. 109
5. see in further detail http://fr.wikipedia.org/wiki/Service_du_ travail_obligatoire
6. Amouroux, *Vol 2*, pp. 32–3
7. ibid, p. 39
8. Article by L. Chabrun in *L'Express* 10 October 2005
9. *La Vie à en Mourir*, pp. 215–9, (abridged)
10. Article by L. Chabrun in *L'Express* 10 October 2005

Chapter 10

1. PRO AIR 9/187 Letter dated 29 October 1942 ref CS15803/ ASP1
2. Papon pursued a high-profile civil service career after the war, untroubled by his record of collaboration until 1997 when, after seventeen years of legal manoeuvres, he was tried for crimes against humanity for his part in the deportation of Jews, and found guilty. He was released on grounds of ill health in 2002.
3. see http://news.bbc.co.uk/2/hi/europe/7984436.stm
4. quoted in Cumming, p. 11
5. ibid, (abridged)
6. PRO DEFE 2/458 Minutes of first *Starkey* conference
7. PRO/AIR 20/4801
8. Cumming, p. 26
9. ibid, pp. 17, 19
10. Amouroux, *Vol 2*, p. 58
11. Cumming, p. 32
12. See http://www.raf.mod.uk/bombercommand/diary.html (updated 6 April 2009)
13. Cumming, pp. 7–80

14. Florentin *Quand les Alliés*, p. 265
15. Photographs of PRO (AIR 40/905) shown in Cumming, p. 131
16. Florentin *Quand les Alliés*, p. 232
17. Principal sources for this chapter are Cumming, Florentin *Quand les Alliés*, pp. 227–33 and D.J. Bacon (Major, USAF) *Second World War Deception – Lessons Learned for Today's Joint Planners* Air Command and Staff College, Maxwell AFB 1998
18. Florentin *Quand les Alliés*, p. 233
19. ibid, p. 604
20. ibid, pp. 609–10

Chapter 11

1. Article by R. Chaussois in *La Voix du Nord* 3 November 1993, (abridged)
2. Amouroux, *Vol 2*, p. 87
3. *La Vie à en Mourir*, p. 265
4. C. Pinaud, *La Simple Vérité* Paris, Julliard 1960 (abridged)
5. *La Vie à en Mourir*, pp. 307–11
6. see http:www.requis-deportes-sto.com
7. *Résistants contre SS 1943–1944*, pp. 1485–89
8. French verb *agir*, meaning 'to act'
9. Chaussois article (abridged)
10. Florentin, *Quand les Alliés*, p. 314–5 (abridged)
11. *La Vie à en Mourir*, p. 330
12. Extract from photostat of Gestapo file in family's possession reading, *Ein besonders gefährlicher Agent, mit allen Mitteln kaltzustellen. 1,000,000 Fcs Lohne wem derjenigen verhaftet oder ausliefert.*

Chapter 12

1. H. Tafforeau *Une Journée Particulière* Villeurbanne, Editions André Odemard, 2009
2. http://perso.wanadoo.fr/d-d.natanson/collabo.htm
3. see www.raf.mod.uk/bombercommand/apr44.html

4. Florentin *Quand les Alliés*, p. 403
5. Extract from R.-G. Nobécourt *Rouen Désolée 1939–44* Paris, Medicis 1949, quoted in Florentin *Quand les Alliés*, p. 404
6. Florentin *Quand les Alliés*, p. 404–5
7. Tafforeau, pp. 43–50 (abridged)
8. Amouroux, *Vol 2*, p.99
9. Final figures quoted in Tafforeau, p. 30
10. She was burned at the stake there by the English on 30 May 1431
11. Full details of the Boulanger *réseau*, the betrayal, arrest and sequel can be found on http://www.defense.gouv.fr/onac/content/download/114855/1000864/file/panneau_expo_ONAC_1-2.pdf
12. http://www.raf.mod.uk/bombercommand/diary.html
13. idem, (abridged)
14. idem, (abridged)
15. Florentin *Quand les Alliés*, p. 450–59 quoting Railkhès *Rouen pendant la Guerre* and Nobécourt *Rouen Desolée*
16. M. Lindsay *So Few Got Through* London, Arrow 1970, p. 66
17. H. Probert *Bomber Harris, his Life and Times* London, Greenhill 2006, p. 292
18. The Churchill–Eisenhower–Roosevelt exchange is taken from W.S. Churchill *The Second World War*, Vol V, pp. 465–8 (abridged)
19. National Archives TNA AIR 37/102, quoted by Professor Andrew Knapp (see Acknowlegements)
20. Lemesle's diary was published in Nobécourt *Rouen désolée*, quoted in Amouroux *Vol 2*, pp. 116–121

Chapter 13

1. Extract from *Kriegstagebuch des Seekommandants Seine-Havre* quoted on http://lehavre1944.free.fr/2bomb0644.htm
2. Amouroux, *Vol 2*, p. 101
3. Florentin, *Quand les Alliés*, pp. 491–2
4. ibid, p. 492 (abridged)
5. ibid, pp. 515–6
6. Bennett and Bennet, pp. 197–8
7. The German designation was *S-Boote*, meaning 'fast boats' but these small craft were generally called E-boats by the Allies.

Roughly the counterpart of British MTBs and MGBs and US PT boats, they were faster than their RN counterparts, especially in rough weather, and played a considerable part in harassing the Allied invasion fleet.

8. Unpublished diary of Paul Latrille
9. D. Stafford *Ten Days to D-Day* London, Little Brown 2004, p. 308
10. *La Vie à en Mourir*, pp. 329–30
11. Florentin *Quand les Alliés*, pp. 562–3
12. Stafford, pp. 29–30, 283, 305–9
13. Florentin *Quand les Alliés*, pp. 563–4
14. Maj-Gen Essame *Normandy Bridgehead* London, Macdonald 1971, p. 144
15. http://perso.wanadoo.fr/d-d.natanson/collabo.htm
16. Florentin *Quand les Alliés*, pp. 565–72
17. R.J.Aldrich *Witness to War* London, Corgi 2005, pp. 701–3, abridged
18. ibid, pp. 713–4, abridged

Chapter 14

1. J. Keegan *Six Armées en Normandie* Paris, Albin Michel 1984, pp. 181–2
2. *Résistants contre SS 1943–1944*, pp. 1470–5
3. Extract from *L'Enfer du Havre* by J. Guillemard, quoted in Amouroux, *Vol 2*, pp. 115–6
4. M. Moynihan *War Correspondent* Barnsley, Pen & Sword 1994, p. 64, (abridged)
5. Moynihan, pp. 66–7
6. Florentin *Quand les Alliés*, pp. 580–2
7. Keegan, p. 211
8. Lindsay, p. 31
9. ibid, p. 59
10. Florentin, *Quand les Alliés*, p. 607
11. Maridor's remains were re-buried after the war in the Ste-Marie cemetery of Le Havre.
12. D.J. Willis *The Incredible Year* Ames, Iowa State University Press 1988, pp. 27, 28, (abridged)

Chapter 15

1. see http://news.bbc.co.uk/2/hi/europe/7984436.stm
2. Lindsay, p. 74
3. Knapp, quoting Wildermuth's special interrogation by Canadian 1st Army in National Archives ref TNA WO 223/72
4. Amouroux, *Vol 2*, p. 110, (abridged)
5. Many of them were *résistants de dernière heure* or last-minute patriots, who had not been active before it became obvious that the Allied invasion would not be driven back into the sea.
6. Aldrich, pp. 729–30, (abridged)
7. For a very full account of the siege and reduction of the pocket, see www.lehavre1944.free/2bomb0944.htm
8. E. Florentin *Le Havre 1944 à feu et à sang* Paris, Presses de la Cité 1985, p. 74
9. Aldrich, p. 731, abridged
10. Aldrich, p. 829
11. Florentin *Le Havre*, p. 131
12. *Le Petit Havre*, 2 September 1944, (abridged)
13. Lindsay, p. 73 (author's italics)
14. Florentin *Le Havre*, p. 131
15. ibid, p. 119
16. ibid, pp. 120–1, 127

Chapter 16

1. Knapp cites TNA WO 233/67/12483 in National Archives and a signed statement by Maj E. S. Scott, present at the parley, deposited with Imperial War Museum
2. Some sources say forty-eight hours
3. Acronym of Pipe Line Under The Ocean
4. Shulman's interrogation of Wildermuth is quoted in Florentin *Le Havre 1944*, p. 143
5. Accessible on www.raf.mod.uk/bombercommand/sep44. html
6. Florentin *Le Havre*, pp. 150–64
7. ibid, p. 165
8. ibid, pp. 174–7

Chapter 17

1. ibid, pp. 182–191
2. www.raf.mod.uk/bombercommandsep44.html
3. Florentin *Le Havre*, p. 217
4. Amouroux, *Vol 2*, pp. 129–30
5. A modified tank designated Assault Vehicle, Royal Engineers
6. National Archives TNA WO 231/23/121483, quoted by Knapp
7. Florentin, *Quand les Alliés*, pp. 591–2

Chapter 18

1. Turretless versions of the Canadian Ram tank
2. Lindsay, p. 79
3. ibid
4. Florentin, *Le Havre*, pp. 543–5
5. Article by B. Esdras-Gosse in *Havre Matin* 13 September 1944, abridged
6. Details of casualties and damage are taken from *Les Victimes Civiles en Haute Normandie* Le Havre, Centre de Recherches d'Histoire Quantitative 1997 and *Le Port du Havre, situation au lendemain de la Guerre* Le Havre, Port Autonome du Havre 1950
7. Amouroux, *Vol 2*, p. 124
8. National Archives reference TNA WO 231/23/121483, quoted by Knapp
9. H. Probert *Bomber Harris – his life and times* London, Greenhill Books 2006, p. 300
10. *Archives Municipales de la Ville du Havre*, Fonds Contemporains, memorandum H4/14/4 dated 16 February 1945, quoted by Knapp
11. Florentin, *Quand les Alliés*, p. 607–8
12. See www.cyanopale-histoires.com
13. National Archives TNA AIR 37/1034, quoted by Knapp (author's italics)
14. D. Lormier *La Poche de Royan* Saintes, Les Chemins de la Mémoire 2002, p.21. Some sources give a total of forty-six German dead.
15. P. Lelaurain *Le Musée de la Poche de Royan* Vauclin 1996, p. 19

Chapter 19

1. For a more detailed account of the investment of Dunkirk, see www. nasenoviny.com/DunkirkEN1944_45.html
2. Extracts are edited translations from the original German entries reproduced in the bilingual edition of *Le Journal de Vice-Amiral Friedrich Frisius, commandant de la "forteresse" de Dunquerque* Wimille, Punch Editions 2002, pp. 45–159
3. By this he means the *Soldatensender Calais* transmissions in German, whose news was printed the following day for air-dropping over German positions out of range. After the fall of Calais, the station changed its callsign to *Soldatensender West*. Allied psywar units on the perimeter also broadcast by loudspeaker news intended to lower the defenders' resistance and also interviews with deserters encouraging comrades to follow their example.
4. The air raids recorded in Frisius' diary do not figure in the Bomber Command Campaign Diary or the US Eighth Air Force Combat chronology, but since his diary was updated virtually every day, there is no reason to suspect that he invented them. It is, of course, possible that Dunkirk was an alternative target or even a target of opportunity for aircraft originally despatched elsewhere.
5. It had been 'open for business' from 26 November

Epilogue

1. W.S. Churchill *The Second World War*, *Vol IV*, p. 250 (author's italics)
2. Corrigan, p. 387

Index